Capitalism and the Political Economy of Work Time

John Maynard Keynes expected that around the year 2030 people would only work 15 hours a week. In the mid-1960s, Jean Fourastié still anticipated the introduction of the 30-hour week in the year 2000, when productivity would continue to grow at an established pace. Productivity growth slowed down somewhat in the 1970s and 1980s, but rebounded in the 1990s with the spread of new information and communication technologies. The knowledge economy, however, did not bring about a jobless future or a world without work, as some scholars had predicted. With few exceptions, work hours of full-time employees have hardly fallen in the advanced capitalist countries in the last three decades, while in a number of countries they have actually increased since the 1980s.

This book takes the persistence of long work hours as a starting point to investigate the relationship between capitalism and work time. It does so by discussing major theoretical schools and their explanations for the length and distribution of work hours, as well as tracing major changes in production and reproduction systems, and analyzing their consequences for work hours.

Furthermore, this volume explores the struggle for shorter work hours, starting from the introduction of the ten-hour work day in the nineteenth century to the introduction of the 35-hour week in France and Germany at the end of the twentieth century. However, the book also shows how neoliberalism has eroded collective work time regulations and resulted in an increase and polarization of work hours since the 1980s. Finally, the book argues that shorter work hours not only means more free time for workers, but also reduces inequality and improves human and ecological sustainability.

Christoph Hermann is a senior researcher at the Working Life Research Centre in Vienna and a lecturer at the University of Vienna, Austria.

Routledge frontiers of political economy

Are capitalist economies nearing the end of a long-term trend toward shortening the work week? Even with the enduring financial crisis, working time is getting longer and employment or job sharing is becoming passé. This book examines the root causes of the trends and issues with work time using a pluralist approach – assessing theory, history, and public policy from a comparative perspective. Fresh new arguments for shortening working time to promote self-determination, equality, and an ecologically sustainable society, are offered.

Deborah M. Figart, *Professor of Education and Economics,*
The Richard Stockton College of New Jersey, USA

Capitalism and the Political Economy of Work Time

Christoph Hermann

Routledge
Taylor & Francis Group

LONDON AND NEW YORK

First published 2015
by Routledge
2 Park Square, Milton Park, Abingdon, Oxon OX14 4RN

and by Routledge
711 Third Avenue, New York, NY 10017

Routledge is an imprint of the Taylor & Francis Group, an informa business

British Library Cataloguing in Publication Data
A catalogue record for this book is available from the British Library

Library of Congress Cataloging in Publication Data
Hermann, Christoph.
Capitalism and the Political Economy of Work Time/Christoph Hermann.
  pages cm. – (Routledge frontiers of political economy)
  1. Hours of labor. 2. Capitalism–History. 3. Economic history. I. Title.
  HD5106.H47 2014
  331.25'7–dc23   2014018646

ISBN: 978-0-415-81023-4 (hbk)
ISBN: 978-1-315-74577-0 (ebk)

Typeset in Times New Roman
by Wearset Ltd, Boldon, Tyne and Wear

Printed and bound in Great Britain by
TJ International Ltd, Padstow, Cornwall

Contents

PART IV
Conclusions   155

Figures

Tables

Acknowledgments

This book has profited immensely from discussions and exchanges with colleagues and friends both in and outside academia. I am particularly indebted to Greg Albo, who extensively commented on my dissertation which formed the basis for this book. I am also grateful to Sam Gindin, Ursula Huws, and Steffen Lehndorff, with whom I have longstanding and continuous discussions on work time and related issues, as well as Ulrich Brand, Markus Wissen, and Birgit Mahnkopf for their support and critical input on my ecological thinking. Beverly Silver provided me with an institutional home for finishing the dissertation during a sabbatical in Baltimore. Many more played a crucial role in providing me with encouragement and emotional support, including, most importantly, my partner Sandra Eder to whom this book is dedicated.

1 Introduction

The Great Recession, which shook the world economy in 2007, and despite some signs of recovery still causes widespread unemployment in 2014, has brought the contested nature of capitalism back to the center of academic and political attention. Two observations are particularly revealing for the relationship between capitalism and work time: we are far away from the 15-hour week predicted by John Maynard Keynes in his well-known essay "Economic Possibilities for our Grandchildren," written in the midst of the last major crisis – the Great Depression. What is more, and in direct contrast to the Great Depression when trade unionists and progressive politicians in the United States and elsewhere fought for a 30-hour week to limit unemployment, shorter work hours were not on the political agenda during the recent crisis – even though short-time working has proved a viable tool to avoid job losses in countries such as Germany. If anything, the crisis has increased pressure on those who still have a job to work longer and more flexible hours – and, ultimately, for more years before retirement.

The starting point of this book is the observation that despite the partial move to the 35-hour week in France and Germany, work time reductions have slowed down markedly since the 1970s. In some countries (full-time) work hours started to increase in the 1980s and 1990s, but more often it was per capita hours that have grown during the last three decades – after decreasing during the postwar period. Given the end of the secular decline in work hours, this book raises a number of questions regarding the role and nature of work time in capitalist societies: why did work hours not decrease to the extent one might have expected from the dramatic gains in productivity and living standards achieved over the past 150 years? Why did work hours decrease up to the 1970s, but thereafter stagnated in most countries and even increased in some cases? Why did work hours become more flexible, and why did flexibilization promote polarization? Why is unpaid domestic labor still mainly carried out by women in spite of the major increase in female employment rates since the 1960s? Finally, why are shorter work hours no longer on the political agenda despite high unemployment and a looming ecological crisis?

This book argues that in order to understand the development of (paid and unpaid) work time in the past 150 years, it is essential to understand the contradictory and contested role of work time in capitalist societies. The book, hence, takes a political economy perspective on work time rather than a purely economic, sociological, or political scientific approach. Following the traditional political economy approach of Karl Marx, and others, it combines theoretical reflections with historical enquiries and a thorough examination of the present situation. Specific attention is paid to the development of production and reproduction systems, as well as to the struggle for shorter work hours and the impact of neoliberalism on working lives. The different perspectives on work time are also reflected in the structure of the book. *Capitalism and the Political Economy of Work Time* encompasses four major parts: the first part deals with work time theories; the second part explores the links between work time, production, and reproduction; the third part captures major struggles for shorter work hours, including the struggle for the eight-hour day and 35-hour week; the fourth part concludes with an examination of the impact of neoliberalism on work hours and discusses the role of work time in capitalist societies, including the link between shorter work hours and human and ecological sustainability.

The first part of the book presents major theoretical approaches and their explanations for the length and distribution of work time. Chapter 2 covers the neoclassical, Weberian and institutionalist schools of thought. Despite different explanations for the length and distribution of work time, they share the assumption of that capitalism is characterized by a certain degree of rationality and stability. In contrast, the approaches covered in Chapter 3 – "Marxist, post-Marxist and feminist theories" – point to major contradictions in capitalist social systems. Chapter 4 provides a discussion of the different views of major controversies such as the self-chosen or socially constrained nature of work time; the role of living standards, productivity, and the search for surplus labor; the impact of institutions and social struggles on the development of work hours and the emergence of country-specific differences in work time; the role of work sharing in the fight against unemployment, as well as the tension between paid, unpaid and socially necessary work time.

The second part explores changes in production and reproduction systems and their impact on work time. Chapter 5 describes changes in industrial production following from the shift from Fordism to post-Fordism and lean production and consequences for work hours, while Chapter 6 analyzes the various fragmentations in work time spurred by the highly diverse character of the service economy. Chapter 7 leaves the world of paid work and explores the transformation of household labor, which affects the hours women spend in paid employment.

The third part of the book focuses on struggles for shorter work hours. Chapter 8 describes the struggles that led to the introduction of the ten-hour day between the middle and the end of the nineteenth century, the eight-hour day after the First World War, and the 40-hour week in the interwar period and after the Second World War. Chapter 9 presents the main features of the introduction of the 35-hour week in Germany and France in the 1990s and early 2000s, as well as the rise of part-time work as an alternative to collective work time reductions and the introduction of paid leave periods in Sweden and Denmark.

The fourth part of the book provides some conclusions with respect to the role of work time in capitalist societies. Chapter 10 explores the impact of neo-liberalism on the length and distribution of work hours. It argues that in the last decades the granting of concessions and exemptions from collective work time norms, the erosion and decentralization of collective bargaining, the flexibilization and individualization of work hours, as well as the workfarist restructuring of welfare states, have caused a surge and polarization of work hours. Chapter 11 brings together the insights from preceding elaborations and discusses the relationship between capitalism and work time. By doing so it specifically addresses the persistence of long work hours, the need to strengthen solidarity against the market, the simultaneous compression, extension, and variation of work time in capitalist societies, the challenge to promote worker as opposed to employer flexibility, the role of more free time as an alternative to more consumption, and the question of necessary social labor time. The book ends with a list of arguments for a 30-hour week.

Part I
Work time theories

2 Neoclassical, Weberian, and institutionalist perspectives

Introduction

This is the first of two chapters that deal with theoretical approaches to work time. Work time plays an important role in the history of political economy and in social theory more generally. The leading question that this and the following chapter attempt to answer is how different theoretical schools explain the length of the work day and the development of work time. The presentation of major ideas necessarily implies some extent of condensation and simplification as it is impossible and perhaps unnecessary to follow every single strand of the respective approaches. It also means that the approaches are constructed, and that not all scholars cited in the respective schools of thought would actually agree with the labeling; some, perhaps, unconsciously, use arguments from different theoretical backgrounds. There is also some overlapping of arguments between different schools of thought, such as between the Weberian and the institutionalist approaches, or between institutionalist and feminist debates. However, in spite of all the difficulties and shortcomings the construction of labels is indispensable to reconstruct a debate.

This chapter covers three major perspectives on work time from the neoclassical, Weberian, and institutionalist schools of thought. As a common ground the neoclassical, Weberian, and institutionalist approaches assume a certain degree of rationality and stability in capitalist social systems, even though they disagree over where the length of the work day is determined: on the individual or the collective level. In contrast, the three approaches presented in the following chapter all assume that capitalist social systems are characterized by major contradictions which have an important effect on the dynamic of work hours. The chapter starts with the neoclassical approach and then proceeds to the Weberian and institutionalist perspectives on work time. The chapter ends with a summary of the main arguments.

Neoclassical perspectives

Neoclassical economists assume that the length of the work day or work week is determined by individual choice.[1] Workers choose their work hours in order to maximize personal utility. The rational behavior of utility-maximizing individuals makes it possible to make some predictions about the development of work hours even though they are the result of individual preferences. There are several competing explanations in the neoclassical school of thought when it comes to the factors determining those individual decisions. On the whole the view prevails that average workers tend to reduce work hours with growing incomes or living standards.

In the neoclassical discourse the question of work time is discussed as the problem of labor supply. Stanley Jevons argued that workers choose between the utility of consumption and the disutility of work. While workers derive pleasure from the consumption of commodities purchased by the wages obtained for working a certain number of hours a day or week, work itself is perceived as "painful exertion" or "negative utility."[2] Yet the utility of consumption and disutility of work do not increase proportionally with the duration of the work day. Instead, the marginalist strand within neoclassical economics, of which Jevons was a leading representative, argued that marginal utility – which is the utility derived from the consumption of an additional unit of the same good – only rises up to a certain point, after which is starts to fall. Maximizing utility in this framework means consuming until the point of the highest marginal utility – or, as common sense would phrase it, consuming until one is satisfied.[3]

Jevons thought that the disutility of work develops in the same manner. The pain first increases and then diminishes after a certain point in the work day. In Jevons's words, "[a]t the moment of commencing labor it is usually more irksome than when the mind and body are well bent to the work."[4] The combination of the utility of consumption and the disutility of work must henceforth result in a particular instance where the marginal utility of consumption and the marginal disutility of work add up to the highest possible degree of pleasure for the individual worker. According to Jevons this is the point where workers naturally stop working – "if we pass the least beyond this point, a balance of pain will result: there will be an ever-decreasing motive in favor of labor, and an ever-increasing motive against it."[5] Jevons acknowledged that the painfulness or disutility of work can vary with the nature, content, and intensity of work, but he insisted that in general "fatigue always rapidly increases when the speed of work passes a certain point." He therefore recommended working at "such a rate ... to recover all fatigue and recommence with an undiminished store of energy."[6]

While sharing the view that "the exercise of our powers is usually attended by the painful feeling of distress and fatigue," Austrian economists were uncomfortable with the idea that labor is associated with disutility.[7] As David Spencer notes, "Austrian economists had fought hard to repel the labor theory of value, and they were not about to reintroduce labor as a causal factor in the explanation of subjective value."[8] Instead they argued that the "toil and trouble of labor" should be considered as cost to be paid for gaining utility from consumption – very much like costs for iron, coal, and other means of production. In another twist, the "pain cost" of labor was considered an "opportunity cost." As David Green points out, the laborer stops work at a certain hour, not simply because he is tired, but because he wants some opportunity for pleasure and recreation.... By devoting our efforts to any one task, we necessarily give up the opportunity of doing certain other things which would yield us some return; and it is, in general, for this sacrifice of opportunity that we insist upon being paid rather than for any pain which may be involved in the work performed.[9]

In another turn the opportunity cost of working was replaced by the opportunity cost of leisure. According to Philip Wicksteed the

irksomeness of the labor by which we earn money is not really the only thing that we have to set against the advantages the money secures. It is only a negative expression of one element in the desirability of rest or leisure.[10]

In other words, workers resist a lengthening of the work day not because of the accelerating pain associated with putting in longer hours, but because of the associated loss of leisure time.[11] With the opportunity cost theorem, leisure becomes a good which is exchanged for other goods purchased from wage income. Essentially workers have to choose between leisure and other commodities.[12]

The view that the number of hours a worker chooses to work depends on the opportunity cost of leisure became widely accepted among neoclassical economists. However, consent about the nature of choices still did not imply agreement on what maximizing marginal utility of leisure meant for the actual length of the work day. In this regard there were still two opposing views. Frank Knight argued that workers who already enjoy an optimal degree of utility from leisure and consumption, and who want to preserve the optimal equilibrium, will respond to an increase in wages by spending parts of the additional income on buying free time rather than on purchasing more commodities: "[i]nsofar as men act rationally they will at a higher rate divide their time between wage-earning and non-industrial uses in such a way as to *earn more money*, indeed, but to work *fewer hours*."[13] Behind this conclusion stood the very simple observation that "the expenditure of money also requires time and energy which must be saved from the work period."[14] In other words, workers need time to consume.[15]

Perhaps the conclusion that workers are inclined to reduce work hours with growing incomes and living standards was as much based on empirical observations as on theoretical considerations. Already Jevons had noted that "the English laborer enjoying little more than the necessaries of life, will work harder the less the produce; or, which comes to the same thing, will work less hard as the produce increases."[16] The conclusion allowed neoclassical theory to account for the widespread work time reductions that took place at the end of the nineteenth and at the start of the twentieth century. As Chris Nyland notes,

the working classes' insistence that a legal limit be placed on the work day made it difficult for the marginalist tradition to retain a concept of the worker as an individual forever seeking to maximize the length of time spent at work in order to gain more income. What was needed was an acceptable theory that would explain why hedonistic beings might choose to reduce the length of time they are willing to labor.[17]

In addition, the conclusion that workers who earn more tend to work less, gave employers a much-welcomed argument for rejecting demands for higher wages because workers would respond to this by working fewer hours.

However, the widely shared view that workers tend to reduce their work hours with growing incomes has not gone unchallenged. Lionel Robbins argued that this assumption is only true if the demand for income is invariable, unaffected by the amount of money gained from performing work – or, in his words, "if the demand for income in terms of effort would be inelastic."[18] In reality workers would typically value income in terms of effort, and the higher the income per unit of effort, the greater their willingness to spend additional effort or work hours. In other words, a higher wage rate lowers the costs of income in terms of effort, while at the same time making it more costly to consume leisure. This argument was consistent with the observation that workers were eager to work overtime if it was paid at a higher rate than regular hours. Robbins therefore argued that a wage rise did not automatically cause a fall in work hours. The effect on work hours, instead, was dependent on "the elasticity of demand for income in terms of effort."[19]

John Hicks later combined the conflicting views, and argued that "a fall in wages may sometimes make the wage-earner work less hard, sometimes harder." On the one hand, a reduced wage rate "make[s] the effort needed for a marginal unit of output seem less worthwhile"; on the other, the lower wage urges workers to "work harder in order to make up for the loss in income."[20] The two countervailing tendencies are known as "income" and "substitution" effects, and have become the standard explanation of labor supply in neoclassical economics. According to the income effect workers can be expected to reduce work time with growing incomes (because of the growing utility of leisure), whereas the substitution effect induces workers beyond a certain wage level to put in more rather than less work (because of the growing cost of leisure). In order for work hours to fall the income effect must outweigh the substitution effect.

As a special variation of the same theme, neoclassical economists also discussed the effect of taxes on the supply of labor power. Following the income effect, Arthur Pigou argued that a tax increase has the positive effect of encouraging workers to put in more work "[s]ince income is taken away from taxpayers the marginal utility of money to them is raised but the marginal disutility of work is unchanged. Thus, unless they are somehow impeded, they will increase the amount of work done."[21] By arguing that a cut in wages forces workers to put in more work hours, Pigou comes close to the Marxist argumentation that work hours are dependent on the value of labor power (see below). For some neoclassical economists Pigou's defense of higher taxes did not sit well with their general criticism of state interventions. In more recent times a number of critics have emphasized the substitution effect and have argued that a tax rise may actually discourage workers from supplying their labor power.[22] This is thought to be particularly true for high income earners, who tend to be disproportionally affected by an increase in taxes. The debate then moved further to the question of how to determine an optimal tax rate that guarantees a maximum supply of labor power (as opposed to a tax rate that is based on considerations of social justice and solidarity).[23]

Still, the general assumption in the neoclassical literature is that work hours tend to fall with growing income; it is only beyond a certain relatively high wage rate that they start to increase again.[24] While originally a neoclassical concept, the assumption is widely accepted in the field of economics, and shared by economists from various (heterodox) backgrounds.[25] Labor economist Lloyd Reynolds summarizes the view as follows:

> Over the long run ... changes in hours reflect worker preferences. The main reason why weekly hours have fallen from about sixty at the turn of the century to around forty at present is that most workers find the increase in leisure preferable to the higher incomes they could earn on the old schedule. If and when most workers conclude that a four-day or a thirty-hour week yields a better balance between income and leisure, management and union policies will shift in that direction.[26]

Weberian perspectives

Although sharing some fundamental concepts with marginalist theory, including the assumption of rationally calculating and acting individuals, Max Weber came to quite opposite conclusions when it comes to explaining the length of the work day and week.[27] First of all, workers do not choose their work hours. Actual work hours are instead the result of production requirements as well as of administrative rules and cultural norms. Second, the actual length of the work day depends on the intensity of the work. After a certain point in the work day work performances start to diminish due to the workers' growing physiological and psychological exhaustion. For employers longer hours become less profitable, encouraging them to shorten the work day: the higher the intensity of work, the shorter the work day. And because higher intensity is often linked to higher productivity, work hours can be expected to fall in line with growing productivity.

The notion of rationality plays a crucial role in the Weberian thinking. The emergence of (Western) capitalism was on the one hand linked to the spread of new and increasingly exact calculations and accounting methods, and, on the other, to bureaucratic organization, fueling specialization, growing division of work, and technological innovation. The result was not only the development of a rational, and thus highly productive industrial organization, but also "the rational capitalistic organization of (formally) free labor."[28] With respect to time in general, and work time in particular, the drive towards greater rationality is symbolized by the spread of clock time as "a time that is standardized, context free, homogenous, and divisible into infinitely small units."[29] The installation of the factory clock and the definition of work time as something different from non-work time became a defining feature of industrial capitalism and replaced more variable and porous notions of time based on growing seasons, changing daylight, religious festivities, etc. As Barbara Adam notes,

> where before the capacity of a person to work a piece of land in one day would be the determinant of the measure, now "man-hours" are calculated on the basis of universally applicable units of time. In industrial societies time has become the measure of work where work was the measure of time in earlier historical periods.[30]

As a result, time has not only become an instrument of control – especially in the form of the stopwatch – but in the relation between work time and output – that is, as measurement of productivity – also a measure of social progress.

A rational organization of labor not only demanded bureaucratic organization, but also a set of rules and norms that guaranteed optimal work performance in order to make sure that maximum output is achieved with minimal input. Weber discussed the factors influencing work performance in an essay on the "Psycho-physics of Industrial Labor," using empirical data from research of selected companies.[31] One of the determining factors (besides the quality of basic materials, alcoholism, trade union membership, etc.) was the number of hours workers are required to labor. Weber showed not only that work performances vary over the workday, but also that performances started to diminish after a certain point as result of the workers' growing exhaustion. Furthermore, in contrast to other factors, exhaustion can only be partly influenced by the workers themselves and depends a great deal on the speed and intensity of work. Still, Weber observed that workers anticipating the end of the work day tend to adjust their performance during the course of the day to make sure that they are not over-exhausted and can recover before the next work shift.[32]

Using evidence from a German glassworks company where the introduction of the eight-hour day was followed by a significant boost in productivity, Weber argues that shorter work hours are almost always a sign of higher work intensity: shorter hours

> mean a physiological extra-claim and therefore a physiological extra-exhaustion ... of workers calculated per unit of work time.... It goes without saying that with shorter work time over-work is not necessarily more easily bearable than in the case of longer hours.[33]

By focusing on workers' fatigue and physical exhaustion, Weber followed Jevons's observation that work is associated with "painful exertion." The important difference to Jevons's argumentation, however, is that for Weber the painful exertion, which tends to increase with longer work hours, becomes the sole explanation for the end of the work day. According to Weber the prospect of higher incomes and of more consumption is not a strong motivation for workers to put in more hours. On the contrary, Weber notes that past increases in piece-rates have shown that workers reduce rather than expand the amount of work because they can earn the same with less effort: a "man does not 'by nature' wish to earn more and more money, but simply to live as he is accustomed to live and to earn as much as it is necessary for that purpose."[34] Some workers may work longer, but not because of the expected gains in consumption. Rather they do so because they perceive their job as "an absolute end in itself" or as "a calling."[35]

By presenting shorter work hours as a rational response to growing work intensity, Weber followed the work of Lujo Brentano, a German economist who, like Weber, was a member of the German Association for Social Policy (Verein für Socialpolitik). Yet Brentano went a step further and argued that productivity is enhanced not only by elevated work performances, but also by the introduction of new and more efficient technology. Higher wages and shorter work hours are the "cause and precondition for enhanced productivity" because they lead to "the application of long-time available and superior production methodology." In contrast, lower wages and longer hours are "reasons for technological backwardness."[36] The argument that shorter hours induce employers to rationalize production and improve productivity was highly influential in the German trade union movement after the First and Second World War. It also played an important role in other countries, including France, where proponents of the 35-hour week argued that part of the additional costs would be covered by the expected productivity gains (see Chapter 9). Gerhard Bosch and Steffen Lehndorff summarize this position as follows:

> Work time reductions provide the impetus for further innovation, since labor becomes scarcer.... On the one hand, firms are likely to look for labor-saving technical processes, with positive effects on investment activities; on the other, they will tend to modernize their entire system of work organization in order to increase labor productivity. Numerous technical and organizational innovations would have been inconceivable without this spur to productivity.[37]

Weber and Brentano, as proponents of the French 35-hour week, sought to convince capitalists that it was in their best interest to limit the work day (as members of the Verein für Socialpolitik they were social reformers rather than socialist revolutionaries). Weber argued that it was not workers who, with their struggles for shorter work time, enforced the long-term fall in work hours; it was employers realizing that long hours are less profitable, and who had voluntarily, albeit reluctantly, shortened the work day.[38]

In stark contrast to the Marxist approach discussed below, workers in the Weberian view are not much more than passive subjects facing a range of social constraints. "The pace of activities in large-scale organizations," Sandro Serge notes, provides ... a direct or indirect constraint on much of modern everyday life, whose tempo is set or regulated by administrative rule.... Since bureaucratic structures are indispensable ... they stabilize the existence of ordinary people by means of binding rules ... and order the lives of all those who work for them, during work hours and in the course of time.[39]

However, some Weberians notice growing conflicts between different time cultures and time constraints.[40] For example, while the market demands for evermore flexibility, people need a minimum level of synchronization and coordination to coordinate their lives.[41] Michel Lallement distinguishes between a "material rationality" dominating the sphere of production, and a "formal rationality" governing societies at large.[42] He also notes that the two rationalities increasingly contradict each other, and the resulting conflict is mainly felt by women: "[m]any investigations of contemporary modes of living indicate that it has become problematic, especially for women, to reconcile more and more contradictory times, those of work, family, school, public services, friends, leisure etc."[43]

The Weberian assumption that work hours tend to fall with growing productivity became the dominant view on the development of work time in the postwar decades. Such eminent social scientists as John Maynard Keynes and Jean Fourastié were convinced that technological progress would allow for a radical shortening of the work day and week. While accepting the utility-maximizing framework, Keynes predicted that in 100 years time the standard of living in progressive countries would be between four and eight times higher than in the 1930s, while work time would be limited to three hours per day or 15 hours per week.[44] Writing in the mid-1960s, Fourastié still calculated that if productivity continued to grow at the existing rate then technological progress would allow for the introduction of a 30-hour week in most parts of the industrialized world by the year 2000.[45] With decreasing work hours, leisure was expected to increase, resulting in what some scholars in the 1960s described as the arrival of a "leisure society."[46]

In the 1990s, with the internet revolution on its way, skepticism emerged about the automatic adjustment processes inherent in the Weberian view of rational capitalism. Given the enormous labor-saving potential of new information and communication technologies, a number of critics warned of the possibility of a "jobless future" or a "world without workers" if no countermeasures were applied.[47] Jeremy Rifkin, a major proponent of this view, argues that

the new high-technology revolution could mean fewer hours of work and greater benefits for millions. For the first time in modern history, large numbers of human beings could be liberated from long hours of labor in the formal market place.... The same technological forces could, however, as easily lead to growing unemployment and global depression. Whether a utopian or dystopian future awaits us, depends to a great measure, on how the productivity gains of the Information Age are distributed.[48]

Other Weberians indentified the 1970s crisis as a turning point, distinguishing an earlier period of "organized" and perhaps "rational" capitalism with a new phase of "disorganized," "postmodern" and partly "irrational" capitalism.[49] While the first period was characterized by concentration, coordination and standardization facilitated by large-scale bureaucratic organizations – "big business," "big government" and "big unions" – the latter experienced a move towards deconcentration, deregulation and flexilibization. Large industries, some of them state-owned, were broken up and split into smaller pieces. The smaller units were further downsized, sold, or privatized and some pushed into bankruptcy – all with the objective to reinvent the beneficial power of markets. Within firms, bureaucratic control was pushed pack in favor of markets, facilitated by the establishment of cost- and profit-centers, as well as growing recourse on outsourcing as alternative to in-house production. At the same time trade unions and other mass organizations lost their appeal as workers and consumers were looking for increasingly individualistic life-styles. Some researchers argue that with the shift to disorganized capitalism clock time, a structural force in organized capitalism lost some of its imperative and was complemented by new logics of time such as "real time" and "internet time."

Manuel Castells believes that with the arrival of the Information Age a new principle of capitalist rationality surfaced – the network.[51] The network structure promotes growing individuality and autonomy at work, which, in turn, must lead to increasing flexibility and diversity in work hours. "Networkers" are perceived as genuine "flextimers." Castells shares this view with another strand of scholars who explain the rise of flexible work hours primarily by an increasing desire for individual work hours, as well as by the spread of new and less formal management techniques and working cultures.[52] Again, another strand of literature has pointed to the impact of globalization and the emergence of an internet-based "24-four hour economy" which, in turn, demanded the creation of the "24-hour on-call worker." The changes amount to a "blurring of the lines between work, social life, family life and personal life," questioning

> the socio-cultural temporal rhythms that evolved over the last two-hundred years, such as weekends, nine-to-five workdays, family time, prescribed holiday times, and so on ... as the need for extreme flexibility carries the economy and the temporality of the network into almost every aspect of our lives.[53]

The fact that workers increasingly take work home when they leave their offices, or work at home instead of working in the office, has stimulated a lively debate among German sociologists about the "blurring of boundaries between work and personal life."[54] However, even Castells has to admit that his increasingly autonomous "networkers" and "flextimers" suffer from growing exhaustion and increasingly long work hours.[55]

Institutionalist perspectives

Another strand of literature focuses not so much on capitalist rationality and technological progress, but on the role of social norms and institutional arrangements in determining the development of work time. Institutionalists share many assumptions with Weberians, making the separation between Weberians and institutionalists somewhat arbitrary. However, institutionalists tend to differ in their emphasis on the continuity of work hours, facilitated through the standard employment relationship, and the persistence of country- and gender-specific differences.[56]

Morris Copeland, early on, attacked the neoclassical position that explained work hours as the result of individual choice. Copeland, instead, insisted that the "factory-system has standardized the work time." In addition, time has been affected by "business policy, and often by trade-union or government policy."[57] Joan Robinson shared his critique. While accepting the general view that workers tend to reduce their work hours with rising incomes, Robinson noted that "[t]he choice between earnings and leisure is not, in modern conditions, left entirely, or even mainly, to the preference of the individual, but is standardized by collective decisions, legal or customary."[58] The result is social norms and institutions that not only reflect collective decisions, but also impose constraints on future choices.[59] Jill Rubery and Damian Grimshaw summarize the institutionalist view as follows: "[S]ocieties make choices at particular points of time as to how to structure the institutions of their economic and social life, but once these institutions are in place they have long lasting consequences."[60] Institutionalists concede that institutions are changing, but even if faced with similar pressures they do not necessarily converge to a common pattern: "[I]nstead these pressures will lead to a modification and change of societal institutions, but the particular form of the response will reflect the country's own societal logic."[61]

The variety of institutions, which in one or other form impact the length and distribution of work hours, form what in the institutionalist literature has been described as a national work time regime. Jill Rubery, Mark Smith, and Collete Fagan define a work time regime as a "set of legal, voluntary and customary regulations which influence work time practice." Work time regimes in turn "limit or extend variations in work hours for full-timers, promote or discourage part-time work and unsocial hours working, and influence the terms and conditions under which overtime, unsocial hours or atypical work contracts are undertaken."[62] The regulation of daily, weekly, and yearly work hours forms the core of the work time regime. Regulation of work time takes place at four levels: at the national level through the universal application of national legislation (in some countries also through nationwide social partner agreements); at the sector- or industry-level through collective bargaining between interested organizations from capital and labor; at the plant- or company-level through single-employer bargaining; and at the individual level through the employment contract concluded between an employer and an employee.[63] In principle, the European Work Time Directive constitutes a fifth, supranational, level of regulation. In practice the directive has only a very limited impact, since most European countries have significantly lower national standards (Britain would be affected but for reasons discussed in Chapter 10 the effects are moderate at best). The four remaining levels also overlap, with collective agreements typically overruling lower standards in individual contracts, and legislation in the same way overruling collective agreements. However, there are a growing number of exemptions which give individual and company agreements priority over sector agreements and statutory regulations (as a result of the crisis-related changes, company agreements now have precedence over sector agreements in Greece and Spain).[64]

The relevance and strength of each of these levels of regulation vary considerably. Some countries rely primarily on collective agreements at industry- and plant-level to determine work hours, while in others statutory norms and legal interventions are more important than collective bargaining.[65] Countries, furthermore, differ in the extent to which they impose maximum work time limits (through legislation of collective bargaining) or rely solely on overtime premiums to be paid after a certain number of hours.[66] Rubery and her colleagues show that although actual work hours differ from statutory or contractual hours, the national systems of regulation do have an impact on the hours usually worked. The connection is particularly evident in the extremely long work hours that can be found in those regimes that lack maximum work time limitation.[67]

Work time regulation in the narrower sense is complemented by a series of other, mostly welfare-based, state institutions, which have an indirect influence on the length and distribution of work time, especially that of female workers. Such factors include access to parental leave schemes, the availability of childcare facilities, the right to stay at home and take care of a sick child or another dependent family member, the right to switch to part-time, etc. Cultural norms such as the extent to which mothers of young children are expected to interrupt their career and stay at home with their children, also play a role. "Gender," as Rubery and her colleagues note, "has an independent effect on work time patterns, shaping the overall work time regime and gender differences within it. However, there is strong evidence for an independent effect for both national work time regimes and for gender differences."[68]

The institutionalist approach to work time is informed by broader institutionalist debates on the varieties of capitalism, comparative welfare state models, and comparisons of care regimes, as well as comparative industrial relations research. David Soskice and Peter Hall have introduced the distinction between "coordinated market economies" and "uncoordinated" or "liberal market economies."[69] While coordinated market economies rely on coordination and cooperation between major economic actors – resulting in long-term accumulation strategies and heavily regulated labor markets – liberal market economies have stronger preferences for markets and competition, promoting flexibility and highly fluid labor markets. With regard to work hours, coordinated market economies support collective regulations while liberal market economies tend to favor individual work time arrangements – with the effect that coordinated market economies tend to have shorter work hours than their liberal counter-parts.[70] Although the researchers emphasize that coordinated and liberal market economies are (Weberian) ideal types that do not exist in a pure form in the real world, the notion of liberal market economies is more-or-less identifiable with those countries that are commonly labeled Anglo-Saxon (Australia, Canada, the UK, and the US); while coordinated market economies comprise a wide range of different economies, including Germany, Sweden, and France.

Based on a study of work time changes in 14 industrialized countries in the mid-1990s, Gerhard Bosch and his colleagues indentified two basic forms of work time flexibilization, largely overlapping with the typology put forth by Hall and Soskice.[71] Regulated flexibilization prevails in coordinated market economies with highly centralized industrial relations systems or compensatory state interventions; whereas liberal market economies with their rather fragmented company-based bargaining systems tend to favor unregulated forms of flexibilization. While in the former case collective norms persist, even though they are adapted to allow for greater variation in daily, weekly or yearly work hours, in the latter variations work hours are based on the erosion of collective norms and the expansion of individual agreements, often with no work time limitations. Not surprisingly, unregulated flexibilization tends to promote longer work hours. Peter Hall and David Gingerich found that from 1980 to the early 2000s coordinated market economies have reduced work hours considerably more quickly than their liberal counterparts.[72] The much slower reduction of work hours in liberal market economies was linked to a much faster shrinking of bargaining coverage and a shift towards company bargaining.[73]

In a different typology, David Coates distinguishes between liberal, state-led, and consensual or negotiated capitalism.[74] While the category of liberal capitalism largely corresponds to liberal market economies à la Hall and Soskice, negotiated capitalism exists in countries with strong social partnership traditions. Many issues are decided in autonomous negotiations between the employer and employee interest groups. State-led capitalism is introduced as a third category to account for countries with strong state traditions and state agencies intervening in various ways in the private economy, including the adoption of statutory labor standards. Examples of the latter category include France and Japan.[75] Dominique Anxo and Jacqueline O'Reilly use a similar concept and distinguish between "negotiated," "statist" and "externally constrained voluntarisic" work time flexibilization.[76] Systems of negotiated flexibility are characterized by the prevalence of social partner negotiations on flexible work hours, while the state provides a minimum framework in the form of maximum work time legislation. Government intervention is rare because highly coordinated employer organizations and trade unions usually find a compromise that is acceptable for both sides. In contrast, in the statist system it is the state that takes the initiative, regulates work hours, and even promotes greater work time flexibility. Externally constrained voluntarism refers to the situation in Britain where legislation has traditionally been absent from industrial relations. Yet in the 1980s collective organization and bargaining has seriously been constrained by the adoption of a number of anti-trade union laws.

While for a long time negotiated work time systems seemed to be the pace-maker for shorter work hours, after the introduction of the statutory 35-hour week France stands at the forefront of work time reduction in Europe, whereas German unions were unable to extend the 35-hour week into eastern Germany (see Chapter 10).[77] However, for Anxo and O'Reilly, even more interesting is the fact that negotiated and statist systems still display a standard work time – as can be seen in one or two major peaks in the distribution of average weekly work hours – while in Britain the concept of standard work time no longer appears to exist.[78] In France 50 percent of workers put in around 40 hours a week in the mid-1990s; in Germany the figure was 30 percent, while in Britain the propor-tion was only 10 percent.[79] The British labor market, instead, is characterized by a high percentage of men working very long hours and of women working very short hours.

The distribution of time plays a particularly important role in those work time regimes that build on Gøsta Esping-Andersen's welfare state models and the subsequent feminist critique. Esping-Andersen differentiates between social democratic, liberal, and conservative welfare states.[80] In a nutshell, social demo-cratic welfare states are the most developed because they go the furthest in pro-viding for a social existence independent from paid labor. Liberal welfare states also provide a set of general tax-funded benefits, but only on a limited level to those who can prove that they are in need. Conservative welfare states, in con-trast, provide decent benefits but depend on previous contributions paid from wage income. Social democratic welfare states can mainly be found in northern Europe, while the conservative type dominates in continental Europe. The United States and Britain display variations of the liberal model.[81]

Brian Burgoon and Phineas Baxandall follow Esping-Andersen's welfare state typology and argue that there are not only "three worlds of welfare capit-alism" – the title of Esping-Andersen's book – but also "three worlds of work time."[82] The assumption is that more developed welfare states have a more equal distribution of work time. To measure the distribution of work time the research-ers not only look at average annual hours worked per person in employment, but also on average annual hours per working-age individual (including unemployed, welfare recipients, etc.). Their hypothesis is that social democratic welfare states combine a low number of hours per employee with a high number of hours per working-age person, indicating a relatively equal distribution of work time. Conservative welfare states are expected to display a high number of hours per person in employment but a low number per person of working-age, while liberal welfare states should score high on both. The empirical evidence supports the assumption that in liberal welfare states workers not only work longer, but there are also more persons in employment. This is especially true for the United States and Canada, and to a lesser extent for the United Kingdom. The differenti-ation is less clear between social democratic and conservative welfare states: social democratic welfare states, indeed, have a high number of hours per working-age person but the number of hours per employee is not much different from those in conservative welfare states.[83]

In reality the picture is more nuanced than suggested by Burgoon and Baxandall. It is true that social democratic welfare states display a more equal distribution of work hours between men and women, but Swedish workers do not work shorter hours than their colleagues in France or Germany. And when it comes to the distribution of work hours "conservative" France has much in common with "social democratic" Sweden. In France a high proportion of women work full-time, resulting in a relatively small gap between male and female work hours. "Liberal" Britain, on the other hand, is closer to "conservative" Germany than "liberal" US. In the United States, too, many women work full-time while in Britain and Germany they tend to work part-time.

Recent institutional literature combines Andersen's welfare state models with Jane Lewis's breadwinner states and broadens the focus of analysis to account for changes in female labor market participation over the life course.[84] Weak male breadwinner states, in Lewis's typology, encourage women's employment on equal terms with men's employment and provide a number of social services to support this goal. Modified male breadwinner states compensate parents for bringing up children; strong male breadwinner states provide limited support for both working mothers and mothers who stay at home to take care of their children. While Sweden is an example of a weak male breadwinner system, France qualifies for the modified version and Britain has a strong male breadwinner state.

Inspired by Lewis's typology, Dominque Anxo and his colleagues distinguish between four different life course models:[85] The "Nordic universal breadwinner model" is based on high and continuous female labor market participation over the life course. Women with small children stay in employment but may reduce their hours from full-time to long part-time hours. In France's "modified breadwinner model" some women exit the labor market when they have children, while the majority work full-time or long part-time hours. In both cases, the provision of public childcare plays a crucial role in facilitating the continuous employment of women.[86] The rest of Western Europe, including Britain, falls under the "maternal part-time work model." Some married women also leave the labor market when they have young children, but most switch from full-time to part-time work, or return after a break on a part-time basis.[87] The fourth model is the the "Mediterranean exit or full-time model." In southern Europe married women with young children tend to leave the labor market and become full-time housewives, but when they keep their jobs they continue to work full-time.[88]

Welfare states models also have an impact on domestic work. According to Tanja van der Lippe the hours spent on domestic work are lowest in social democratic welfare states (with an average of 23.2 hours per week), followed by liberal welfare states (28.4 hours). Domestic work is considerably longer in conservative welfare regimes (34.4) and particularly long in Mediterranean regimes (50.7).[89] In terms of the distribution between men's and women's share in domestic labor, the difference is highest in conservative welfare states.[90] This is confirmed by the findings of Claudia Geist, who looked at the impact of welfare regimes on the distribution of household responsibility.[91] Conservative welfare states exhibit the highest rates of inequality.[92] However, while social democratic countries generally display a comparable high share of equality, liberal countries show considerable variation in this regard.[93] While in the US and Canada more than 30 percent of respondents note that the responsibility for household labor is shared equally, in Australia and New Zealand the proportion is around 20 percent.[94]

Summary

Neoclasscial economists explain the length of the work day by individual choice. Workers base their decisions on the trade-off between consumption acquired from work-based income, and free time. Even though the actual length of the work day is the result of individual decisions, neoclassical economists make some predictions with regard to the development of work time. In general they assume that work hours tend to fall with growing living standards. Weberians have a different explanation for the secular fall in work hours. Weber argued that workers can only expend a certain amount of labor power per day. When the work day is long they will lower the pace of work in order to make it to the end of the work day. This means that a shortening of the work day must not necessarily reduce output. The same may be produced in less time when work is more intense. The result is an improvement in productivity. Weberians assume that work time tends to fall with growing productivity. Institutionalists share a number of commonalities with Weberians. However, while Weberians focus on productivity, institutionalists stress the role of work time regulation and associated institutions (e.g., welfare systems) in determining the length and distribution of work time. The sum of institutions and regulations which have an effect on work time amount to what institutionalists call national work time regimes.

Notes

1 Neoclassical economists differ from classical economists, who perceived the question of labor supply mainly in terms of population dymanics. See Philip *et al.* (2005: 79).
2 The following pages draw heavily on Spencer's work on labor supply controversies within neoclassical economics. See Spencer (2003a: 505–13, 2003b: 235–50).
3 Hunt (2002: 252–3).
4 Jevons (1888: 173).
5 Ibid.
6 Ibid.: 197. Spencer argues that in contrast to the Austrian school, and following neoclassical economists, Jevons acknowledged that some sorts of labor could be pleasurable. But most work was naturally painful; see Spencer (2009: 71).
7 von Böhm-Bawerk (1923: 80–1).
8 See Spencer (2004: 392). Eugen Böhm-Bawerk not only rejected Jevons's theory of disutility; he also disagreed that workers can freely choose the hours they want to work. Over this specific question Böhm-Bawerk actually joined sides with Marx by arguing that hours of work are fixed by capitalists. See West (1983: 272).
9 Green (1894: 222).
10 Wicksteed (1910): 524.
11 Spencer (2009: 78).

12 Ibid.: 76. See also Wolff and Resnick (1987: 61–4). In contrast to the neoclassical assumption, leisure is hardly a good in quite the same way as any other good: leisure is limited to 24 hours a day, seven days a week, 365 days a year, and a certain number of years per life. Even more important: leisure cannot be stored. What can be stored is money which may allow the worker to buy leisure at a later point, but the worker may not reach the point when she or he has planned to use the savings to enjoy more free time. In other words, leisure, as labor power, is a fictitious commodity in the Polanyian sense.

13 Knight (1921: 117–18).

14 Ibid.

15 But, as Prasch (2008: 86) points out, they also need money to enjoy their free time: "Leisure worthy of the name is generally a 'joint product' of free time and purchasing power."

16 Jevons (1888: 181–2).

17 Nyland (1989: 17).

18 Robbins (1930: 127).

19 Ibid.

20 Hicks (1946: 117).

21 Pigou (1947: 83–4).

22 Prescott (2004).

23 Mankiw and Weinzierl (2009).

24 Prasch (2008: 85).

25 See Galbraith (1969: 243) and Robinson (1947: 121–2).

26 Reynolds *et al.* (1974: 34).

27 In fact Weber compared utility-maximizing individuals to managers, managing their lives as if they were companies; see Weber (1988: 394).

28 Weber (1930: 21).

29 Adam (1990: 112).

30 Ibid.

31 Weber (1988).

32 Ibid.: 142.

33 Ibid.: 139. The glassworks company, Zeiss, voluntarily introduced a nine-hour day in 1899; and an eight-hour day in 1900.

34 Weber (1930: 59–60).

35 Ibid.: 59–60. Weber notes that a calling is an attitude that is by "no means a product of nature. It cannot be evoked by low wages or high ones alone, but can only be the product of a long and arduous process of education."

36 Brentano (1893: 35–7).

37 Bosch and Lehndorff (2001: 213).

38 Weber (1988: 139–40).

39 Segre (2000: 154).

40 Rifkin (1987).

41 Nowotny (1994: 106–13).

42 Lallement (2003: 60–2).

43 Lallement (2008).

44 See Keynes (1963: 363). Joan Robinson criticized Keynes for sticking with the neoclassical labor supply model, despite its obvious deficiencies; see Spencer (2006: 467–8).

45 Fourastié (1965).

46 Dumazedier (1967).

47 See Aronowitz and DiFazio (1994) and Aronowitz and Cutler (1998).

48 Rifkin (1995: 13).

49 See Offe and Keane (1985), and Lash and Urry (1987).

50 See Urry (1994: 131–49), and Hassan and Purser (2007).

51 Castells (1996: 195–200).
52 Hörning *et al.* (1995).
53 Hassan (2003: 236).
54 Wolf and Mayer-Ahuja (2002).
55 Castells (1996: 441–5).
56 Bosch (2006: 47–8).
57 Copeland (1931: 70) provides an early and pointed critique of the neoclassical approach.
58 Robinson (1947: 121).
59 Philip *et al.* (2005: 82).
60 Rubery and Grimshaw (2003: 38).
61 Ibid.: 39.
62 Rubery *et al.* (1998: 72–3).
63 Anxo and O'Reilly (2000: 62–3).
64 Hermann (2014a: 118).
65 Anxo and O'Reilly (2000: 62–3).
66 Rubery and Grimshaw (2003: 166–7).
67 Rubery *et al.* (1998: 74–6).
68 Ibid.: 89.
69 Hall and Soskice (2001).
70 Ibid.: 21.
71 Bosch *et al.* (1994: 26–9).
72 Hall and Gingerich (2009: 167).
73 Ibid. The OECD notices in 1998 that "countries where collective bargaining is more developed … have shown a faster decline in work hours." The only exception in the OECD's 12 country sample is Sweden, where work hours have tended to increase since the 1980s, OECD (1998: 167).
74 Coates (2000).
75 Ibid.
76 Anxo and O'Reilly (2000: 70–6).
77 Lehndorff (2001).
78 Anxo and O'Reilly (2000: 67–8).
79 Ibid.
80 Esping-Andersen (1990).
81 Ibid.
82 Burgoon and Baxandall (2004).
83 Ibid.
84 Lewis (1992).
85 Anxo *et al.* (2006).
86 Ibid.: 102.
87 Ibid.: 102, 108.
88 Ibid.
89 van der Lippe (2010: 50, Table 3.3).
90 Ibid.
91 Geist (2005).
92 Ibid.: 30.
93 Ibid.
94 Ibid: 31, Table 3.

3   Marxist, post-Marxist, and feminist perspectives

Introduction

This chapter continues with the presentation of major approaches to work time. It covers Marxist, neo- and post-Marxist as well as feminist perspectives on the determination and development of work hours. All three approaches share the common understanding that capitalist social systems are characterized by major contradictions or fault lines – between capital and labor, capital accumulation and ecological sustainability, as well as between men and women and the gender-specific distribution of work. All three approaches, furthermore, assume that these tensions have an impact on the determination and development of work time. The chapter starts with the Marxist approach and then moves on to post-Marxist perspectives and to feminist thinking about work time.

Marxist perspectives

For Marxists the essential distinction is not between work time and non-work time, but between necessary and surplus work time. Surplus labor time is the difference between the time necessary to produce the commodities consumed by the working class for its reproduction, and the time workers spend at work. Surplus labor time depends on the length of work day and the intensity of work. It is appropriated by capital and turned into profit. Thus, while capitalists have an interest in expanding surplus labor time, workers have an interest in restricting it, usually by limiting the time they spend working. For Marxists, accordingly, the length of the work day is determined by class struggle, rather than by changing living standards, productivity, or institutional traditions.

Work time plays an essential role in Marxist political economy, one that goes beyond the determination of labor supply and the length of the work day. For Marx, as for other classical economists, labor power is the source of value of commodities produced and exchanged in capitalist societies, and work time is the measure of value.[1] Yet Marx differs from the classical school by distinguishing between necessary and surplus labor time. Necessary labor time reflects the amount of work time which is necessary to produce the means of existence that the working class needs in order to reach a certain socially defined standard of living.[2] Surplus labor time is the difference between necessary labor time and the number of hours the working class actually spends at work.[3] As legal owners of the commodities produced by workers, capitalists appropriate surplus labor time and turn surplus value into profit by selling the resulting output at a price that is higher than the value of labor power paid to their workers.

By introducing the concept of necessary and surplus labor time, Marx sets out to reveal the exploitative nature of the capitalist mode of production. The existence of surplus labor time, while obvious in pre-capitalist societies when serfs were forced to work particular days of the week or month for the landlord in addition to working the soil for their own reproduction, became increasingly blurred with the arrival of the "free" wage laborer, "free" markets, and the separation of workers from the means of production. Thus, whereas in pre-capitalist societies necessary and surplus labor existed "side-by-side" as two parts which are accurately marked off, under capitalism the two parts "glide into each other" in the sense that the laborer "in every minute works thirty seconds for himself and thirty seconds for the capitalist."[4] The result, however, is the same insofar that in both cases one class pays tribute to the other class.[5] And a process whereby one class appropriates wealth from another is commonly defined as "exploitation."[6]

With respect to the work day, the distinction between necessary and surplus labor means that for one part of the work day the worker labors for the satisfaction of his own needs and the other part for the profit of the capitalist. Marx further argues that while the part the worker labors for his or her own reproduction is more-or-less fixed, the part claimed by the capitalist is variable.[7] Accordingly, the length of the work day tends to vary in line with the duration of surplus labor, rendering it "not a fixed, but a fluent quantity."[8] This does not mean that there are no limits. The lower limit is set by the necessary part of the work day. If the worker only worked the hours necessary for his/her reproduction, "the work day would exchange for its own product, so that capital could not realize itself and hence could not maintain itself as capital."[9] The upper limit is set by physical and psychological needs; that is, by the time needed for the worker to recover his/her potential to continue working the next day. Social needs such as the need for communication, education, and emotional exchange can also play a role. However, while the lower limit is fixed the upper limit is of a "very elastic nature" (which constitutes an important analogy with nature – see below).[10]

Before the introduction of what Marx called a normal work day, capitalists persistently tested the elasticity of labor power; 16 hours and longer work days were no exception; neither was the deployment of child labor despite the negative consequences early work experiences had on the ability of workers to continue to supply their labor power in later years (see below for an analogy between the exploitation of labor power and natural resources).[11] Capitalists were in a position to test the elasticity of labor because initially the labor contract was concluded for a work day rather than for a specific number of work hours.[12] In the absence of legally binding rules, capitalists drove the end of the work day up to and beyond the natural limit, while workers, receiving little more remuneration than needed for basic survival, tried to limit hours to those that were necessary.[13] The result was a conflict of interest, based on "right against right." And, as Marx points out, "between equal rights, force decides."[14] Thus, while productivity and living standards play a role in the development of work time, Marxists assume that the length of the work day is ultimately decided by social conflict; that is, by the "struggle between collective capital, namely the class of capitalists, and collective labor, that is, the working-class."[15]

Despite dangerously long work days, Marx did not accuse capitalists of moral inadequacy like many of the social reformers of the nineteenth century did. In Marx's view the drive towards longer work hours did not depend on "the good or ill will of the individual capitalist." Rather than being the fault of individual capitalists, long hours were the result of the systemic imperative of competition.[16] Capitalists who accepted shorter work days at the expense of higher profits – risked being taken over or driven out of business by more profitable capital.[17]

While competition prevents capitalists from cutting work hours, it also makes sure that individual workers are lost when they test the power of capital (except in cases where they have certain scarce skills urgently needed by capital). As Marx notes, "the history of the regulation of the work day ... proves conclusively that the isolated worker, the worker as 'free' seller of his labor power, succumbs without resistance once capitalist production has reached a certain maturity."[18] In order to confront capital, "workers have to put their heads together" and "[act] as a class."[19] The introduction of the ten hour work day in mid-nineteenth century Britian is a telling example: capitalists resisted the demand for shorter work hours – with the "scientific" support of bourgeoisie economists – even though the introduction of a normal work day was in capital's uttermost interest.[20] Workers, too, were not able to make progress as long as they acted individually. It was only through the formation of collective "shorter hours" committees, and the alliance with other social groups – some of which supported shorter hours not so much because they liked workers but because they disliked capitalists – that enough pressure could be build to compel the British Parliament to adopt the famous Factory Acts. The result was that legislation "for the first time ... saw itself compelled to control directly and officially the labor of adults."[21]

The establishment of the normal work day put an official end to work time, but it did not prevent capital from maximizing surplus labor. Capital has two ways to increase surplus value despite the limitation of the work day: first, it can increase the work time expended in capitalist production by increasing the number of workers employed, so that "the real work day is simultaneously multiplied instead of only lengthened."[22] Second, capital can also increase surplus value by increasing the amount of commodities produced in a normal work day; that is, by increasing the "productiveness of labor."[23] This is usually achieved by substituting machines for labor and by making work more intense. Thus, as Marx points out, "the shortening of hours of labor creates, to begin with, the subjective conditions for the condensation of labor."[24] Condensation leads to a "closer filling up of the pores of the work day" and a "heightened tension of labor power."[25] As a result, the "denser hours of the ten hours' work day contains more labor, i.e., expended labor-power, than the more porous hours of the twelve hours' work day."[26]

Marx also notes that the fact that more labor is expended in a shorter amount of time means that the quantity of labor cannot only be measured in terms of its duration; in addition labor now "acquires a measure of its intensity or of the degree of its condensation or density."[27] For workers this means that the struggle over surplus labor must not only focus on the length of the work day. It should also address the intensity of work. The problem is that there is no objective measurement of work intensity.[28] Productivity (output per working hour) is often used as a proxy for work intensity, but in theory productivity can also increase without an intensification of work. Workers occasionally demand measures that protect them from the expected work intensification that usually accompanies a reduction in work hours.

While Marx calls the surplus value created by a prolongation and multiplication of the work day *absolute surplus value*, the reduction of necessary work time and the corresponding decrease in the value of labor power constitutes an increase in *relative surplus value*.[29] The increase in relative surplus value corresponds to what in mainstream theory is described as a growth in productivity. However, while Weberians and others welcome an increase in productivity because it allows the economy to produce the same amount of output with less work effort, Marx insists that the object of all development of the productiveness of labor is not to produce the same output with less effort, but "to shorten that part of the work day during which the workman must labor for his own benefit, and by that very shortening, to lengthen the other part of the day, during which he is at liberty to work gratis for the capitalist."[30] The goal, in other words, is to cheapen the commodities used by workers for their reproduction, and by that very cheapening increase the proportion of surplus claimed by capital.[31]

The dramatic shortening of necessary work time, or the spectacular increase in productivity, distinguishes capitalism from earlier economic systems and from systems that existed along with capitalism. Yet the reason is not the alleged superior rationality. The reason is that the same forces that prevent individual capitalists from reducing the work day compel them to adopt the newest production technology in order to assure that the work time inherent in their commodities does not exceed average necessary work time – since failing to do so results in a loss rather than a profit.[32]

Marx agrees with Weber when he argues that a reduction of work time brings about an intensification of work, and that consequently a point must be reached where the extension of the work day and the intensity of the labor mutually exclude each other in such a way that "the lengthening of the work day becomes compatible only with a lower degree of intensity, and a higher degree of intensity only with a shortening of the work day."[33] But Marx strongly doubts that capitalists themselves will voluntarily shorten the work day as productivity grows. As Alfredo Saad-Filho points out, there is a contradiction between the collective interest of capital and the interests of individual capitalists. While collective capital profits from a limitation of work time because shorter hours protect the source of surplus value, boost productivity, and help to preserve economic stability, individual capitalists may lose potential to extend surplus value.[34] As a result, work hours and productivity can increase simultaneously. Marx specifically refers to the Industrial Revolution in Britain which led to a rise rather than a fall in work hours, as might have been expected from the introduction of new machinery and the following leap forward in productivity. Yet instead of encouraging capitalists to shorten the work day, new machinery induced them to make their workers stay longer.

The reason was that longer work days allowed for longer machine operating times. And capitalists prolonged machine operating times in order to shorten the period necessary for the amortization of the new investments. Thus, far from bringing about shorter work days, new machinery has a tendency to "sweep away every moral and natural restriction on the length of the workday."[35] However, the problem is not machinery as such. The problem is the fact that the machinery is owned by capitalists. In the hands of capital, "the most powerful instrument for shortening labor time, becomes the most unfailing means for placing every moment of the laborer's time ... at the disposal of the capitalist."[36] This was the experience of the Industrial Revolution until the introduction of the normal work day. After the introduction of a compulsory work time limit, capitalists invented new and increasingly flexible shift systems in order to keep their machines running.[37]

Marx not only insists that capitalists themselves do not reduce work time if not forced to do so by the working class (even if it is in their own interest), he also fundamentally disagrees with Weber's notion of capitalist rationality. In Marx's view, the capitalist production process is not only contradictory because it is based on class exploitation, but also the fact that one class consumes less than it produces causes a host of problems for the realization of surplus value – and, consequently, recurring social crisis with disastrous effects for workers who depend on their jobs as their only source of income. With regard to work time, the contradictory nature of capitalism causes capital to constantly create as much labor as possible while at the same time reducing necessary labor to an absolute minimum; or "to make human labor (relatively) superfluous, so as to drive it, as human labor, towards infinity."[38] The result is a persistent compression and extension of time, which is not only felt by those without employment, but also by those workers who still have a job. As a result of the crisis-prone development of capitalism, work hours also depend on the changing rate of accumulation, with total hours rising during boom phases and declining during the following recessions.[39]

While compulsory work time reduction can curb capital's tendency to expand the total sum of work time, the introduction of a normal work day creates a new problem for surplus maximization. Although mechanization and automation of the production process extends the proportion of surplus labor time in relation to necessary labor time, the substitution of constant for variable capital at the same time reduces the amount of labor expended in the capitalist production process and henceforth shrinks the source of surplus value (labor power is the only source of surplus value since in a state of perfect competition all material ingredients exchange exactly for their value). In Marx's words, the growing deployment of machinery "converts what was formerly variable capital, invested in labor power, into machinery which, being constant capital, does not produce surplus value."[40] The result is a general tendency for the rate of surplus value, or profit, to fall in line with growing technological progress.

In this situation capital can still fall back on the second strategy of increasing absolute surplus value – the multiplication of work days. Yet the multiplication of work days depends on an expansion of production, which, again, depends on growing commodity markets and the commodification of previously uncommodified spheres of life. This was essentially what happened during the long postwar boom: the potential reduction of necessary work time following from a dramatic increase in productivity, was balanced by an expansion of consumption. In other words, although each commodity embodied a radically shortened amount of labor time, the growing number of commodities made sure that the total sum of surplus value was not diminishing. For this strategy to work, however, wages had to rise. Since the value of labor power is not only equal to necessary work time but also to wages, expanding the total sum of the wages paid to the working class results in a stabilization of necessary work time despite an increase in productivity (given that all wages are spent on consumption). Yet the same competitive pressures which prevent capitalists from reducing work hours make them hesitant to increase wages – even if it is in their own interest. While capitalists depend on affluent consumers in order to sell their products, they want their own workers to earn as little as possible. It required strong trade unions, influential working class parties, and a viable and available communist alternative in Europe and Asia to secure rising living standards during the postwar decades.

The French Regulation School has called the postwar mode of mediating capitalist contradictions Fordism. In this system "[a] social norm of working-class consumption is formed, which becomes an essential determinant of the extension of the wage relation, as a fundamental modality of relative surplus value."[41] Retrospectively, capital maintained profits by accepting rising worker living standards; that is, by enabling them to buy houses, cars, and other mass-produced goods. Thus there is a connection between income and work hours, but not necessarily a positive one from a Marxist point of view:

[T]he systematic propensity of capitalists to encourage consumption rather than a reduction of work hours can be explained by their need to expand incessantly the mass of production (mass of surplus labor) while compressing, in relation to it, the number of workers employed (the total time of necessary labor).[42]

On the other hand the stagnation and decline in (real) wages which followed the end of the postwar boom has caused workers to compensate for the decline in the value of labor power by putting in more work hours.[43] As described in Chapter 10, this not only refers to individual work hours, but especially to paid hours put in by working families. As Samuel Bowles *et al.* note,

> average hours per capita declined fairly steadily until the early 1960s – as workers and households were able to take advantage of the rising wage and salary income. Average hours rose in the mid 1960s when real earnings growth began to slow down. They have risen most rapidly since the mid 1970s as households have tried to stave off the squeeze of real earnings.[44]

The postwar boom was not only exceptional for the unprecedented growth in living standards that accompanied it, it was also exceptional for the historically low rates of unemployment. While exceptional growth rates are primarily responsible for low unemployment, repeated work time reductions in this period also contributed to the confinement of the "structural excess of labor power," or what in the postwar decades was defined as "technological unemployment."[45] Weberians make a similar argument when they assume that work hours decrease in line with growing productivity. However, while Weberians assume that work hours decrease automatically, Marxists insist that both shorter hours and lower unemployment are the result of workers' struggles. As described in Chapters 8 and 9, trade unions not only fought for shorter work hours to ensure more free time for their members, they did so also as a way of tackling unemployment.

Beverly Silver, in her world history of labor unrest, distinguishes between Marx-type and Polanyi-type worker struggles. The first category is directed against capitalist exploitation – that is, the act of surplus extraction – while the second category is aimed at limiting the negative consequences of the establishment of markets, most notably the market for labor (impressively described by Karl Polanyi in this major work *The Great Transformation*).[46] The struggle for shorter work hours fits into both categories. Workers not only demanded shorter hours to resist exploitation, but also to fight unemployment by sharing available work among a larger group of workers (see Chapters 8 and 9). In the latter case, shorter work hours are a form of labor market regulation. As such they are part of a broader movement against commodification. The commodification of labor power entailed a process in which workers had to be stripped of all forms of social security. Only when the evolving proletarians had no alternative to selling their labor power were they willing to accept the harsh conditions of capitalist labor markets. Initially, workers were hired on a daily basis and had no support when they were sick or old. It was only through the establishment of protective regulations that proletarians were able to (re)gain a certain degree of security (in Karl Polanyi's terminology, markets were re-embedded).[47] To the extent that they limit market mechanisms, such regulations – including the establishment of a normal work day – amount to a gradual decommodification of labor power (bearing in mind that labor power must always be a commodity in capitalism).[48]

Yet while standardization of work hours is part of a decommodification process (work hours are determined outside the market), current attempts to make work hours more flexible can be interpreted as a move towards recommodification (work hours are made more responsive to market forces).

Neo- and post-Marxist perspectives

While classical Marxists perceived the struggle for shorter working hours primarily as a means to limit capitalist exploitation, neo-Marxists like André Gorz saw the reduction of work time more as a way out of the accelerating alienation inherent in the capitalist mode of production as well as consumption. Hence, for Gorz and other neo-Marxists the struggle for higher wages may reduce the rate of exploitation but in contrast to the struggle for shorter work hours it does not hinder capitalist accumulation and therefore does not challenge capitalist domination. Post-Marxists advocated shorter working hours as a means of breaking with the ever-expanding capitalist cycle of production and consumption, a cycle which not only fuels alienation but also destroys natural resources and the environment.

Class struggle did not translate into a radical shortening of the work day, as one might expect from Marx's writings. Neither did the growth in productivity and the increase in living standards. In the 1960s and 1970s (male) workers in many countries were still working 40 hours a week, and before the arrival of the postwar crisis many were putting in additional overtime hours. Trade unions have often favored wage increases over shorter work hours, reflecting their members' alleged preference for consumption.[49] In the 1960s Gorz and other neo-Marxists started to advocate shorter work hours as a means to free labor from the double alienation caused by work and consumption – with both processes greatly accelerating in the last phase of the postwar expansion. Gorz (as Marx) saw as the root of alienation the separation of workers from the means of production and capital's subsequent control over labor and the production processes. Alienation intensified during the postwar decades, fueled by an increasing division of labor. As a result, unskilled and semi-skilled workers became mere "adjuncts to the machinery," while skilled laborers remained "passive operators" in the accumulation process.[50] Gorz argues that it is precisely because workers are denied their creative potential at work that it is here that they feel most isolated; the only place left for them to develop their potential is in the sphere of non-work, in the realm of consumption:

> It is on the basis of their initial pre-conditioning, that neo-capitalism is able to play upon passive, individual consumer-needs, offering ever more complex and sophisticated ways of satisfying them, developing the need to *escape*, and selling the means of forgetting, of distraction from the pressures of industrial organization.[51]

Gorz concludes that the struggle against exploitation must become a conscious struggle against the social consequences of exploitation – a struggle against the false priorities, the waste and deprivation imposed on society by affluent consumption: "to struggle against the exploitation of labor is necessarily to struggle against the purposes of which labor is exploited."[52]

Gorz vehemently contested the view that workers prefer higher wages over shorter work hours in order to be able to spend more money for consumption. Instead, he interpreted workers' wage claims as "revolts against the systematic mutilation of the workers' personality, against the stunting of his professional and human faculties, against the subordination of the nature and content of his working life to technological developments." Workers demand as much money as possible to "pay for the life wasted, the time lost, the freedom alienated in working under these conditions."[53] And they demand more money – rather than more free time – because that was the preferred objective of trade union bargaining. Trade unions, in Gorz's view, have little interest in shorter work hours because they represent workers at the workplace – and not at home.[54] Employers, on the other hand, have a strong interest in maintaining and expanding workers' consumption in order to sustain economic growth. To fuel growth in capitalist societies, wage earners cannot simply reduce their work hours; instead they "must work and earn beyond their felt needs, so that a growing proportion of income may be spent on consumption determined by no need."[55]

As a result, wage demands present a dead end for workers' struggles for emancipation. Gorz is very outspoken in this regard:

> Wage claims as such allow industry to manufacture a new proletariat: a lobotomized proletariat, whose eight hours of daily degradation and work against the clock leaves them with only the weary desire to escape – an escape which manipulators of leisure and culture sell them on credit in their homes while they convince them that they are living in the best of all possible worlds.[56]

Yet far from creating the best possible world, production in capitalism serves the accumulation of profit. The purpose, in other words, is to produce objects "which can be sold for a maximum profit, no matter what their usefulness or lack of it."[57] The focus on profit, accordingly, not only determines what is produced but also how it is produced. While "creative work is stunted by considerations of financial profitability, millions of work hours are squandered, in the process of neo-capitalist competition, on often minor but always expensive modifications to consumer goods."[58] Thus, Gorz concludes that it is "impossible to break this vicious circle by confining politics to a quantitative level of consumer demands."[59]

While initially Gorz emphasized the need for workers' self-control in the sphere of production, he increasingly argued for the reduction of work time as a means to break out from the vicious circle of work and consumption: "In their free time individuals cease to be workers; the desire for free time is precisely the desire for self-definition through other activities, values and relationships than those of work."[60] The promotion of free time has two crucial effects: on the one hand it restricts affluent consumption to what Gorz calls fundamental or felt needs; on the other it creates room for autonomous activities and production which is not subordinated to the goal of maximizing profit and thus is driven by the desire for use values rather than exchange values. Thus the demand to work less frees up time, but it does not necessarily mean more rest: "It means the right to do many more things for ourselves that money cannot buy."[61] To promote such autonomous activities Gorz in his later work emphasized the need to combine a policy of work time reduction with the provision of a guaranteed basic income available for those who are not in paid employment.[62] Gorz is very clear about the nature and consequences of his proposals: "It is a negation and rejection of law and order, power and authority, in the name of the inalienable right to control one's own life."[63]

In the 1970s, the capitalist obsession with growth was fundamentally shaken by two consecutive oil price shocks. Although the restriction of oil and the following price increases were caused by political events, it demonstrated the extent to which the Western growth and consumption model was dependent on access to cheap oil. Around the same time a group of intellectuals known as the Club of Rome published a widely read report in which they argued that the limited availability of natural resources, including oil, meant that the established growth model could not go on forever.[64] Gorz, early on, took up the growing ecological concerns and argued that a reduction in work time was not only the key to limit workers' alienation. In connection with the resulting restriction of affluent consumption and the expansion of autonomous use-value-oriented activities, shorter work hours were also essential for the establishment of an alternative, ecologically sustainable, social model: a "policy of free choice of work hours, expanded possibilities of self-determined activity and democratization of economic decision-making are the only paths which lead in freedom to a more frugal, ecological sustainable consumer model."[65]

Although Gorz advocated a policy of self-restraint he did not criticize affluence per se – at one point he even condemned the "poverty of affluence" in Western consumer societies.[66] Instead he argued for a different form of satisfying human needs: "It is possible to live better by working and consuming less, provided we produce more durable things as well as things which do not destroy the environment or create insurmountable scarcities once everyone has access to them."[67]

In the 1980s the demand for shorter work hours became part of an emerging ecological agenda, and as such started to resonate with progressive groups outside the labor movement, including the newly formed Green parties in Europe. Apart from Gorz, another post-Marxist writer who championed the reduction of work time as a means to promote a sustainable economic development, was Alain Lipietz.[68] Yet while Gorz demanded a reduction of work hours without a reduction in wages, Lipietz argued that a reduction in hours would partly have to be paid for by a consequential loss in income (although he also argued for an increase in the statutory French minimum income rate).[69] As Lipietz notes, "the biggest obstacle to happiness is not a lack of 'having' but a lack of 'being'," and he therefore argues that "we must learn to produce and consume in moderation."[70]

In the subsequent debates on sustainable development the reduction of work hours was less advocated as a means to liberate workers from the double alienation of work and consumption, and more as a method to discipline workers and limit the destructive effects of their excessive consumption behavior. In a book entitled *Sharing the Work, Sparing the Planet*, Anders Hayden notes that "consumption levels in the North have led to global problems such as a build-up of greenhouse gases, the depletion of the ozone layer, exhaustion of fisheries, unprecedented species extinction, the loss of forests and more." His solution to the problem is clear:

> [T]he affluent in the North need to begin taking responsibility for finding ways of reducing our resource consumption. Perhaps the most obvious response to this issue is to say that people in the North must simply reduce their material standard of living.[71]

The ecologist critique of consumerism partly converged with a critical approach that can be traced back to the work of Thorstein Veblen. In contrast to Marx and Weber, who assumed that living standards were constant or changing only gradually, Veblen observed a tendency of rising consumption associated with a desire to conform to a specific social group and move up the ladder of social status.[72] Veblen, furthermore, noted that a lot of this consumption was conspicuous and wasteful, going far beyond the elementary physical wants that have long been provided for.[73] In the late 1960s, John Kenneth Galbraith noted that work hours have increased rather than declined, as might have been expected from rising living standards. He argued that long work hours, including large amounts of overtime, are the result of the industrial system's capacity to persuade people that goods are more important than leisure.[74]

Some 20 years later, Juliet Schor provided a similar critique in her widely read book *The Overworked American: The Unexpected Decline of Leisure*. She argued that the unexpected decline in leisure is the result of an insidious work-and-spend cycle.[75] In her later publications she increasingly emphasized the disastrous effects of consumerism on the environment and the resulting ecological crisis.[76] Based on a large-scale empirical study, she argued that countries with shorter working hours tend to have lower carbon dioxide emissions. Hence, "reduced working hours could contribute to sustainability by decreasing the scale of both production and consumption."[77] Schor shares a lot of the Marxist critique voiced by Gorz and others. The difference is that she believes in the possibility of overcoming consumerism and the ecological crisis without abandoning capitalism, while Gorz was convinced that the combination of shorter hours and less consumption threatens "the linchpins of a social order established nearly two centuries ago."[78]

While acknowledging the disastrous effects of consumerism, some ecologists, who continued to call themselves Marxists, insisted that the problem is not the workers' consumption but capital's exploitation of labor and nature. Paul Burkett, among others, emphasizes similarities in the treatment of labor power and nature as resources in the capitalist production process (in a chapter entitled

"Marx's Work-Day Analysis and Environmental Crisis").[79] Marx argues that capital, in its "were-wolf hunger for surplus labor ... oversteps the merely physical maximum bounds of the work day."[80] He further notes that

> capital cares nothing for the length of life of labor power. All that concerns it is simply and solely the maximum labor power that can be rendered fluent in a workday. It attains this end by shortening the extent of the laborer's life, as a greedy farmer snatches increased produce of the soil by robbing it of its fertility"[81]

By doing so, capital not only accepts the worker's "physical and mental degradation" and her "premature death" but also risks destroying the very source of its wealth, surplus labor.[82]

Capital treats nature very much like labor. As with labor power, nature needs time to reproduce itself, but in both cases the limit is highly elastic (in Polanyi's terms both are "fictitious commodities"). Thus, Burkett notes, "capital abuses the elastic limits of the laborer's recuperative powers as much as it abuses the absorptive capacity and resilience of particular ecosystems, in both cases leading to the vitiation of natural forces."[83] The analogy can already be found in Marx's writings on labor and land. As Marx notes, the future can be "anticipated and ruined in both cases by premature overexertion and exhaustion."[84] In both cases, however, capital was able to postpone the destructive effects of its practices by tapping new pools of resources – new labor power and new land – while ultimately only social struggles waged by non-capitalists can save capital from self-destruction:

> [T]he limiting of factory labor was dictated by the same necessity which spread guano over the English fields. The same blind eagerness for plunder that in the one case exhausted the soil, had, in the other, torn up by the roots of the living force of the nation. Periodical epidemics speak on this point as clearly as the diminishing military standard in Germany and France.[85]

In order to prevent the environmental collapse, struggles for sustainable development can therefore not restrict themselves to demanding for the introduction of adequate market incentives. Instead, environmental struggles, like the struggle for a compulsory limitation of the work day, must contest "the blind rule of the supply and demand laws" (the political economy of the bourgeoisie) and propose as an alternative a "social production controlled by social foresight" (the political economy of the working class).[86]

Feminist perspectives

As for Marxists, for feminists the crucial distinction is not between work time and non-work time; but for these the distinction between necessary and surplus labor time is equally unsatisfying. Instead, feminists have emphasized the existence of unpaid labor provided by women in family households. Not all non-work time is automatically leisure. The reproduction of labor power not only demands for periods of rest and recovery, but also involves the performance of a number of activities that are as exhausting, and sometimes as cumbersome or painful, as paid labor. Such activities include cleaning, the purchase of commodities, laundry, and the preparation of meals, as well as the provision of emotional support for and the caring of children and parents. In the case of male workers who live within families, many of these activities are carried out not by the laborers themselves, but by female household members, perhaps the brunt of it being borne by their spouses. In turn, the number of hours women spend in paid employment is dependent upon their reproductive duties as wives, mothers, and daughters.

Interestingly, the issue of domestic work received increasing attention as more women entered the labor markets of the 1960s and 1970s. As recalled by Susan Himmelweit, the promotion of the concept of unpaid work enabled the feminist movement to address a number of related issues including the recognition of the value of women's work within the household, the explanation of the absence of women from the labor market and much of public life, and the significance of women's reproductive work to the economy as a whole, as well as the discrimination and disadvantaging of women in paid employment: "What all these aims had in common was a desire to validate and make visible the contribution of women made in the home, by recognizing it as 'work'."[87]

The exclusion of women from paid work – women only worked for money until they were married or gave birth to their first child – made sure that hardly anybody imagined that "the terms applied to men's employment outside the home should apply to women's activities in the home."[88] However, with growing female labor market participation in the 1960s and 1970s the distinction became increasingly blurred. When two sorts of activities are carried out by the same person, and when they share a series of common characteristics – women were often employed in jobs with tasks similar to those faced in family care – it became difficult to explain why similar activities on one occasion counted as work and were paid, and on another did not count as work and were unpaid. As Himmelweit notes, "when women's paid labor visibly enters into society's division of labor through the market, the fact that their unpaid labor in the home is part of a household-based division of labor is also, if not so transparently, posed."[89] And if one accepts, as increasingly was by social scientists of the 1960s and 1970s, that at least part of household activity qualifies as work, the work day of women has two parts – the time spent on paid work outside the home and the time spent on domestic labor at home. For women, thus, the number of hours they put in doing their paid jobs is directly linked to the number of unpaid hours they spend working at home – rather than following from a trade-off between income and leisure, the intensity of work, or the struggle between capital and labor. As a result of their domestic responsibilities, women frequently work part-time and/or interrupt their careers and even leave the labor market and become full-time housewives.

Neoclassical economists acknowledged that not all non-work is automatically leisure, but upheld their utility-maximizing paradigm.[90] To do so, they substituted the family for the individual. The family in neoclassical terms is seen as an "economic unit, which shares consumption and allocates production at home and in the market."[91] Accordingly it is no longer the individual worker who contemplates the trade-off between more income and more commodities – it is the family, with the additional possibility of substituting home-produced goods for commodities purchased on the market. The important difference to an individual utility function is that an increase in income obtained by one partner may result in an increase of time spent outside the market by the other partner. As Jacob Mincer notes

> an increase in the market wage rate for some family members makes both the consumption of leisure and the production of home services by that individual more costly to the family, and will as a matter of rational family decision encourage greater market labor input by him (her).[92]

As it is usually the male partner who receives higher compensation in the labor market, it is perfectly rational in this system of thought that men put in long hours while women stay at home and take care of the household.

For neoclassical economists higher male wages are the result of higher productivity following from higher investment in human capital (education), greater work experience, and the performance of longer hours. Lower female efficiency is the result of lower education, frequent interruptions in employment, and less work experience, as well as a lower commitment to the job. The fact that frequent interruptions and less commitment may have more to do with women's domestic responsibilities hardly occurred to neoclassical economists – and if it did occurr, as occasionally in Gary Becker's writings, they failed to draw adequate conclusions.[93] Becker argues that the sexual division of work follows not from more, or less, but from different investments in human capital.[94] Women tend to invest in human capital that raises "household efficiency" whereas men invest in human capital that increases "market efficiency."[95] Due to their specific "comparative advantages" it is only rational that men specialize in the market sector and women in the household sector. Although Becker emphasizes that "differences in efficiency are not determined by biological or other intrinsic differences" his argumentation remains biologically determined because the alleged female investment pattern still follows from the biological function of child bearing and rearing.[96]

For Marxists, the fact that women perform unpaid labor in working class households posed other important questions: are women reproducing men creating surplus value claimed by capital, with the result that they are also exploited by capital? Or are women performing domestic labor being exploited by their male partners?[97] The search for answers to these questions stood at the heart of the "domestic labor debate" in the 1970s and 1980s.[98] From the various contributions to the debate three main positions can be identified. The first position conceives unpaid domestic work as a hidden part of the capitalist wage-labor relation. In this view unpaid domestic work is an unpaid extension of the work day acquired by capital. As Mariarosa Dalla Costa and Selma James note, the wage commands "a larger amount of labor than appeared in the factory bargaining."[99] However, as Wally Seccombe adds, to the extent that the wage form mystifies capitalist exploitation of the male laborer – he receives only part of the value of labor power – it also obscures domestic labor's relation to capital: "The fact that the product of her labor is embodied in another person does not allow for a clear perception of its appropriation by capital, and consequently of her relation to capital."[100] Accordingly the family functions as "a distributive mechanism through which wages can be imagined to extend to the nonwaged, underwaged, not-yet-waged, and no-longer-waged."[101] Yet the family not only allows capital to pay only for a fraction of the real work day; it also absorbs economic shocks and other irregularities in the wage-based economy.[102]

A second position challenges this view and argues that women performing domestic work do, indeed, create value – but use value, not exchange value. The products of domestic work are "not directed towards the market but are for immediate consumption within the family."[103] Although it is true that the working class housewives contribute to the (re)production of labor power, the sale of which guarantees their existence and through this process participate in social production and exchange, what mediates this participation and this exchange is not the market but the marriage contract.[104] By creating use values for family reproduction, women, furthermore, perform necessary labor even though the labor does not qualify as necessary labor in the sense of Marx's concept of socially necessary labor.[105]

Marx's concept of socially necessary labor only reflects the average abstract work time embodied in commodities consumed by the working class. This caused him to argue that the real wage must be fixed for a given level of subsistence.[106] Yet as Jean Gardiner points out, "a historically determined subsistence level ... can be achieved by varying the contributions to it of commodities purchased out of wages on the one hand and domestic labor performed by housewives on the other.[107] In other words, an increase in domestic work can save money which otherwise would have been spend in the market.[108] Gardiner subsequently argues that necessary labor is in fact variable and that unpaid domestic labor can, indeed, have an impact on surplus labor – but not as an extension of the work day, rather the effect is "keeping down necessary labor to the level that is lower than the actual subsistence level of the working class."[109]

A third position holds the view that domestic labor is performed outside capitalist value relations as part of a patriarchal mode of production. This has important consequences for the female work day. According to Nancy Folbre, in the history of capitalist development it is not uncommon that non-capitalist modes of production have existed alongside the capitalist one (e.g., feudalism and capitalism). Folbre defines a patriarchal mode of production as a

> distinctive set of social relations, including but by no means limited to control over the means of production that structures the exploitation of women and/or children by men within a social formation that may include other modes of production, none of which is necessarily dominant.[110]

The marriage contract, like the employment contract, is a contract concluded between free individuals. But as much as the employment contract obstructs exploitation in capitalist production, so does the marriage contract in patriarchal reproduction. In both cases one party receives more than it gives to the other: "To say that a class is the beneficiary of a transfer of surplus labor time is to say that its members consume more embodied labor than they perform."[111] As Folbre further points out, "numerous time-budget studies showing that women work much longer than men, when household as well as wage labor are taken into account, suggest that patriarchal exploitation can be analyzed in quantitative terms."[112] For the length of the female work day this means that it also, and perhaps even primarily, depends on the exploitation of women by their male partners and their ability to resist such abuse.[113]

From the Marxist-feminist analysis of unpaid domestic labor, it follows that the struggle over surplus labor time cannot be separated from the struggle over compensation and distribution of social labor time. However, because non-wage labor is mainly carried out by women, here women struggle against men rather than labor against capital. The gender struggle over the extent and distribution of paid and unpaid work time takes place on two different levels: within the family as distribution of household responsibilities between men and women (this can result in the hiring of a paid home helper who takes care of the domestic work); or on the terrain of the welfare state where private and non-waged but necessary work can be transformed into waged and public employment. Parts of reproductive work, as a result, are not only socialized in the sense that such work is provided outside the household (through the market); it is socialized in a deeper sense as it has been transformed from a private to a public responsibility. As Elisabeth Hagen and Jane Jenson note, "social services, including the provision of care for the elderly, childcare and other services for dependants, mitigated the traditional family responsibilities of women and allowed them to work outside the home for wages."[114]

In this regard the Nordic welfare states made the greatest progress during the postwar period. They not only have a high proportion of women in paid employment, paid and unpaid work time is also more evenly distributed between men and women than in other welfare systems (see Chapter 7). At this point the feminist approach to work time converges with institutional approaches described above which explain the varying length and distribution of work hours by different family and welfare state arrangements. On the other hand, some feminists who remained close to the Marxist framework noted that rising female employment rates during the postwar decades were not only an act of emancipation; from the 1970s onwards, increasing female labor market participation was also a response to stagnating or falling real wages.[115]

Summary

For Marxists the length of the work day is primarily determined by class and social struggles. The reason is that for Marx work is not only the source of income to be spent for consumption (what he calls necessary work time), it is also the source of surplus value and of capitalist profit. As a result workers want to reduce the work day to the necessary part, while capitalists have an interest in extending it to maximize profits. Marx acknowledges that the intensification of work allows capital to press out more surplus value in a shorter amount of time. But in contrast to Weber, who assumes that employers would voluntarily shorten the work day, Marx argues that competition prevents individual capitalists from reducing work time. Instead it is the workers, through their collective struggle, who compel capital to limit work time. Neo-Marxists question the assumption that growing working class strength automatically results in shorter work time and emphasize the role of consumption in inducing workers to put in longer than necessary hours. Rather than falling in line with growing living standards, increasing consumption makes sure that work hours remain long despite substantial gains in productivity. Post-Marxists make unnecessary or conspicuous consumption responsible for the environmental crisis and propose the consumption of free time as an ecological sustainable alternative. For feminists the length of the work day is neither determined by rising living standards, nor by growing productivity and class struggle. For women the number of hours they spend in paid employment depends on the number of unpaid hours they work at home. This has two consequences: first, the combined work days of women tend to be longer than those of men (meaning that women are not only exploited by capital, but also by their male partners). Second, in order to reconcile their paid job with their unpaid family responsibilities many women work part-time rather than full-time.

Notes

1   Heinrich (2001).
2   See Marx (1967: 217); and Philip (2001: 29).
3   See Marx (1973: 399). Harvey (2000: 20) labels it as "the difference between what labor gets … and what labor creates."
4   See Marx (1967) and Marx (1973).
5   In Marx's words, "[w]herever a part of society possesses the monopoly of the means of production, the laborer, free or not free, must add to the working-time necessary for self-maintenance an extra working-time in order to produce the means of subsistence for the owners of the means of production"; ibid. (1967): 235.
6   See Resnick and Wolff (2006: 144). See also Saad-Filho (2002: 46–8).
7   Marx did not necessarily believe that the living standard of the working class did not change. Michael Lebowitz argues that Marx did so, in *Capital*, to focus on the link between the augmentation of relative surplus value and improvements in productivity. Marx planned to give up this assumption in a book on wage labor, planned but never completed. See Lebowitz (2003: 44–50).
8   Marx (1973: 324).
9   Ibid.: 324.
10 Marx (1967: 232).
11 Ibid.: 237.
12 In pre-capitalist modes of production, darkness imposed a natural limit to the work day. It was only with the invention of factories and modern artificial lightning that workers could be forced to work almost around the clock.
13 Marx (1967: 235).
14 Ibid.

15 Ibid.
16 "Free competition brings out the inherent laws of capitalist production, in the shape of external coercive laws having power over every individual capitalist" (ibid.: 270).
17 As Lebowitz (2003: 82) notes, "capital's tendency to increase the workday ... is manifested through the efforts of individual capitals to lower their costs of production relative to other individual capitals in the context of competition."
18 Marx (1967: 299).
19 Ibid.: 302.
20 Senior William Nassau was a prominent English economist. Nassau vigorously argued against the introduction of the ten-hour day. He argued that profit is made in the last hour of the work day and that a one hour reduction would therefore eliminate profit and destroy the whole of British industry. Marx ridiculed Senior's argumentation as "Senior's Last Hour" in a specific section of *Capital*.
21 Marx (1967: 282).
22 Marx (1973: 386).
23 Marx(1967: 324).
24 Ibid.: 406.
25 Ibid.: 410.
26 Ibid.
27 Ibid.
28 However, there are various subjective measurements based on individual judgments.
29 Marx (1967: 19, 315).
30 Ibid.: 321.
31 Lebowitz (2003: 107).
32 See Marx (1967: 319). As John Weeks notes, "socially determined normal labor time exists 'behind the backs' of each capitalist, and without entering the consciousness of capitalists regulates their production." See Weeks 1981: 48).
33 Marx (1967: 409).
34 Saad-Filho (2002: 109).
35 Marx (1967: 408).
36 Ibid.
37 In more recent years, the interest in greater (fixed) capital utilization has led to a decoupling of operating times and working hours. As a result, countries can compensate shorter work days with longer operating hours. See Lei Delsen (2007).
38 Marx (1973: 399).
39 Botwinick (1993: 74–5).
40 Marx (1967: 407).
41 Aglietta (1979: 152). See also: Fine (1998: 180–6).
42 Basso (2003: 211).
43 Botwinick (1993: 73). See also Bowles *et al.* (1990: 38).
44 Bowles *et al.* (1990).
45 Hinrichs *et al.* (1982).
46 Silver (2003: 17–20).
47 See Polanyi (1957: 251) and Castel (1995).
48 Albritton (2007: 42–3).
49 See Gorz (1982: 134):

> Since its birth, the labor movement has always struggled to reduce work time. Marx considered it as the "fundamental imperative".... Workers of the whole world were called upon by their trade unions to refuse to do more than eight hours a day from 1 May 1906. Three quarters of a century later, it is the struggle to free time that the labor movement made the least progress.

50 Gorz (1966: 318).
51 Ibid.: 349.

52 Gorz (1969: 56).
53 Gorz (1966: 319).
54 Gorz (1989: 15).
55 Ibid.: 119.
56 Gorz (1966: 320).
57 Ibid.: 344. Gorz argues that Marx was well aware that "capitalism needs to shape subjects for the objects to be marketed"; see Gorz (1969: 70). But he could not have imagined the ability to "raise the level of consumption without raising the rate of satisfaction"; see Gorz (1989: 115).
58 Gorz (1966: 344).
59 Ibid.: 349.
60 Gorz (1989: 16).
61 Gorz (1982: 2–3).
62 Gorz (1999: 80–5).
63 Gorz (1982: 11, 133).
64 Meadows *et al.* (1972).
65 Gorz (1994: 42).
66 Gorz (1980: 41):

> The connection between "more" and "better" has been broken. "Better" may now mean doing with less. It is possible to live better by working and consuming less, provided we produce more durable things as well as things which do not destroy the environment or create insurmountable scarcities once everyone has access to them. Social production should be reserved for those things which remain useful to each when distributed to all – and vice versa.

67 Ibid.: 41.
68 See Lipietz (1992: 77–91). While Lipietz broke with what he calls Marxist productivism (see the debate in the Journal *Capitalism, Nature, Socialism* (2000) Volume 11, No. 1 and 2), Gorz became a post-Marxist insofar as in his later work he rejected substantial parts of Marxist value theory. See also Hermann (2009: 275–89).
69 Gorz (1994: 102–17).
70 Ibid.: 85.
71 Hayden (1999: 14–15).
72 See Veblen and Banta (2007: 70–1). Interestingly, Veblen argues that the superior owning classes show their wealth by refusing to work and celebrating leisure. It is only in the lower classes, whose wealth depends on actual labor, that (conspicuous) consumption becomes more important as a means of social differentiation than leisure. See ibid.: 57.
73 Ibid.: 75.
74 Galbraith (1969: 365–7). Galbraith consequently argued that the move towards shorter hours demands an emancipation of workers from the management of their wants. Particularly striking in this regard is the development of a leisure industry. With the leisure industry even free time becomes a commodity that has to be paid for through income gained from working.
75 Schor (1991); see also and Schor (1998), and Bowles and Park (2005).
76 Schor (2010).
77 Knight *et al.* (2012: 11).
78 Gorz (1982: 11, 133).
79 Burkett (1999: 133–43).
80 Marx (1967: 265).
81 Ibid.: 265.
82 Ibid.: 270.
83 Burkett (1999: 135).
84 Marx (1969: 309).

85 See Burkett (1999: 142–3), and Marx (1967: 239).
86 Marx (1983: 362).
87 Himmelweit (1995: 1).
88 Ibid.
89 Ibid.: 8.
90 Mincer (1980: 43):

> The logical complement of leisure time is work broadly construed, whether it includes remunerative production in the market or work that is currently "not paid for". The latter includes various forms of investment in oneself and the production of goods and services for the home and the family.
>
> See also Mincer and Polachek (1980: 169)

91 Mincer (1980: 43).
92 Ibid.
93 Becker (1991), 77:

> Whatever the reason for the traditional division – perhaps discrimination against women or high fertility – household responsibilities lower the earnings and affect the jobs of married women by reducing their time in the labor force and discouraging their investment in market capital.

94 See ibid., especially Chapter 2, "Division of Labor in Households and Families."
95 Ibid.: 39.
96 Ibid.: 32. See also Humphries and Rubery (1984: 334–5).
97 Gardiner (2000: 82).
98 The debate started in the early 1970s and continued until the mid-1980s. For a summary see the appendix of Fine (1992: 169–91). See also Himmelweit (2000).
99 Dalla Costa and James (1972: 28).
100 Seccombe (1974 [1975]: 20).
101 Weeks (2011: 121).
102 Ibid.
103 Coulson *et al.* (1975: 62).
104 Ibid.: 62–3.
105 The reason is that Marx analyzed the reproduction of the working class from the perspective of capital and not of the working class. Since its products are not produced for the market, domestic work is private production and as such is of no interest to capital. See Himmelweit and Mohun (1977).
106 Gardiner *et al.* (2000: 27).
107 Gardiner (1975: 54).
108 Lebowitz (2003: 149).
109 While concrete labor exists as hours and minutes, abstract labor exists as dollars and cents. Through exchange, concrete labor time becomes "abstracted" and through this abstraction time becomes money. Wage labor and domestic labor cannot be added because the latter only exists as concrete labor, not abstracted through market exchange and therefore not denominated in money terms. See Lebowitz (2003).
110 Folbre (1987: 320).
111 Ibid.: 331–2.
112 Ibid.
113 Folbre (1982: 324).
114 Hagen and Jenson (1988: 9).
115 Humphries and Rubery (1984: 342).

4 Causes and consequences

Debating work time theories

Introduction

This chapter brings the different theoretical perspectives together and debates the strengths and weaknesses in the explanation of the length of the work day and the development of work time. Rather than discussing each approach separately, the different assumptions of the neoclassical, Weberian, Marxist, post-Marxist and feminist approaches are presented and criticized with respect to five major controversies: the self-chosen or socially constrained nature of work time; the role of living standards, productivity, and the search for surplus labor; the impact of institutions and social struggles on the development of work hours and the emergence of country-specific differences in work time; the role of work sharing in the fight against unemployment; as well as the tension between paid, unpaid, and socially necessary work time.

Self-chosen or socially constrained work hours

The neoclassical approach to work time stands out from the other approaches because it is the only one that seriously argues that individuals in capitalist societies are free to decide about the number of hours they want to work. All the other approaches argue that social constraints play an important role in deciding the actual length of the work day – including production requirements, institutions, and norms such as work time legislation and collective agreements, competition and exploitation, consumption patterns, as well as the burden of unpaid domestic labor. The idea that workers start and end work as they wish may be conceivable for a pre-industrial era, and it may hold for certain categories of jobs such as professionals and self-employed workers, but the vast majority of laborers in industrial and post-industrial capitalism, characterized by an advanced division of labor, have little choice. They are working according to a regular – that is, a pre-fixed – work time schedule in order to make sure that production is not halted or services interrupted because some workers take time off, say, to spend a sunny day at the beach. Ironically Eugen Böhm-Bawerk, one Marx's fiercest critics, agreed with Marx that work hours are determined by capitalists and not by workers.[1]

In stark contrast to the idea of freely chosen work hours, Edward P. Thompson shows in his highly influential essay "Time Work-Discipline and Industrial Capitalism" how workers in the nineteenth century were disciplined to conform to increasingly tight and rigid work time standards.[2] With the emergence of the manufacturing system, workers were literally forced to abandon traditional and irregular work time practices – what may be called pre-industrial flexibility – and adjust to regular and predictable work time routines. "Under modern factory conditions," as Mark Blaug notes, "labor services are generally sold in lump amounts; the laborer may have to work far in excess of the point at which the marginal utility of income equals the marginal utility of effort."[3] But it is not only work organization that has an impact on work hours. Macroeconomic conditions, too, impose certain constraints on the choice of work time. In post-industrial capitalism workers may even work less than they wish to because they can only find a part-time job. In Canada, for example, more than a fourth of all part-time workers would rather work full-time if an adequate position became available.[4] The availability of work not least depends on economic growth and the rate of unemployment.[5] Thus, David Spencer is right to insist that "in the real world, most workers do not have the option of deciding when and how long they work."[6]

Rather than freely choosing individual work hours, Weberians and institutionalists depict workers as largely passive subjects, coping with a number of constraints that emanate from production requirements, work time regulation and social norms. In the case of consumption patterns they are even portrayed as victims of an accelerating work-consumption cycle. Weberians acknowledge that individuals work different hours, but they do so mainly because of their social status – such as the status of a manager – rather than because of individual preferences. Accordingly, in the Weberian and institutionalist view the move to flexible work hours is the result of a new mix of constraints caused by the globalization of production systems, the spread of new skills, and the transformation of traditional family norms. For institutionalists, existing institutions mitigate some of the constraints so that the resulting work time arrangements can still differ considerably from country to country.

Marxists also acknowledge the constraints emanating from production systems, including the introduction of 24-hour shift systems that allow capital to extend the operating time of costly machinery. Yet in contrast to Weberians and institutionalists, Marxists emphasize the contradictory nature of these constraints, including capital's simultaneous drive to extend and compress work time – which cannot only explain the increasing flexibilization, but also the polarization of work hours. For Marxists, furthermore, competition plays a crucial role in enforcing work time constraints on both capitalists and workers. Most importantly, Marxists do not see workers as passive subjects. On the contrary: workers have the power to withstand the constraints and impose a work day that at least partly reflects their own needs and desires. Yet to do so they must act collectively, as part of a wider class struggle. As long as they act individually, workers are not only passive subjects but also victims of capitalist exploitation. Accordingly, differences in individual work hours are mainly understood as differences in the rate of exploitation.

A major problem, which the Marxist approach has difficulty explaining, is that a number of workers stay on at their workplaces without being compelled to do so by their bosses. Weberians argue that for some workers their job is a passion and a source of intrinsic satisfaction. However, while Weber thought that this was only true for a small group of privileged workers, many – if not most – workers find positive aspects to their jobs. Work is not only toil and exertion; it is also a collective experience and allows individuals to gain acceptance, recognition, and commendation. The more interesting, challenging and satisfying the job, the more time workers are willing to spend at work – and this is not only true for mentally stimulating work.

Writing in the 1970s and 1980s, neo- and post-Marxists have clearly underestimated the ability of capital to adopt new forms of work organization, such as team and project work, in order to make work more satisfying, while at the same time increasing the rate of exploitation. They have also underestimated the ability of capital to create new needs and modify existing demands, sustaining consumption growth even in the most affluent societies.

Interestingly all approaches conceive work mostly as a negative experience.[7] Only feminists perceive paid employment as an improvement to unpaid domestic work – but not so much because of the interesting content of work than because it makes women less dependent on their male partners. Women even accept the intensification, casualization, and alienation associated with paid work in order to gain economic independence and to overcome the social isolation of domestic work. For feminists the main work time constraint is the unpaid domestic labor that women carry out in addition to their paid jobs. The neoclassical idea that male and female family members are balancing paid and unpaid work according to various utilities derived from family income, leisure, and self-production is as unrealistic as the idea that workers can choose work hours independently of production requirements. The various attempts to explain the fact that women mainly deal with unpaid domestic work while men leave the household to pursue paid employment (lower wages, lower or different investments in human capital, less work experience, etc.) are nothing other than excuses for the gender-specific division of labor and the related patriarchal mode of social domination that constrain female choices.

Feminists and institutionalists agree that welfare states play an important role in defining the work day of women, especially over the life course. And there are few doubts that the support provided by the Scandinavian welfare states – including comprehensive and affordable childcare facilities – plays a key role in sustaining the Northern countries' extraordinarily high female employment rates. However, in connection with welfare state retrenchments and with the stagnation and decline of (real) wages, the opportunity to work outside the home has sometimes turned into a constraint. While initially women took up paid jobs to break free of the patriarchal family, many of them now have to work to make ends meet.

Living standards, productivity, and the search for surplus labor

Although neoclassical economists argue that work time is decided individually, they still make some predictions on the development of work hours based on the allegedly rational behavior of individual workers. The main assumption is that work hours tend to fall with growing incomes – at least up to a specific (and rather high) income level. While for large parts of the postwar period there indeed seemed to be a positive link between rising living standards and falling work hours, a closer look shows that work hours at several points in time were reduced during times of extraordinary economic hardship – such as in the years after the First World War, in the 1930s, and in the first half of the 1980s (mainly as a measure to tackle unemployment). It is also important to note that over the long run work hours were falling much more slowly than living standards were increasing. Between 1870 and 1998 GDP per capita increased by seven times, while work hours only halved.[8] In other words, if a reduction in grain prices is held responsible for the introduction of the ten-hour work day in mid-nineteenth century Britain, the dramatic increase in living standards in the twentieth century should have caused work hours to fall beyond the eight-hour day and the 40-hour week.[9] The relationship becomes particularly distorted in the last decade of the twentieth century when work hours and GDP per capita have increased simultaneously in countries such as the United States.

The income effect, furthermore, cannot explain national differences in work hours. According to the neoclassical approach those countries with the highest living standards can be expected to have the shortest work hours. This may have been true for the postwar period when the United States was not only the richest country, but also the frontrunner with regard to work time reductions; yet the correlation between higher living standards (measured as GDP per capita) and shorter work hours has become much less clear in the latter part of the twentieth century, and in the 1990s the relationship has even reversed.[10] While the US is still a country with one of the highest living standards in the world, it is now also the one with the longest work hours. As Linda Bell and Richard Freeman note,

> the fact that Germans would choose to work more hours when their incomes were lower than American incomes in the 1960s fits nicely with the standard income effects in labor supply. The fact that Germans have reduced their desire for hours as their incomes have risen in the 1970s and 1980s is also consistent. What is odd is that in the 1990s, with comparable living standards, Americans and Germans are so different, so extreme in their preferences.[11]

According to Joseph Stiglitz "the anomaly is not just that America's seemingly higher wages have not resulted in substantially more leisure, but actually in less.[12]

Economists have spent considerable time and resources to explain the apparent work time puzzle. Bell and Freeman, for example, have argued that workers tend to work longer hours in countries with higher earning inequalities compared to those with a more equal income distribution.[13] More recently Samuel Bowles and Yongjin Park have also argued that inequality induces people to put in longer work hours.[14] However, high income inequality may be the result rather than the cause of long work hours. For the OECD, the particularly long hours put in by high income earners is an important factor in explaining accelerating income inequality in Europe and North America.[15]

Another explanation is different consumption patterns. Richard Freeman and Ronald Schettkat have proposed that the work time gap between the US and Germany can be explained by variations in home and market production.[16] Americans work longer hours to earn more money to buy goods on the market, whereas Germans spend more time to produce goods at home.[17] The extent of home production in Germany, in turn, explains the low female employment rate compared to that in the US. Here, too, the fact that American families more often eat prepre-pared food, or eat out, may be the result rather than the cause of long work hours (with mostly negative consequences for the diet of American children).

The substitution effect can also hardly explain country-specific variations in work hours. According to Edward Prescott "virtually all the large differences in the US labor supply and those of Germany and France are due to different tax systems."[18] However, while taxes may explain some of the difference between the US and Europe – US workers have to work more because the state does not earn enough taxes to provide for comprehensive public services – they hardly explain variations within Europe. As Alesina *et al.* show, countries with similar

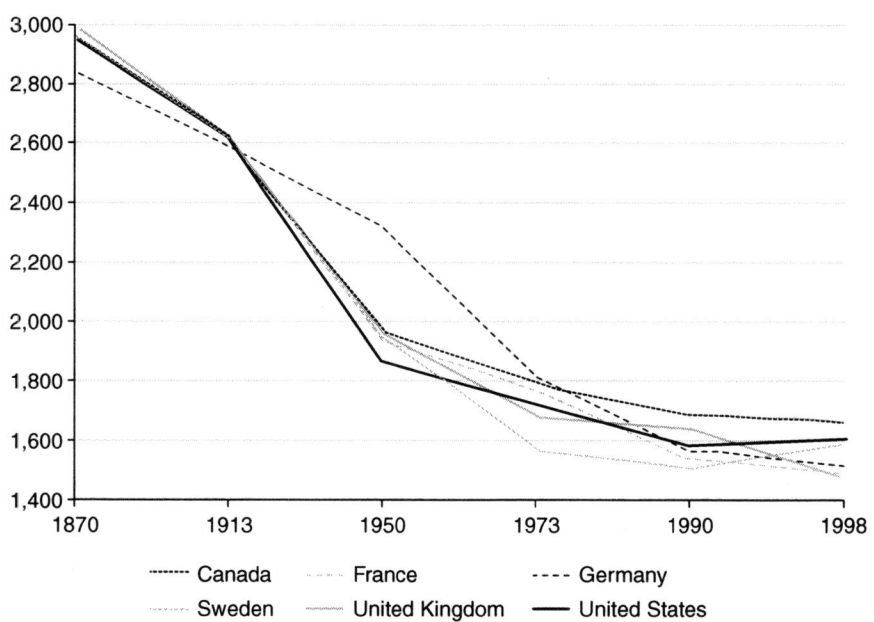

Figure 4.1 Average yearly work hours (1870–1998) (source: Maddison 2001).

marginal tax rates have quite different work hours. According to their data, Portugal has a comparably low marginal tax rate, but laborers there work relatively short hours, whereas Austria has high tax rates and long hours.[19] In stark contrast to Prescott's explanation, a number of authors follow Pigou's when they argue that a decline in real wages has compelled American workers to put in longer hours to maintain their living standards. Median wages for American males in their thirties were 12 percent lower in 2004 than they were in 1974.[20] Hence, "US workers are forced to bear an increase in the sweat, weight and length of work time ... to combat the stagnation or fall in real wages."[21]

Weberians assume that work hours tend to fall with growing productivity. While this has become the dominant view of the development of work time during the postwar decades, the evidence is inconclusive. Marx had argued that before the introduction of a compulsory ten hour workday in the mid-nineteenth century, work hours and productivity increased simultaneously for at least half a century. More recent historical research confirms that the technological innovations which led to the First Industrial Revolution in England and elsewhere were actually followed by a rise in work hours, as employers extended work hours to shorten pay-off periods for new investments.[22] Assumptions about a straightforward correlation between increasing productivity and shorter work hours must also be questioned by the fact that the majority of developed capitalist countries saw the most dramatic fall in work hours between 1913 and 1950, while the same countries experienced peak growth in productivity between 1950 and 1973.[23] The data supports the assumption that work time reductions force employers to increase productivity rather than the other way round.

Even when growing productivity leads to decreasing work hours, it is far from clear that the resulting shortening of the work day fully reflects the growth in output per work hour. Between 1870 and 1998 average labor productivity (measured in GDP per hour worked) increased 15 times in the United States and 18 times in Europe, while work hours per person in employment were cut by little more than half.[24] In other words, each person in employment today would have to work fewer than 200 hours a year to produce the same amount of GDP per capita as in 1870, or less than 600 hours a year or 12 hours per week to reach the level of 1950.[25] Clearly productivity is only one of several factors influencing the development of work hours and, as more recent experience from the US shows, it is far from being the determinant force.[26] While productivity gains reached record growth rates in the manufacturing sector in the second half of the 1990s, work hours went up rather than down. Pietro Basso, thus, hits a nerve when he asks, "how shall we explain the fact that in the past half-century ... labor productivity has more than doubled in the United States while work hours have grown somewhat longer, not shorter?"[27] According to Saad-Filho "reductions in the workweek generally fail to keep pace with technical progress, because capitalists tend to resist against measures that reduce the rate of exploitation." And as he further notes, "the success of attempts to curtail labor time depends upon the strength and political leverage of the working class, whilst the state of technology is an important, but secondary influence."[28]

For Marxists the development of work hours is the result of capital's search for surplus labor and the ability of the working class to resist capitalist exploitation, both as extension of the work day and intensification of work. In other words, work time is the result of a continuous class struggle. The Marxist approach is confirmed by the collective, cyclical, and contingent nature of work time reductions. The decrease in work hours did not evolve as a constant process but rather took place in a number of waves such as the introduction of the eighthour day after the First World War, the 40-hour week in the 1930s and after the Second World War, as well as in some countries the 35-hour week in the 1990s. The linkage to class and social forces can also explain country-specific variations as well as the recent increase in work hours in the US and other countries. In a comparison of work hours in the United States and Europe, Alesina and colleagues have found that trade union members work shorter hours on both continents. The authors conclude that "Europeans today work much less than Americans because of the policies of the unions in the '70s, '80s and part of the '90s and because of labor market regulations."[29] A study by Orsetta Causa also

Table 4.1 Development of work time, productivity, and GDP

	1870	1913	1950	1973	1990	1998
	1998=100%					
Canada						
Work time	178	175	118	108	101	100
Productivity	7	17	40	76	90	100
GDP per employee	12	27	47	82	91	100
France						
Work time	196	172	128	118	102	100
Productivity	4	9	17	53	87	100
GDP per employee	8	15	22	63	89	100
Germany						
Work time	187	170	152	119	103	100
Productivity	6	11	15	56	83	100
GDP per employee	11	19	23	66	85	100
Sweden						
Work time	186	164	123	99	95	100
Productivity	4	10	27	65	86	100
GDP per employee	9	16	33	68	82	100
UK						
Work time	200	176	131	113	110	100
Productivity	9	19	37	62	78	100
GDP per employee	19	28	38	66	86	100
US						
Work time	184	162	116	107	99	100
Productivity	7	15	37	69	87	100
GDP per employee	12	24	42	73	86	100

Source: Maddison (2001), own calculations.

confirms that high unionization rates and strict labor market regulations tend to have a negative impact on average work hours.[30] Guilia Faggio and Stephen Nickel also note that employment protection has a negative impact on work hours; unionization rates, however, do not. The authors particularly stress the case of Sweden which has high unionization rates and sector-wide bargaining coverage, while having longer hours than France and Germany.[31] Yet as described below, Sweden is an exception as here the trade union interest in shorter work hours was much lower than in France and Germany because work time reductions are not seen as an adequate measure to tackle unemployment. However, by assuming that under capitalism the living standard of the working class changes only modestly, Marx has seriously underestimated the appeal of higher wages as an alternative to shorter work hours. In the past trade unions have repeatedly opted for more income rather than more free time.

Institutions and social struggle

For institutionalists, institutions are a key factor in determining the length of the work day and work week. Institutions such as work time legislation, collectively agreed work hours, and the welfare state can, indeed, explain country-specific variations in work hours, as well as the distribution of work time between men and women. However, if seen isolated from class and social struggles they can hardly explain the shift in work hours and the reversal of country-specific work time trends. Britain and the United States are both representatives of what the varieties of capitalism school calls liberal capitalism. As such both countries have comparably long work weeks (although the UK differs from the US insofar as British workers enjoy much longer vacations). However, both countries were also forerunners in the battle for shorter work hours during certain phases of capitalist development.

Britain was the country with the shortest work hours in the second half of the nineteenth century. On the continent the establishment of the six-and-a-half day work week (with half of Saturday becoming free time) was announced as the introduction of the "English work week."[32] In the same way the United States led the struggle for shorter work hours for several decades after 1945. Large sections of the American workforce enjoyed a 40-hour week by the end of the 1950s, while workers in most parts of Europe were still putting in 48 hours a week. Workers in Germany and other countries had to wait until the 1970s to catch up to their American counterparts. The catching-up process at the same time shows that national models do not develop independently of each other. They are part of a capitalist world system. Longer work hours, usually in combination with lower wages, allow technologically less developed countries to compete with the leading capitalist forces. Of course the absence of maximum work time legislation made it easier to exploit decreasing trade union power to expand work hours in liberal market economies such as the United States and the United Kingdom. But for 100 years the labor movement in Britain was strong enough to win shorter work hours through collective bargaining. The

Trade Union Congress believed that they did not need legal protection when the British Parliament discussed the introduction of new laws establishing the eight-hour day and 48-hour week after the First World War (see Chapter 8).

For Marxists, institutions play an important role in determining the work day and explaining country-specific differences in work hours. However, for Marxists institutions such as work time legislation, collectively agreed work hours, and the welfare state reflect specific class and social compromises, and as such are closely linked to class and social struggles. Institutions have some degree of autonomy vis-à-vis day-to-day struggles, but in the long term they adjust to major changes in the balance of class and social forces. In Germany, for example, sector-wide collective agreements are still the main instrument to regulate work hours. However, decreasing trade union membership and an increasing number of companies leaving the employer organization have severely weakened the effectiveness of collective regulations (see Chapter 10). Furthermore, work time regulations may continue to exist but they become an instrument for work time flexibilization. Virtually no country has withstood the drive towards more work time flexibility.

Despite the difficulties in accounting for major shifts in the development of work hours, the institutionalist emphasis on the life course perspective and related changes in work hours has added a new perspective to the development of work time which is largely absent in the Marxist and neoclassical approaches. By doing so it has also brought important insights for the feminist and socialist struggle for shorter work hours. A reduction of the work day or week is only one aspect of the struggle for emancipation from capitalist accumulation and patriarchal domination. At least as important, from the life course perspective, are extended periods of paid leave which give workers the possibility to pursue interests beyond work, including spending more time with their children. Over this point the feminist life course perspective converges with the post-Marxist approach which sees paid breaks as early but important steps to break out from the never-ending work-consumption cycle.

Work sharing against unemployment

Following the Weberian approach, work time reductions play an important role in counterbalancing growing productivity. Through shorter worker hours, so the assumption goes, the shrinking amount of work is shared among a larger group of workers, thus avoiding "technological unemployment." As described in Chapters 8 and 9, the idea of work sharing has been highly influential in the struggle for shorter work hours, arguably as important as the perspective of more free time. Even Keynes, the theorist of demand-led growth, acknowledged that full employment can be reached by consuming more or working less. In a letter written at the end of the Second World War he notes that "personally I regard the investment policy as first aid. In the U.S. it almost certainly will not do the trick. Less work is the ultimate solution (a 35 hour week in the U.S. would do the trick now)."[33] Marxists have also advocated work time reduction as a measure to share employment and to limit the "reserve army of labor." Ecologists, furthermore, argue for work sharing as an alternative to environmentally damaging growth. In contrast, neoclassical economists strongly reject the idea that work time reduction can solve the unemployment problem. In neoclassical thinking unemployment is the result of inappropriate wage demands or skill mismatches but has nothing to do with work hours. If anything, restriction on work hours may even create unemployment by disturbing the optimal labor market equilibrium. Interestingly, the Swedish economist Gösta Rehn has also strongly rejected the idea that work time reductions can have an effect on employment. According to Rehn,

> theory as well as experience have shown that unemployment has nothing to do with normal weekly work time. Unemployment can be equally high or low in a country with a forty or with a forty-eight hour week. The level of unemployment depends on other factors such as the stimulation of the level of demand, labor market programs, and competitiveness of the national industry or the impact of currency exchanges.[34]

Rehn's assumption has been highly influential in Sweden where work time reduction never played a major role in full employment policies.

A number of studies have investigated the effects of work time reductions on unemployment. In France, for example, the shift from the 38 to the 35-hour week is estimated to have created 350,000 additional jobs (see Chapter 9). However, as already noted by Brentano in the early twentieth century, the employment effect of work time reductions is significantly curtailed by a boost in productivity accompanying the shift to shorter work hours (the resulting increase in labor costs induces employers to introduce labor-saving technology or/and introduce more efficient forms of work organization). Hence the employment effect of past work time reductions was often smaller than expected.

Paid, unpaid, and socially necessary work time

When it comes to the length and distribution of work time, most approaches limit their considerations to the realm of paid work. It is only fairly recently that unpaid domestic work has become a major focus of academic debate. As mentioned before, feminists have pointed out that the work day of a woman usually does not stop when she has finished her paid shift. They have also pointed out that the number of hours women work outside the home is dependent on the time she spends maintaining the household. Feminists have also argued that unpaid domestic work is essential for human reproduction even though it is not paid and not accounted for in the Marxist concept of necessary work time. As Jean Gardiner *et al.* note, "the value of labor power is not synonymous with the labor time embodied in the reproduction of labor power."[35] Duncan Foley concedes that "an important part of reproduction is carried out outside the capitalist relations of production";[36] and in developed capitalist societies, the "most important part of this extra-capitalist labor is household production and domestic labor."[37] In order to account for the fact that necessary work can be waged and non-waged, Foley introduces the concept of social labor time, encompassing necessary waged and unwaged, as well as unpaid surplus labor time.[38] Surplus labor time remains the difference between necessary and actual work time. However, surplus labor time cannot only be increased by extending the work day and/or by shortening the proportion of necessary labor, but also by transforming waged labor into non-waged work.[39] This, for example, is the result of welfare state cuts shifting reproductive work back into households where it is carried out as unpaid labor by female household members.

Notes

1 West (1983: 279).
2 Thompson (1967).
3 Blaug (1968: 314).
4 OECD data, available at: http://stats.oecd.org/Index.aspx?DataSetCode=INVPT_I.
5 Philip *et al.* (2005: 79).
6 Spencer (2009: 72).
7 For Marxists, work per se is not negative. Marx saw work as a means of self-development and self-realization. It is only under capitalist relations of production and the resulting separation of the producers from the means of production that workers are alienated, exploited, and frustrated. See Spencer (2009: 48–50).
8 Figures are based on data drawn from Maddison and the Organisation for Economic Co-operation and Development. See Maddison (2001: 345–56).
9 The repeal of the Corn Laws in 1846 was followed by a fall in the price of bread and the following rise in living standards spurred the introduction of the ten-hour day in 1848. The Corn Laws, indeed, played an important role in facilitating the adoption of the ten-hour day, not because of the increase in living standards, but because the British land aristocracy was looking for revenge after the industrialists' repeal of the tariff; they subsequently supported the working classes in their struggle for shorter working hours. For the rather inconclusive relationship between income and work hours in the second half of the nineteenth century see Huberman (2004).
10 However, this situation is far from new. Huberman argues that already between 1870 and 1913 countries with the same level of income worked different work hours (ibid: 986).
11 Bell and Freeman (1994: 15).
12 Stiglitz (2008: 50).
13 Bell and Freeman (1994: 24–5). See also Bell and Freeman (2000).
14 Bowles and Park (2005: 403)
15 OECD (2011: 32).
16 Freeman and Schettkat (2002). See also Schettkat (2003).
17 Freeman and Schettkat (2002).
18 Prescott (2004: 13–15) argues that "in these countries [Germany, France and Italy] if someone works more and produces 100 additional euros of output, that individual gets to consume only 50 euros of additional consumption and pays directly or indirectly 60 euros in taxes."
19 Alesina *et al.* (2005: 67, Figure 6); see also Faggio and Nickell (2007: 417).
20 Sawhill and Morton (2007: 5).
21 Basso (2003: 36).
22 Voth (2000: 286ff).

23 Figures are based on data drawn from Maddison (2001: 345–56).
24 Ibid.
25 Ibid.
26 While an OECD study found a positive correlation between the level of productivity and average working hours in a sample of 26 countries, the correlation was essentially zero within a group of the eight most productive countries. The OECD concludes that in these countries obviously "many factors, in addition to productivity, also affect hours per worker"; OECD *Employment Outlook* (2004: 28).
27 Basso (2003: 103).
28 Saad-Filho (2002: 109).
29 Alesina *et al.* (2005: 30).
30 However, the study has also revealed that work time regulations mostly affect men and that a high union density tends to increase the work hours of women. Causa (2009).
31 Faggio and Nickell (2007: 435).
32 Fridenson (2004: 58).
33 Keynes, "Letter to T.S. Eliot, 5 April 1945" in Moggride (1980: 384).
34 Rehn (1973: 333–4).
35 Gardiner *et al.* (2000: 34).
36 Foley (1986: 41).
37 Ibid.
38 Ibid.: 42.
39 Huws (2013: 84–5).

Part II

Work time, production, and reproduction

5   From Fordism to lean production

Introduction

This is the first of two chapters which trace changes in production patterns and their impact on work time. Following a Marxist framework, the two chapters attempt to show that the transformation of production systems is not simply the result of technological innovation, changing market structures, and the need to outperform competitors; the main purpose is to uphold and expand the proportion of surplus labor time. However, different strategies to expand surplus labor time have different consequences for the length and distribution of work time. While this chapter focuses on changes in the manufacturing sector, the following chapter deals with the more diverse world of service work. The chapter starts with an account of the Taylorist–Fordist production model and the related efforts to control and compress work time. The following section deals with the shift to post-Fordism and the need to increase work time flexibility. The chapter ends with an analysis of lean production as the ultimate approach to squeeze out time from increasingly flexible workers.

Fordism

In pre-industrial societies the length and variation of the work day was largely determined by cultural norms and social habits. Frequent festivities and spontaneous absenteeism presented serious obstacles for the capitalist goal of surplus maximization. Steven A. Marglin has argued that the shift from the putting-out to the factory system was not only due to an increasing division of labor (as proposed by Adam Smith), but even more so due to capital's desire to improve control over workers, including control over the duration and variability of work time.[1] Edward P. Thompson shows in his essay "Time, Work-Discipline and Industrial Capitalism" how proletarians following traditional notions of time had to be compelled and disciplined to adjust to the newly emerging industrial order of time.[2] The new order was imposed by the introduction of bells, clocks, and clocking in, as well as work rules and threats of fines for lateness and absenteeism.[3] Yet while the factory system divided the week day into work time and non-work time, the deployment of time during the work day was still largely left to the workers. "Capitalists," as Ed Andrew notes, "bought the laboring time of workers, but their ability to dispose of it in the most productive or profitable fashion was limited by the monopoly of industrial know-how in the hands of skilled workers."[4]

In the late nineteenth century many industries were organized as internal contracting systems, with the work itself being arranged and carried out by gangs of workers, with internal forms of hierarchy and control.[5] Yet as André Gorz notes, the "maximization of control was a precondition for the maximization of exploitation."[6] Based on his experience as a shop floor worker in the steel industry, Frederick W. Taylor concluded that "most of the shops in this country ... [are] really run by the workmen and not by the bosses."[7] Taylor subsequently set out to change the power relations in the factory. Instead of relying on the initiative of workers to apply their skills and experience to accomplish the requested tasks, Taylor took the lead, redesigned work processes, and told his workers how to do their jobs.[8] The role of workers was consequently reduced from the prime agents of production to the mere followers of management's orders. The separation of conception and execution of work became the key to the establishment of a greatly enhanced mode of control in the factory and, consequently, to a new regime of surplus extraction. "Taylorism," as Greg Littler notes, "represents a historical switchover from traditional effort-norms to the creation of new social mechanisms for constituting effort standards."[9]

The stopwatch and time and motion studies were the main instruments to redesign labor processes according to what Taylor perceived as scientific principles. By dividing complex labor processes into the simplest possible tasks, and by measuring and comparing different sequences of movements to complete these tasks, Taylor and his disciples were able to define the best way to "turn out each day ... [the] largest possible day's work."[10] The stopwatch became the internal equivalent of the factory clock. The fragmentation of time that first occurred as separation of work time and non-work time was pushed forward and extended into the factory. The fragmentation and standardization of work processes enabled capital to eliminate periods of inactivity, rest time, or hideouts for worker resistance against capitalist exploitation. The result of "the enormous saving of time" was an effective prolongation of the work day without changing its duration.[11] But the stopwatch not only enabled capital to reorganize work processes more efficiently; it also gave managers a tool to increase the pace of work. As one worker noted during a public inquiry into the effects of scientific management, the stopwatch was used as a "whip to lash on workers."[12]

Not surprisingly workers rejected Taylor's methods. They did so not only because of the intensification of work, but also because of the deskilling of previously skilled and autonomous laborers. Taylor was convinced that workers would give up their resistance if they were paid higher wages. And the growth in output, following from the scientific design of labor processes, would enable companies to pay higher wages and still increase their profits.[13] Yet while Taylor was clearly in favor of "first class wages" for "first class men" his attitude towards shorter work hours was ambiguous. In a testimony before US Congress,

Taylor stated that he could not recall a single case in which the scientific restructuring of work processes was followed by an extension of work time, "but I do recall many instances in which the hours of work were shortened."[14] One such occasion was the reorganization of a department for the inspection and shipment of bicycle parts. In addition to sitting the workers further apart (to stop personal conversations during work), he ordered a cut in work hours first from ten to nine-and-a-half, then to nine, and finally to eight-and-a-half hours per day. To his surprise output increased rather than diminished with each reduction. Together with the introduction of piece-rates the outcome was "that thirty-five girls did the work formerly done by one-hundred-and-twenty. And that the accuracy of the work at the higher speed was two-thirds greater than at the former slow speed."[15] However, in the American steel industry, where Taylor spent most his professional career, 12-hour days were not uncommon when Taylor introduced his groundbreaking changes.[16]

In any case, employers rarely followed Taylor's advice when it came to concession-making. Instead of wage incentives and/or work time reductions, it took the defeat of the American labor movement after the end of the First World War to break the workers' resistance and pave the way for the spread of Taylorism, and soon afterwards Fordism. As Mike Davis notes,

> It would be difficult to exaggerate the magnitude of American labor's defeat in the 1919–24 period.... In the interlude of the "American Plan" employers accelerated the attack on worker control within the labor process, the new-production technologies advancing side by side with new forms of corporate management and work supervision.[17]

Henry Ford, in many regards, built on Taylor's work, including the separation of the conception and execution of work, the fragmentation of tasks, as well as the deskilling of the workforce.[18] Ford's engineers made detailed time and motion studies before the introduction of the moving assembly line in 1916.[19] Some authors argue that Taylor focused on the labor process, whereas Ford concentrated on production techniques – "the hardware," in David Hounshell's words.[20] However, Ford's most important innovation was the application of the principle of interchangeability to such a delicate and complex product as an automobile.[21] Whereas previously automobiles were handcrafted luxury goods produced by highly skilled workers, Ford's Model T was made up of a number of interchangeable parts that could easily be put together by a team of semi-skilled laborers. Interchangeability and advanced standardization – the Model T famously was available in any color as long as it was black – enabled Ford's engineers to adapt the principle of flow production to manufacturing processes, while increasing the division of labor and introducing new labor-saving machinery.

To start with interchangeability was used to assign workers specific tasks rather than deploying a group of workers to assemble an entire vehicle – which was the common practice until Ford's groundbreaking innovations.[22] The advanced division of labor, in turn, allowed workers to move from car to car carrying out specific tasks rather than waiting until a car was finished before taking on the next assignment.[23] In a next step Ford realized that even more time could be saved if assembly workers could remain stationary while the cars, instead, moved (Ford used to say that walking was not a paid activity).[24] A prototype of flow production existed in Chicago's meat-packing industry where animal carcasses were fixed on conveyors and moved through the slaughter-houses for further processing.[25] Of course, assembling cars was much more complex than disassembling animal carcasses. Ford started with dissolving the existing departmental structure according to which similar machines were placed in the same location – for example, lathe machines in the lathe department. The machines were instead distributed over different production lines with the result that each line comprised a number of different production steps. Then the different production steps were connected, initially through the introduction of gravity slides, endless conveyors, and ultimately the moving assembly line.[26]

According to Wayne Lewchuck the time necessary to manufacture and assemble an entire automobile decreased from 140 to 70 hours with the initial shift to flow production, and to 39 hours with the mechanization of the production flow.[27] This meant that labor productivity soared by more than 300 percent.[28] The moving assembly line, as Benjamin Coriat has pointed out, converted dead time into productive time.[29] Yet the assembly line not only saved time spent on unproductive activities; it also gave Ford and those other employers who followed his path a convenient tool to increase the pace of work. While Taylor and his disciples used the stopwatch to push workers to work harder, at Ford it was the machine that ultimately set the pace of work.[30] As employers frequently used machinery to speed up work, the assembly line, more than anything else, became the means in the hands of capital for squeezing out more labor in a given time – as envisaged by Marx.[31]

The combination of repeated speed-ups and continuous mechanization and automation made sure that the amount of labor embodied in mass produced automobiles accounted for only a fraction of the time necessary to produce a car in the pre-Fordist era. In 1910 Ford built 30,000 automobiles and was already the largest car producer in America. That number more than doubled in 1912 (while his greatest competitor was still producing fewer than 30,000 cars), and increased by ten times in 1914 (while the second largest producer increased its yearly output to 50,000). The number further soared to reach 1.7 million vehicles by 1924.[32]

The principle of flow production soon went beyond the assembly line and came to dominate the entire value chain. The prolongation of the assembly line took the form of vertical integration, meaning that more and more production steps were concentrated at the same location, and, as far as possible, under the same roof. Ford's River Rouge plant was a point in case. It combined all relevant production steps from steel-making to final assembly, and in the 1930s employed more than a 100,000 workers.[33] Rising fixed costs deriving from growing mechanization and automation were more than set off by ever-larger volumes of goods, dispensing costs over an ever-greater number of output units. To maximize the profitability of increasing use of costly machinery, Ford had moved from a two- to a three-shift system (while most of his competitors remained on the two-shift system).[34] Growing output, in turn, reduced per unit productions costs (including labor costs) resulting in a *virtuous circle* of falling prices and growing demand – or to full exploitation of economies of scale.[35] The unit price for the Model T dropped from $950 in 1909 to $360 in 1916, while output increased over the same period from 13,840 to 585,388 vehicles per year.[36] In the early 1920s, when output reached two million cars per year, prices fell below $290 per vehicle. In 1922, a well-paid American worker could buy a Model T with ten weeks' wages.[37] Not surprisingly, River Rouge was known as "the most expensive factory built at the time to produce the lowest-priced cars."[38]

As with Taylor's scientific management, workers responded to the new strategy of surplus maximization with pronounced hostility. Despite massive immigration from the south, and from Europe, Detroit experienced labor short-ages at the same time as Ford introduced the groundbreaking factory changes.[39] The auto industry was a hire-and-fire industry.[40] Workers primarily showed their resistance by quitting their jobs. The industry suffered from high labor turnover and the Ford plant, due to its particularly intense working conditions, was par-ticularly vulnerable. Turnover rates reached 370 percent in 1913. Each hire cost the company between $50 and $100. In 1913, the costs for hiring new workers accounted for between two and three million dollars.[41] While the workers left their jobs, trade union organizers started to specifically target Detroit's growing auto industry. The Industrial Workers of the World (IWW) organized the indus-try's first mass strike in 1913 with more than 3,500 participants at Studebaker's motor company.[42] In the following summer IWW activists shifted their attention to Ford's Highland Park. According to David Roediger and Phillip Foner, the introduction of the eight-hour work day played an important role in the cam-paign. Union organizers argued that instead of quitting their jobs Ford workers should demand better working conditions, including shorter work hours.[43]

Confronted with the double pressure of high turnover rates and union organ-izers at the door, Ford made a surprising move: he doubled wages to $5 per day and introduced the eight-hour work day in 1914.[44] The day after the announce-ment of the so-called profit sharing plan more than 10,000 applicants stormed the factory gates at Highland Park. Turnover rates dropped by 90 percent, absenteeism fell from 10 percent to less than 1 percent, while the union organ-izers lost one of their major arguments for encouraging workers to join the union.[45] It is no wonder that Ford later noted that "the payment of five dollars a day for an eight-hour day was one of the finest cost-cutting moves we ever made."[46] In 1926, shortly after he had introduced the 40-hour week, Ford argued that "the short work week is bound to come.... The industry of this country could not long exist if factories generally went back to the ten-hour day because the people would not have time to consume the goods produced."[47]

Initially Ford's vision did not find much support among fellow capitalists who cared only for short-term profits. Despite the groundbreaking technological innovations and the dramatic increase in the rate of exploitation, the American economy dipped into the Great Depression by the end of the 1920s. Ford himself gave in and abandoned the 40-hour week in 1929. Given the lack of rational capitalists, it took the mass worker protests and violent clashes of the 1930s to enforce an effective rise in wages and a systematic reduction in work hours (see Chapter 8).

Post-Fordism

Michael Piore and Charles Sabel argued in the mid-1980s that the crisis of Fordism is merely a crisis of mass production. In their view the dominance of mass production did not stem from the greater efficiency of mass production systems, but from the emergence of a big and homogenous market space following the completion of the North American railway system in the second half of the nineteenth century.[48] In contrast to Europe, this market was not divided along different national languages, cultures, and related consumer preferences.[49] Thus, it was not by accident that mass production was invented in the US and because of the scale of their home markets US producers were able to flood European and Asian markets with cheap but highly standardized consumer durables, thereby further extending the scale of their operations. According to the authors, economies of scale reached their limits with more and more saturated consumer markets in the 1960s and 1970s. In the wake of an increasingly fragmented and diversified demand, as in Piore and Sabel's main argument, craft producers could outplay mass producers due to their ability to use the same resources for the production of a variety of highly qualitative goods – that is, in other words, due to their ability to exploit economies of scope.

As predicted by a number of critics, craft production hardly replaced mass production since Piore and Sabel published their thesis.[50] Changes in production systems cannot be reduced to modifications in market structures, even if market structures and production systems are closely interrelated.[51] As Marx has pointed out, competition forces capitalists to persistently break down and overcome existing barriers to capitalist accumulation. Ford not only responded to market needs – even though he was certainly aware of the potential of a "motor car for the great multitude."[52] Ford and other capitalists actively deployed markets as a means to advance surplus labor and turn potential surplus into profits. The shift from craft to mass production was not simply a reaction to the emergence of mass consumer markets (in fact, mass production preceded mass consumption and it took several years before the invention of new technology was followed by the development of a mass consumer culture). Mass production was invented because of its much greater potential for maximizing surplus and, thus, for accumulating profits.

In the early stages of the car industry, automobiles were luxury goods manufactured by skilled workers for upper class consumers.[53] True, these cars were sold at a profit, but given the labor-intensive production model, surplus could only be accumulated slowly. In 1909 (before the introduction of the moving assembly line), an average American auto plant had fewer than 200 workers and made fewer than ten automobiles a week; by 1929 a typical car factory had nearly 1,000 workers and produced more than 400 cars a week.[54] The production of 15 million Model Ts involved the creation of an unprecedented amount of surplus labor – an amount that was certainly out of reach with traditional production methods, no matter how much customers paid for the handcrafted luxury cars.

But the production of a cheap and reliable transport vehicle alone did not do the trick for very long. By 1927, more than half of American families had an automobile in their garage and the other half presumably did not have a garage to put one in.[55] In this critical situation it was Alfred P. Sloan of General Motors who, by producing a range of different models as well as introducing yearly model changes, again overcame another limit to surplus maximization:

> Sloan and his managers came to see that growth would occur not by the production of basic needs or by a "car for the masses" but by selling cars whose appearance, if not features, changed annually.... In this consciously orchestrated economy of change and consumption that stressed style and comfort above utility, mass production as Ford had developed it with the T was no longer suitable.[56]

Sloanist marketing principles were extremely successful: GM not only surpassed Ford as the world's largest car manufacturer in the 1920s – even though GM's Chevrolet of 1923 was almost three times as expensive as Ford's Model T. Continuous diversification and market segmentation, together with a remarkable degree of concentration – three auto firms came to dominate the American market – enabled auto producers to maintain high sales numbers and comfortable prices until the 1970s.[57]

The problem was not economies of scale versus economies of scope.[58] The problem was to find a new way to maintain and expand surplus labor in a situation where a reduction of time per unit of output could no longer be compensated by simply producing more of the same product (production output of American car manufacturers peaked in the 1970s). In some sense Marco Revelli is right when he argues that while Fordism was based on the belief in unlimited growth, post-Fordism follows from the realization that markets have limits.[59] Yet he fails to see that market limitations are only a problem for capitalists insofar as they limit surplus maximization. In other words, the problem was not the limit of markets (what looked like market limits was perhaps the result of accelerating competition with European and Japanese manufacturers flooding the markets with additional goods); the problem was the emerging barrier to the expansion of surplus. And because the goal was surplus maximization a return to craft production was never an option. The solution, instead, was a new approach to mass production, which combined the traditional focus on expanding output per unit of work time with a greater effort to reduce work time per unit of output – or what Harley Shaiken has described as "maximizing machine utilization and reducing the number of workers required."[60] The combination of increasing output per unit of time and limiting time per unit of output allowed for greater product variability while the time expended per unit of output remained low. And the early adoption of this recipe, for several years, gave Japanese car producers a decisive competitive advantage over their American and European rivals (see below).[61]

From the 1950s onwards, American car manufacturers put increasing efforts into limiting work time per unit of output. Many used the conversion from war to peace production in the second half of the 1940s to introduce new and labor-saving technology.[62] At River Rouge employment fell from 84,000 in 1941 to 28,000 in 1961 (as a result of the dramatic job losses, workers demanded a reduction of the work week). However, early forms of automation were still rather rigid, depending on a high degree of product standardization and increasing output numbers. As a result they still fit in the overall Fordist paradigm of expanding output per unit of time, even though the substitution of capital for labor reduced the amount of time per unit of output (the logical outcome of this paradigm would had been the establishment of the workerless factory).

Things started to shift with the invention of microchips. Microchips allowed for the storage and processing of large amounts of information. In combination with automation this meant that the new generation of robots was no longer limited to conducting only a single series of tasks. The new machines could carry out a variety of production sequences.[63] By using the same equipment for the production of a variety of models, or even products, flexible automation helped to balance the fluctuations in demand, while at the same time reducing the volume break-even point (the point where the investment becomes profitable) for each product. This, in turn, made a greater variety of models not only possible but advisable.[64] "Flexible automation," as Ulrich Jürgens *et al.* note, "showed a way out of the dead end of single purpose mechanization, committed to economies of scale."[65] The Ford Motor Company shut down production for an entire year when it replaced the Model T with the Model A.[66] Later on, new models were introduced much faster, but the substitution of old for new machinery could still last for several days if not weeks.[67] With flexible automation model changes reached an unprecedented pace. As a result of the new possibilities, car manufacturers made significant investments in new equipment in the early 1980s, despite a gloomy economic outlook.[68]

While the production technology became more flexible, the organization of work still followed the rather stiff paradigm of fragmentation and standardization (which, however, was highly efficient as long as productivity increased as a result of growing output per unit of work time). In the 1960s and 1970s, the Taylorist organization of work had come under growing pressure. More and more workers were no longer contented by the prospect for growing (mass) consumption to accept the monotony and repetitiveness of work in Fordist factories. Growing frustration and discontent translated into absenteeism, sabotage, wildcatting, and sometimes even official strikes. In the US wildcatting continued after the 1950s as rank-and-file members demanded that union officials bargain for provisions to limit speed-ups in auto worker contracts.[69] However, strike activity picked up significantly in the second half of the 1960s, exceeding by most measures the level of strike activity of the 1930s, and with the exception of 1946 the 1940s. The "rank-and-file rebellion" reached its apex in 1970, when over 66 million work days were lost due to strikes.[70] Among the confrontations to gain national attention was a production shutdown at GM's Lordstown plant in Ohio where 7,000 workers walked from their posts in 1972 after a refurbishment of the factory was followed by another shortening of work cycles.[71]

Lordstown was not an exception. In France, workers protested against persistent overtime and joined students in the mass demonstrations of May 1968, whereas in Italy frustration exploded in a series of militant strikes in the late 1960s, during which Italian workers challenged capital's control over their workplaces.[72] Even in Germany shop floor conflicts accelerated during the 1960s, while Sweden experienced a rapid rise in work days lost to absenteeism and sickness. Capital's immediate response was to push even more vehemently for (rigid) automation – in Italy, Fiat attempted to build the workerless factory – but confronted with falling sales numbers and new technological possibilities, the main strategy for surplus extraction started to shift.[73] As Ulrich Jürgens summarizes,

> [A]t the beginning of the 1970s the pressure for work reform ... was felt by manufacturers worldwide.... Short cycle times, and hence repetitiveness resulting from increased specialization and mechanization introduced for greater efficiency, were regarded as primary cause for this dissatisfaction. The labor rebellion at the General Motors assembly plant in Lordstown ... was regarded as a signal that this type of work was not accepted by workers any longer.[74]

While analyzing recent changes in the German automobile, machine tools, and chemical industries in the early 1980s, Horst Kern and Michael Schumann found a notable departure from the traditional Taylorist division of labor.[75] Manufacturers started to enrich jobs by integrating tasks, introducing teamwork, even on the assembly line, and improve the skills of production workers. Kern and Schumann argued that the changes amounted to the establishment of "new production concepts" signaling a qualitative break with the Taylorist-Fordist production model. Schumann later argued that "the key resources of this concept was the creative potential of each individual, the development of subjectivity, whose abilities were only insufficiently used in traditional enterprise and work organization or, even worse, were completely oppressed."[76] Perhaps the break with the traditional organization of work went furthest in Sweden, where the humanization of work became a prominent issue in the 1970s and 1980s. Workers in Sweden showed their dissatisfaction not so much with strikes than with high rates of sick leave and absenteeism. At the height of the humanization movement a group of nine workers assembled almost an entire vehicle in Volvo's Udevalla plant.[77]

Some authors have argued that the break with the Taylorist–Fordist production model was not such much a response to growing dissatisfaction and resistance. Instead it was a response to new production requirements, in particular the need to increase flexibility, variability and quality of production. In their view the rigid division of tasks had become "sub optimal if not dysfunctional."[78] Growing complexity caused by model mixes, as well as flexible and therefore less reliable technology, demanded unconventional responses to unforeseeable challenges.[79] John MacDuffe and Frits Pil argue that flexible automation per se does not demand for a flexible organization of work: "[R]obots do not require teams to operate effectively, nor multi-skilled workers."[80] But in plants building a variety of different models, workers with problem-solving capacities are an important asset. Thus "the decision to invest in flexible automation and the decision to invest in new forms of work organization are increasingly interconnected."[81] Institutionalists like Wolfgang Streeck adopted the idea that quality production demands for a non-Taylorist organization of work, with added emphasis on workers' involvement and union responsibilities, and incorporated it into the "German model" or the "high road" to flexibility and economic success.[82]

In contrast, critics early on warned that some researchers had drawn too optimistic a picture of the post-Fordist world of work.[83] Harley Shaiken and his colleagues noted that task integration not only enriches work; instead the recomposition of tasks – like the integration of production and quality work – can also be used "to redefine the level of work effort," or, in most cases, to make labor more intense.[84] They argued that in the mass production plants they had visited during the first half of the 1980s the reduction of staff levels was at least as important as the promotion of worker adaptability.[85] Jürgens and his colleagues also argued that a "central goal of job integration was to carry the 'efficiency drive' beyond direct production into the areas of indirect labor."[86] Indirect labor, like maintenance work, only played a subordinate role in the traditional Fordist approach to rationalization in which efficiency was traditionally measured by the number of direct production hours per car.[87] Thus task integration may have been a response to growing worker dissatisfaction, but it was also part of a new wave of rationalization aimed at expanding surplus labor time. This time, however, surplus maximization was based on reducing work time per unit of output, while the volume of output per unit of time was kept high.

What advocates of the progressive competitiveness approach fail to see is that individual capitals not only compete for market shares. At the same time they also compete for the maximum rate of surplus labor time. As Christopher Roberts points out, "individual firms compete through the greater exploitation of labor, and utilization of their own labor and capital – they compete amongst themselves 'indirectly' by advancing their own technique and organization toward the end of surplus value."[88] The ultimate objective of the restructuring process was not the establishment of a flexible and more human production system; the ultimate goal was to re-establish and expand the rate of surplus labor time. And when the ultimate goal is the expansion of surplus labor time there can be no win-win situation for labor and capital. Instead the outcome is always the result of confrontation. The dependence on class power became particularly evident in Sweden where the Udevalla plant was closed in 1993 after a sharp increase in unemployment and the possibility of relocating production outside Sweden shifted the balance of class forces in favor of capital.[89] In Germany, too, researchers found a partial "return to Taylorism" in the second half of the 1990s after globalization and German reunification had pushed up unemployment and weakened the German trade union movement.[90]

Lean production

The search for surplus labor culminated in the invention of lean production. Lean production ruthlessly exploits task integration as well, as workers' responsibility and flexibility, to radically reduce the amount of labor time embodied in lean manufactured commodities. Researchers from MIT's International Motor Vehicle Program (IMVP), investigating Japanese lean production systems in the second half of the 1980s, were not entirely wrong to argue "lean production ... is 'lean' because it uses less of everything ... [including] half of the human effort in the factory," even though this is, of course, a vast exaggeration.[91] Following the post-Fordist paradigm of surplus maximization, lean manufacturers put unparalleled efforts into reducing work time per unit of output. This, as discussed below, has important consequences for the allocation of time and the intensity of work. As Roland Springer notes, "organizational rationalization now means not asking individuals first and foremost to produce more pieces but to carry out additional tasks."[92]

According to the official narrative the roots of lean production reach back to postwar Japan, when Toyota and other manufacturers were struggling to adjust Detroit-like mass production methods to significantly smaller Japanese home markets. Instead of shaping the means of production to create the largest possible amount of output – what is commonly referred to as economies of scale – Japanese manufacturers were eager to use the same production facilities to manufacture not only one, but several products – what is known as economies of scope.[93] The emphasis on economies of scope had two major consequences: first, Japanese manufacturers were looking for alternatives to single purpose mechanization;[94] and second, Japanese management put greater emphasis on avoiding waste – including material resources, work hours, and defective output. In order to limit waste, workers were given a much more active role in the production process.[95] The focus on economies of scope resulted in what many Western observers believed to be a much smarter and more effective production model. However, Japanese producers not only responded to smaller markets (they did not change their production system when they started to conquer the much bigger American and European markets), they also compensated for the lack of resources and consumers by pressing out more surplus labor from their workers.

Particularly appealing from a Western perspective was a process known as *kaizen*.[96] The idea was to use workers' knowledge and experience to constantly improve the production process. Rather than banning workers from thinking about work as practiced in Fordist factories, Japanese manufacturers encouraged and rewarded workers who came forward with suggestions. Workers, in other words, were no longer seen as passive objects but as active agents in a process of rationalization and improvement. According to Martin Kenny and Richard Florida, the harnessing of workers' knowledge was a key element of the competitive strength of the Japanese manufacturing model.[97] Yet while advocates of *kaizen* saw a win-win situation based on workers working "smarter not harder," critics insisted that the real purpose of *kaizen* and other changes was simply to intensify work.[98] Several researchers argued that the time saved by process improvements was instantly used to assign additional tasks to staff members.[99] Joseph Fucini and Suzy Fucini report from a Japanese transplant (a Japanese-run factory) in the US that "in the early phases of the plant's history, workers eagerly contributed suggestions for increasing productivity.... Later, when it became obvious to workers that their suggestions were only increasing their own workloads, enthusiasm for *kaizen* all but disappeared."[100]

In the context of lean production, teamwork, too, was hardly an outflow of humanitarianism. Instead it proved to be a highly effective instrument for saving labor time by burdening the same workload on fewer workers. As James Rinehart and his colleagues have argued, teams not only absorbed indirect duties previously performed by special categories of workers (housekeeping, inspection, repair, stock handling, etc.), but team premiums and peer-pressure also made sure that individual workers would not fall behind, and, if they did fall behind, other team members would make up for them.[101] Yet team spirit can quickly turn into internal accusations when sick or injured workers are not replaced – which, in fact, was often the case since lean manufacturers deliberately underestimated the need for replacement staff. From interviews in a Japanese transplant in Canada the researchers learned that workers started to accuse colleagues of pretending to not be able to come to work. As one respondent stated, "when you're sick or injured you feel guilty because they won't replace you."[102] Even healthy team members, who had problems keeping up with the speed of work, were threatened by their colleagues, as reported by Laurie Graham who worked as an undisclosed observer in a Japanese transplant in the US.[103] Thus, as Pierre Durand sums up, "lack of punctuality, repeated leave of absence, fatigue or poor performance were no longer commented upon or dealt with by the manager, but by the group itself." And as he further notes, "self-imposed group discipline was far more efficient than any other kind would have been in weeding out those who fell below the standard."[104]

While Japanese production systems are known for their break away from the rigid Taylorist division of labor, job enrichment and teamwork did not result in improved working conditions. On the contrary: as Springer, a former manager for Mercedes Benz, argues,

> [T]he main benefits for ... using organizational measures such as job enrichment, job enlargement or even job rotation lie not just in the fact that the intrinsic potential to motivate workers is activated by such measurers; more important is the fact that the redistribution of work improves the individual worker's capacity and overcapacity in the workforce is reduced.[105]

To this end, lean production has embraced a new time regime. Whereas Taylor focused on the improvement of individual work processes, and Ford on speeding up the workflow, the new goal was to accelerate the entire factory. To do so, not only assembly line work but the whole factory was anatomized into simple tasks and then distributed among staff members with the goal of reducing the number of workers necessary to carry out the work.

In this process the stopwatch is replaced by special time study software. The computer allows management to simulate the production process and to test different compositions of tasks. These are assigned with specific time values. As a former shop steward at a British auto plant recalled,

> the person that gives ... the time never has to see the job ... all he knows is the job contains a hundred "gets", fifty "reaches" and X number of yards walking, which he'll give a given value, and all of a sudden there is a time there.[106]

The change from actual performances to abstract values resulted in a significant intensification of work. The intensification caused the same shop steward to note that this development, more than anything else, marked the beginning of the lean era in the factory. The relative independence of planning from actual performance, furthermore, means that there is hardly ever an optimal situation. Instead management is constantly trying to save a few seconds by shifting around tasks. As another shop steward points out, "all they do is go round trying to shave seconds off jobs. Their job is to take a second off here, a second off there.... Someone's got a second shy on his job, you can have this second."[107] Persistent change results in the widespread impression that lean management is a process without an end. And because everything is constantly in flux, it became increasingly difficult to defend established work standards.

The new work time regime has been described as "management by stress."[108] While Taylor eradicated periods of inactivity during the work day, and Ford converted unproductive time into productive activity, Taiichi Ohno, the founder of the Toyota production system, set out to save wasted work time. And he did so by gradually cutting back staff numbers. Lean production, in other words, "saves time by establishing a general lack of time."[109] The success of the Japanese production system, thus, did not so much depend on its innovative character, than on its ability to press out more surplus labor from its workers – or, as Michel Freyssenet puts it, from "fully utilizing the workforce."[110] While in traditional Fordist automobile plants workers actively labored 45 seconds per minute, in a typical lean production factory they effectively work 57 seconds a minute.[111] Tony Smith projected that in a plant with 2,000 workers the additional ten seconds per minute amounted to 2,667 extra work hours per eight-hour shift, or 13,335 extra work hours per five-day work week.[112] "This is equivalent to hiring an extra 333 workers to work a forty-hour week. Or, put another way, the equivalent to each worker performing the equivalent of more than an extra day's labor every five-day week."[113] Following from a historical study on the development of lean production in Japan, John Price confirms that "employees at Toyota and other automakers were put under severe stress through processes of constant rationalization, expanding job tasks, routinization of standard work movements and long work hours."[114] Perhaps the considerable increase in the rate of exploitation would not have been possible without the defeat of the militant elements in the Japanese labor movement, organizing workers after the Second World War, and the establishment of a much more employer-friendly business unionism in the 1950s.[115]

The compression of time and intensification of work did not stop at the factory gates. With *just-in-time* delivery, management by stress was literally passed on in the supply chain. In the traditional Fordist factory, production was centrally planned and coordinated by the planning department. The planning department projected output numbers and according to these projections issued orders for parts and inventories weeks if not months earlier than they were actually needed – what has been described as *just-in-case* delivery. Toyota got its inspiration for just-in-time production from large American retail stores where the "consumer could get the goods that he needed, at the time that he needed them and in the quantity needed."[116] In the second half of the 1950s, Toyota started to apply the same principles for the production of automobiles. As Durand points out, "as in the supermarkets, in the new system at Toyota it was the consumer who put his/her requirements to the fore."[117] And as in the case of supermarkets, the act of purchasing a car created a chain of command in the supply chain reaching back as far as the producers of the basic product ingredients. The flow of production is complemented by an inverse flow of information, with each station in the production process signaling to the preceding station what supply is needed. Because stations respond to a push from the preceding station, rather to centrally administered orders, the changes have been described as a shift from a *pull* to a *push* system.[118]

Just-in-time production not only allowed for quicker and more accurate responses to customers; at the same time it saved lean companies expense on inventories that were previously used as buffers to make sure that production could continue until the arrival of new parts. With just-in-time production parts are delivered on a daily or even hourly basis. This system demands a complex system of cooperation and trust, and the need to meet quotas on very short notice also increases pressure on workers. "The absence of buffer stocks," as Robert Boyer and Jean-Pierre Durand note, "puts enormous stress on workers and supervisors, given each breakdown or problem disrupts the totality of production by interrupting the material flow."[119] To quickly resume the flow of production, or make up for losses due to production breakdowns, workers are frequently required to work overtime. Thus, just-in-time production is not free of buffers – "long and flexible hours are the hidden buffer that are utilized if necessary."[120] Bruce Roberts makes an important point when he notes that "what appears as a shift in the technical system – moving from a push to a pull production system – ends up as changing the social relations of production."[121]

Whereas European manufacturers often use flexible work time systems, including three-shift systems and measures to average out work hours over a year, North American employers traditionally rely on overtime to cope with additional workloads.[122] Writing before the 2007 crisis, Charlotte Yates and her colleagues argued that the drive to a more flexible allocation of labor time has led to increasingly long work hours: "Across the board in the automobile industry, average hours worked crept upwards, with some plants such as the Chrysler minivan plant in Windsor reporting standard forty-eight-hour work weeks for the past five years and more."[123] In a case study on work time organization in a Toyota auto plant in Canada, Mark Thomas found that the production schedule was formally organized around two eight-hour shifts, but if the factory ran at full capacity, ten-hour shifts were scheduled from Monday to Thursday resulting in a 48-hour week. In times of high demand work was further extended into the weekend with the result that work weeks could easily amount to 56 hours.[124] Thus Thomas concludes that "overtime facilitates Toyota's approach to just-in-time production: its commitment to produce what is needed as it is needed."[125]

Just-in-time production was only the start of a far-reaching transformation of modern supply systems. While in the traditional *kanban* system orders and withdrawals were still passed on with written cards along the production line, new information and communication technologies allowed for a much more rapid and accurate exchange of vast amounts of information. From the manufacturing sector, just-in-time production, or what Durand has called the tight-flow system, diffused into other sectors, affecting work in a large variety of workplaces including a large number of service sector jobs.[126] The popularity of tight-flow not only stems from the possibilities to save inventories, but also from its capacity to use time to constrain work. As Durand argues, "tight flow turned time pressure and deadlines into management tools.... Being objectified within the requirements and exigencies of tight flow, time constraints are 'naturalized' and accepted as unavoidable."[127]

The shift from Fordism to post-Fordism and lean production, and the resulting intensification of work, took place during a period of high unemployment and increasingly defensive and weak trade unions. In the United States the total number of trade union members still grew until 1980, even though trade union density had fallen from 34 percent in the mid-1950s to about 25 percent in 1980. With the spread of lean production and other technological innovations, union density decreased further and reached 14.5 percent in 1996. In the private sector, union members accounted for no more than 10.2 percent of the non-agricultural workforce.[128] In Europe and Canada the decline was less dramatic, but still substantial. Even more significant is that trade unions disappeared in sectors which were once the hotbed of industrial unionism. It is not by accident that the majority of the Japanese transplants in the United States are non-unionized, and it is not surprising that many of them are located in the south of the US where there is little or no history of industrial struggles. However, even those plants which were unionized did surprisingly little to resist the conversion to lean factories (notable exceptions can be found in Canada and the United Kingdom). In the wake of the crisis, trade unions focused on attracting investment, and thereby safeguarding jobs. Only over time did it become clear that workers as whole could not win since the whole purpose of lean production was precisely the elimination of jobs.

Summary

In order to increase the amount of surplus value, or to maximize profits, capitalists first had to gain control over the work day and week. A first step was the shift from the putting out to the factory system and the establishment of rules and fines penalizing those who did not adhere to the new work time standard. The factory clock became the symbol of the new industrial order of time. In a next step, control efforts were intensified within the factory with the help of stopwatch and time-and-motion studies. The result was a dramatic intensification of work. But this was only the prelude to an even greater intensification based on a growing division of labor and the introduction of the moving assembly line. The moving assembly line more than anything else symbolized the means for squeezing out more labor, as envisaged by Marx. The changes led to a radical shortening of work time per unit of output, but the fall in necessary work time was more than compensated for by a multiplication of cars, refrigerators, washing machines etc. Since the resulting increase in productivity was mainly based on an extension of output per unit of work time, the Fordist system was fairly compatible with standardized work hours.

With the shift to post-Fordism and lean production, this was no longer the case. Lean manufacturers were striving to combine an increase in output per unit of work time with a reduction of work time per unit of output. In practical terms this meant that lean manufacturers not only turned up the speed of the assembly line, they also cut back time resources spent on support activities and other tasks not directly related to production. The result became widely known as downsizing. With the emphasis on reducing input rather than increasing output, the standardization of work hours became obstacle, and employers increased pressure to make work time more flexible – in Europe mainly through the introduction of averaging periods and work time accounts, in North America primarily through the use of overtime.

Notes

1 Marglin (1996: 33–4).
2 E. Thompson (1967).
3 Ibid. See also Flohr (1981), and Adam (2001).
4 Andrew (1999: 44.)
5 See Nelson (1975: 44–55; Edwards (1979: 30–4); Littler (1982: 165–71); and Bendix (1963: 212–13).
6 Gorz (1976: 169).
7 Taylor (1911: 48–9).
8 Braverman (1974: 113–18). There is a famous story about Taylor teaching a

workman named Schmid, at Bethlehem Steel, how to handle 47 tons of pig iron per day instead of the previously common 12.5 tons (ibid.: 102–6).

9 Littler (1982: 61).
10 Taylor (1911: 15).
11 Ibid.: 24.
12 Adam (2001: 13).
13 In Taylor's view scientific management would made it possible to "give the workman what he most wants – higher wages – and give the employer what he wants – a low labor cost"; see *The Principles of Scientific Management*, 10.
14 Taylor (1947: 23).
15 Ibid.: 95
16 Until 1923, 12-hour work days were fairly common in the American steel industry. See Roediger (1988).
17 Davis (1986: 51).
18 Chinoy (1982: 92).
19 See Ford and Crowther (1926: 125–6.) See also Hounshell (1984: 250–3); and Meyer (1981: 19–20).
20 Hounshell (1984: 252). As a result Ford not only made individual tasks more efficient; he more importantly eliminated a series of tasks by deploying machine power instead of labor power. See Batchelor (1994: 48).
21 The ability to make parts interchangeable greatly improved in the early twentieth century with the invention of new sorts of steel that could be pressed instead of cast. Pressing techniques not only allowed for the production of more parts in the same amount of time; pressed steel parts also freed further time up by not requiring further adjustment from distortions caused during the cooling process. See Hounshell (1984: 224–5).
22 Lewchuk (1987).
23 Ibid.: 46.
24 Coriat (1979: 76).
25 Hounshell (1984: 241).
26 Ibid.: 241–9.
27 Lewchuk (1987: 49).
28 According to Clarence Hooker the number of automobiles produced per worker at the Ford Motor Company increased from 15 cars in 1911 to 39 cars in 1926. This means the number almost tripled in 15 years. See Hooker (1997: 83–4).
29 Coriat (1979: 76).
30 Hounshell (1984).
31 Chinoy (1982: 95), and Marx (1967: 406).
32 Numbers from wikipedia.org/wiki/U.S._Automobile_Production_Figures.
33 Revelli (1999: 53–6).
34 Edsforth (1995: 155).
35 Tolliday and Zeitlin (1992: 2–3).
36 Hounshell (1984: 224).
37 Frieden (2006: 161).
38 Revelli (1999: 55).
39 Meyer (1981: 76).
40 Beynon (1984: 19).
41 Sward (1968: 49).
42 See Klug (1989: 52), and Meyer (1981: 91–4).
43 Roediger and Foner (1989: 190).
44 Meyer (1981: 95–121).
45 Sward (1968: 53).
46 Ford and Crowther (1926: 147).
47 Cited in Edsforth (1995: 156).

48 Piore and Sabel (1984: 40–8).
49 Tolliday and Zeitlin (1992: 30–4).
50 Williams *et al.* (1987).
51 Because of their focus on market conditions, Mark Elam has called Piore and Sabel's approach "neo-Smithian." According to Elam (1994: 50),

> the most powerful forces in their analyses of periods of transition tend to be reduced to *market forces* and the most decisive exercises of economic power to exercises of *market power*. Although the "narrow track" of technological progress is rejected the spectre of market determinism looms large.

52 Henry Ford, cited in Meyer (1981: 16).
53 Cross (2000: 25).
54 Frieden (2006: 161).
55 Cross (2000: 50).
56 Alfred P. Sloan once described diversification as application of "the 'laws' of Paris dressmakers ... in the automobile industry." See Hounshell (1984: 267). He also notes (p. 264) that

> the saturation of the Model T market and the rapid growth of GM's Chevrolet Division were part of a larger movement in the American economy characterized by increased consumer purchasing power.... Sloan and his managers came to see that growth would occur not by the production of basic needs or by a "car for the masses" but by selling cars whose appearance, if not features, changed annually.... In this consciously orchestrated economy of change and consumption that stressed style and comfort above utility, mass production as Ford had developed it with the T was no longer suitable.

57 Cross (2000: 50).
58 If anything, the changes amounted to an integration of economies of scope into economies of scale – as can be seen in the modularization production in which the same parts are used for different products – e.g., the same platform for different cars.
59 Revelli (1997).
60 Shaiken (1985: 144).
61 While in the mid-1960s GM offered its Chevrolet in five basic adaptations, Toyota's Crown was assembled in 48 different combinations of engine, body, and transmission components. Haruhito Shiomi (1995: 38) remarks that "with the inclusion of different interiors, exteriors, and paint colors, a total of 322 finished versions were possible."
62 Ford, for example, opened a largely automated engine plant in Brook Park, Cleveland, in the mid-1950s. See Edsforth (1995: 163–4).
63 MacDuffe and Pil (1997).
64 Shaiken *et al.* (1986: 169).
65 Ulrich Jürgens *et al.* (1993: 62).
66 Hounshell (1984: 263–7).
67 Even if General Motors only reluctantly followed the Fordist path of single-purpose mechanization, the introduction of a new six-cylinder engine in 1929 still caused production to be shut down for three weeks. See ibid.
68 Malsch (1988: 70–1).
69 Moody (1988: 83–86).
70 Ibid.
71 See Jürgens (1997: 262). See also Chinoy (1982: 97).
72 See Silver (2003: 52–3). See also Armstrong *et al.* (1984: 271–90), and Bellofiore (1999: 20).
73 See Gorz (1999: 29). See also Bellofiore (1999: 22).
74 Jürgens (1997: 262).

75 Kern and Schumann (1990); Kern and Schumann (1987). See also Dankbaar (1988).
76 Schumann (2003: 51).
77 See Berggren (1992: 164–5). See also Sandberg (1995).
78 Jürgens *et al.* (1993: 372).
79 Kern and Schumann (1990: 49).
80 MacDuffe and Pil (1997: 250).
81 Ibid.
82 See Streeck (1987: 298). See also Lipietz (1997).
83 Among others, editors and authors of the British journal *Marxism Today* were hailing the "new times" associated with the arrival of post-Fordism and flexibility. A critical position in the ensuing debate was taken by Anna Pollert and her colleagues. See for example two volumes: Pollert (1991); and Gilbert *et al.* (1992). For a summary of the debate see Macdonald (Fall 1991).
84 Shaiken *et al.* (1986: 178).
85 Ibid.
86 Jürgens *et al.* (1993: 127).
87 Ibid.
88 Roberts (2002: 93–4.)
89 Gorz (1999: 35).
90 Springer (1999).
91 See Womack *et al.* (1991: 13). For a profound critique see Williams *et al.* (1992).
92 Springer (1997: 275).
93 Womack *et al.* (1991: 48–53).
94 Ibid.: 52–3. Toyota developed special techniques that allowed them to change dies more quickly than was possible in traditional mass production systems and, subsequently, to produce different models on the same line. See Shiomi (1995: 39–40).
95 IMVP researchers were stunned to find a cord at every workstation during their visits to Japanese auto plants in the early 1980s. The cord enabled every worker to stop the line. In North American plants only senior line managers had the power to hold up production. See Womack *et al.* (1991: 56–7).
96 Kenney and Florida (1993: 39).
97 Ibid.
98 See Rinehart *et al.* (1994: 155–7). See also Graham and Stewart (1995).
99 See Graham and Stewart (1995) See also L. Graham (1994: 137–8) and Fucini and Fucini (1990: 161).
100 Dassbach (1999: 119).
101 Rinehart *et al.* (1997: 93).
102 Ibid.: 102.
103 L. Graham (1994: 135–7).
104 Durand (2007: 50).
105 Springer (1997: 275).
106 This and the following quotes are from a roundtable discussion with shop stewards in Liverpool in 2002. They are published in Stewart (2009: 92–3).
107 Ibid.: 96.
108 Parker and Slaughter (1995).
109 Lehndorff (1997: 5).
110 Freyssenet (1997: 306).
111 Smith (2000: 60).
112 Ibid.
113 Ibid.
114 Price (1994: 83).
115 Ibid.
116 Ono (1988: 25–8).
117 Durand (2007: 30).

118 Skorstad (1994: 434). See also Wood (1989), and Tomaney (1994).
119 See Boyer and J Durand (1997: 115–16). See also Durand (2007: 32).
120 See Berggren (1992: 175–6). See also Altman (1995: 346–8), and Lehndorff (1997: 73–4).
121 Roberts (1995: 201).
122 Lehndorff (2000).
123 Charlotte Yates *et al.* (1991: 537).
124 Thomas (Autumn 2007: 116–17).
125 The plant was not unionized and the company expected employees to work all posted overtime. Job applicants were routinely asked to "indicate willingness to work beyond their regular work day and work week." See ibid.
126 Durand (2007: 200).
127 Ibid.: 45.
128 Moody (1997: 182–3).

6 The fragmented world of service work

Introduction

This chapter analyzes the organization of work time in the service economy. Compared to the manufacturing sector, employers in the service industries or providers of service jobs rely on a much broader range of strategies to increase surplus labor time. An important trend that has been fueled by the shift from production to services is the expansion of part-time employment. In other service areas such as software development the prevalent work time trend is the application of long work days, including large amounts of overtime work. However, in both the production and service sectors the flexibilization of work time is not so much the result of market changes and the nature of work, than of capital's interest in maintaining and expanding surplus labor time. The chapter starts with a section on the service economy and the spread of part-time work. This is followed by an analysis of the new economy and the promotion of increasingly long work hours.

The service economy

The success in reducing the amount of work time inherent in mass- and lean-manufactured commodities encouraged capitalists to expand into other areas of surplus creation in order to counter the decline of labor expended in industrial production. In the late 1960s and early 1970s, Daniel Bell and Alain Touraine predicted the arrival of the post-industrial society based on the production and consumption of services rather than of tangible goods.[1] According to the authors, workers would profit from the changes as deskilled blue-collar assembly line work would be replaced by highly skilled white-collar jobs. After it became clear that the reality did not match the expectation – industrial production did not wither away and many of the newly created service sector jobs were low skilled and badly paid – the discourse shifted from the arrival of the post-industrial society to the rise of the service economy.[2] The statistics showed that a growing number of jobs shifted from the secondary (production) to the tertiary sector (services). By the end of the 1990s almost 65 percent of employment in the OECD countries was in services, and in a number of countries the proportion was more than 70 percent; value added in services accounted for a figure between 55 and 75 percent. Since in the United States more than 70 percent of workers were employed in services, and the service industries together accounted for 70 percent of value added, the size of the service sector was widely perceived as an indicator for economic progress and power.[3]

Of course statistics can hide as much as they reveal. The problem with the service sector is that it is a residual category comprising a large variety of activities that simply do not fit into other categories.[4] Another problem is that part of the rise of the service economy has not been the creation of new service sector jobs, but the result of outsourcing from the industrial sector following the disintegration of large business conglomerates. A number of activities that were previously carried out by staff employed by industrial corporations such as security, building maintenance, cleaning, and catering, were outsourced and provided by external businesses – all of which counted in the statistics as service companies (as discussed below, outsourcing was part of a strategy to place growing pressure on wages). Later, more sophisticated services such as information technology, logistics, and even customer service (call centers) were outsourced to external providers. At the same time, industrial companies which had developed specific services for their own production, established them as separate entities and started to offer these services to other producers (including, for example, specialized IT services). They are part of what is commonly classified as business services – one of the fastest growing parts of the service industry.[5]

There are some concerns that the shift from production to service may be the result of statistical classifications rather than a qualitative transformation of the economy. Jonathan Gershuny has argued that households tend to spend less on services and more on consumer durables, partly because consumer durables replace services (washing machines, for example, replace dry cleaners).[6] Despite the statistical ambiguities, there is a characteristic shared by most services: in services, labor costs make up a greater part of production costs than in industrial production. Services, in other words, are particularly labor-intensive and the high degree of labor intensity means that more labor time is expended per unit of output than in industrial production. The result is a reduced productivity gain in the service sector, or what William Baumol has described as the "cost disease" of personal service.[7]

Despite major advancements in fragmentation, standardization, and automation of service sector work, especially through the application of new information and communication technology, output cannot easily be increased in the service sector. The main reason is that service sector workers deal directly with customers and each customer needs a minimum of time to be dealt with – especially if they do not behave according to the standard manual. Even call center agents cannot simply cut off callers if they are not satisfied with the standard answers (they are usually passed on to an alleged supervisor). In some services, such as healthcare and education, a successful service delivery even depends on a close interaction between the service provider and the service user in a process described as co-production. "The 'front line,'" as Steffen Lehndorff argues, is still different from the industrial assembly line, in that the pace of work on the front line is not solely determined by the requirements of production, but is influenced, at least in principle, by the fact that the worker is interacting with human beings.[8]

This does not mean that there is no room for productivity growth in services. Yet the main strategy is not to increase output per unit of time; the main strategy is to limit work time per unit of output. And since there is only limited potential for substituting capital for labor, the main method is the application of flexible work hours.

In the early 1980s the British Institute of Manpower Studies (IMS) gained widespread attention for developing the model of the *flexible firm*. Based on interviews with managers and trade unionists in 72 companies, John Atkinson and his colleagues identified four ways that firms might cope with increasingly unpredictable market outlooks.[9] Of the four strategies, two became particularly important in the following debate about the best way to improve a firm's adaptability. While functional flexibility captures the ability to adapt a constant workforce to changing tasks and challenges, numerical flexibility refers to the capacity of an organization to adjust the size of the workforce, or the number of work hours, to changes in orders or demand.[10] The two modes of promoting flexibility have important consequences for the quality of jobs. Functional flexibility requires the development of a core of polyvalent workers, who in exchange for their willingness to learn new tasks and confront new challenges are granted a high degree of employment security; numerical flexibility, in contrast, demands the creation of a periphery of low-skilled workers on atypical contracts, who can be easily hired and fired. The idea is that as the market grows the periphery expands; as growth slows, the periphery contracts. At the core, in contrast, only tasks and responsibilities change, rendering the core employment segment relatively independent from short-term market fluctuations.[11]

A number of scholars have criticized the underlying assumption that the creation of the peripheral workforce is necessary to protect core workers. As Anna Pollert notes, "the 'discovery' of the 'flexible workforce' is part of an ideological offensive, which celebrates pliability and casualization, and makes them seem inevitable."[12] In spite of the criticism, the dualism of functional and numerical flexibility has been reproduced in concepts like internal/external or offensive/defensive flexibility.[13] Offensive/defensive flexibility, in particular, suggests that there are two roads to flexibility – a *high road* based on a highly skilled workforce in stable, full-time employment relationships, and a *low road* relying on unskilled laborers with non-standard contracts. Yet the assumption that the core workforce could be shielded from market fluctuations proved premature. Instead, core workers were also subjected to numerical flexibility – although in a different form than peripheral staff. While in the periphery numerical flexibility is secured by the deployment of temporary contracts and agency workers, core staffing levels are mainly adjusted through the use of flexible work hours; that is, variable work time arrangements and part-time contracts.[14] Perhaps the core's exposure to work time flexibility went furthest in the concept of the "breathing enterprise," developed by Volkswagen human resources director Peter Hartz. VW introduced a 28.8 hour work week in 1994 under the condition that work hours could temporarily be extended to 38 hours without the need to pay overtime (see Chapter 9).[15]

Aside from the core-periphery dichotomy, the IMS study revealed another interesting finding, which remained largely unnoticed by its authors. While only one firm from the manufacturing sector planned to expand the use of part-time employment, almost all service sector companies announced that they would extend their number of part-time workers in the near future. Perhaps the IMS sample was not representative, but a number of large-scale quantitative studies have found a greater inclination of service providers to deploy part-time workers. Even the OECD acknowledges that "part-time work is a much more common form of working arrangement in the service sector than in the goods producing sector."[16] The greater use of part-time work is mainly responsible for the fact that average work hours are lower in services than in manufacturing.[17] Of course, the greater incidence of part-time work has to do with the high proportion of women working in these industries.[18] Whereas in the 1960s employers responded to women's needs by offering part-time hours, they nonetheless quickly realized the cost savings associated with the transformation of full-time into part-time jobs.[19]

Based on a study on the development of part-time work in the 1970s and early 1980s in Coventry, England, Veronika Beechey found quite different patterns of part-time deployment in the recession years compared to the earlier period of economic growth: "In the period of expansion management employed part-time women ... because there was a labor shortage relative to wages or because they could not attract full-time labor into particular occupations." Yet when the economy contracted part-time women workers "were employed in certain occupations to extend the length of time during which production was carried out, to provide a flexible labor force over the workday or workweek, and to fill in gaps and cope with overflow."[20] As part of this process, the part-time rate in manufacturing fell between 1971 and 1981, while rapidly increasing in services, particularly the distributive trades (retailing).[21] Furthermore, part-time employment increased while full-time employment decreased, indicating a replacement of full-time jobs by part-time positions.[22] Arne Kalleberg found a similar development in the United States:

> Most of the increase in part-time work before 1970 ... was due to the growth of voluntary part-time work, mainly among women and young people.... Since 1970, virtually all of the increase has occurred among those who would prefer full-time work.[23]

In other words, part-time work changed from an activity that mainly accommodated the needs of the workforce, to one that primarily served the needs of employers.

A large part of the cost saving associated with part-time jobs has to do with the fact that part-time work is mainly carried out by women and that industries with a high proportion of part-time positions are typically poorly unionized. This allows employers to pool part-time workers into specific labor market segments – what segmentation theorists call secondary labor markets – which pay lower wages than comparable jobs held by men in the manufacturing sector.[24] At the same time, employers profit from the fact that part-time work hours can be extended to regular full-time hours (often on short notice) without the need to pay overtime premiums. In addition, part-time hours, and especially very short or marginal part-time hours, in several countries are exempted from employer contributions to social security or the provision of employer-funded healthcare. The cost savings involved in this present a strong incentive for employers to expand part-time work.[25] In the manufacturing sector the situation is different: since there are also costs involved in dividing up labor processes into smaller units and distributing them among a larger number of workers (costs for administration, control, training, for additional equipment, etc.), and since these costs tend to increase with a higher rate of fixed capital, manufacturers typically prefer variable hours or overtime and sometimes even agency workers to the deployment of part-time workers.

But there is also another and perhaps even more important reason why service-providing corporations prefer part-time hours, one that goes beyond labor market segmentation theory. In many services demand fluctuates during the day and week rather than the month and year (although seasonal fluctuations also play a role). A typical day has several peak periods with particularly high volumes of customers.[26] Part-time hours give employers the possibility to temporarily expand staffing levels during peak periods and reduce them after demand has bounced back to the regular level. As Mark Smith *et al.* point out, since the provision of services is more labor-intensive than the manufacturing of tangible goods, "there are relatively greater productivity gains to be made from a closer matching of work time to peaks in service demand."[27] The main advantage of part-time work over other forms of employment is that "it can be relatively easily decreased or increased and can be moved to a different time during the day."[28]

The retail trade is a perfect example. The customer flow in retail stores changes several times during the day, and while the flow is never fully predictable, there are some recurring patterns resulting in repeated peak periods (caused, among other things, by the customers' own work hours). These peak periods are staffed with part-timers, making part-time work the most important instrument of retailers to adjust staffing levels to fluctuations in activity.[29] In addition to fluctuating demand, retailers use part-time workers to cover the so-called unsocial hours in the evenings and at weekends. Grocery stores were replaced by supermarkets, and supermarkets by hypermarkets, in an attempt to maximize retail space. Yet to make the greatest use of the costly infrastructures, retailers started to expand operating hours, with some operating on a 24-hour schedule. The combination of fluctuating demand and extended operating hours meant that the retail trade in the United States and elsewhere was responsible to a greater extent for driving the growth of new part-time jobs that emerged in the 1960s and 1970s.[30] Even today, retail, together with education, health, and social services, is a major contributor to the overall part-time rate.[31]

While part-time rates in retailing are generally higher than in the rest of the economy, within retail companies part-time work is particularly widespread among "front-line" workers – that is, those staff members that interact directly with customers. According to one estimate, up to 95 percent of the workers employed at checkouts in French hypermarkets work part-time hours.[32] Part-timers deployed to cover additional demand are called "time adjusters." Their work time schedules tend to vary considerably from week to week. Time adjusters, furthermore, often work longer than their contractual hours because of unforeseen increases in demand or because a colleague did not show up for work (staffing levels no longer include reserve capacities). In contrast, those part-timers who work the additional hours in the evening, and at weekends, are called "gap fillers." They work unsocial hours but their work hours are more predictable.[33] In some sense retailers take just-in-time production more seriously than just-in-time manufacturers. Labor is not the buffer that keeps the flow going; labor itself becomes a part in the production process that is ordered when needed.[34]

The willingness and ability to put in additional hours if necessary is an implicit requirement in the retail trade and demands a high degree of flexibility on the part of the workers. This often conflicts with family commitments. Mothers typically look for work during the times their children are in kindergarten or in school, while retail stores often operate with changing shift systems and offer part-time hours in the evenings and at weekends when children will be at home. Thus, while many women seek part-time work to combine paid work and unpaid domestic labor, the unpredictability of work schedules in retailing makes it difficult to combine work and family obligations.[35] According to Isik Zeytinoglu and her colleagues the conflict between work and family is a major reason for high stress among women with children employed in the retail trade.[36] In Germany, retail stores make frequent use of marginal part-time work, or what in German are called "mini jobs."[37] As mini jobs pay less than $450 a month, the flexibilization of employment becomes synonymous with the casualization of work. Because they only work for a few hours per week, however, marginal part-time workers are willing (and perhaps even grateful) to put in additional hours. The growing use of part-time work does not mean that full-time work is entirely disappearing. On the contrary: store managers, typically male, tend to work particularly long work hours of up to 60 hours per week.[38]

But the retail trade is not an exception. Similar strategies are applied in other parts of the service economy, including the rather new call center industry. In the last three decades call centers have largely replaced the old customer service departments and are now the main tool for handling customer demands. At the same time, many companies have decided to outsource parts of their customer service activities to specialized call centers (as opposed to "in-house" call centers). In addition to greatly advanced possibilities for supervision – managers can instantly listen to the ongoing conversations of their agents – call centers have the advantage of allowing for a greater division of labor and a standardization of tasks, while customers still think that they are being dealt with individually. For customers the main advantage of call center services is the fact that they can be reached from home or work and that they are available outside regular office hours (during which the callers may themselves have to work).

While most call centers run on an extended operating schedule, some provide a 24/7 service. Another parallel to the retail trade is its fluctuating and not fully predictable customer flow.[39] The permanent registration and monitoring of calls makes it relatively easy to identify periods of over or understaffing; that is, periods when agents wait for new calls or when calls are lost because all agents are busy (calls which cannot be handled are sometimes also directed to external call centers as so-called overflow).[40] Part-time labor, among other forms of flexible employment, is used to make sure "that staff presence reflects, as accurately as possible, the (expected) volume of calls."[41]

Although there are differences between countries and between call centers in the same country, most studies show a high proportion of part-time workers among call center agents, along with other contracts that allow for variable work hours (e.g., freelance contracts). A British study based on four call centers sets the part-time rate of non-managerial staff at 43 percent.[42] An Australian study covering 20 call centers and based on the responses of more than 1,000 call center workers found that approximately 40 percent of the call center agents worked part-time.[43] In Germany, too, the proportion of part-timers in call centers ranges between 40 and 50 percent with work hours tending to be longer in internal than in external call centers.[44]

As in the retail trade, part-timers in call centers are mostly women, and many are students. Part-time workers in call centers, however, do tend to work longer part-time hours (the average of part-time hours worked in German call centers is 20 hours per week), and marginal part-time work is rather uncommon.[45] The reason, perhaps, is that the use of advanced information technology, while allowing for a high degree of Taylorization and control, demands a certain amount of training, increasing the costs for additional hiring, and for high labor turnover. Another important difference to the retail trade is that call center jobs are mentally demanding. While part-time hours allow management to adjust staffing levels to varying call volumes, just as important for the high incidence of part-time work, if not more so, is the fact that few workers are able to do the job for a regular eight-hour shift. As a call center manager notes, "this is really a tough job to do for eight hours a day. I think it's a tough job to do for five hours a day. Eight hours for me is a bit mind-boggling."[46] In a survey of 855 call center agents in Scotland nearly half responded that they dealt with stress at work "quite often" or "all the time." As in the retail trade, workers with care responsibilities felt particularly stressed because of the unpredictability of work hours.[47]

Another service where the introduction of new technology and the fragmentation of work has led to a fragmentation of time, is post delivery. A few years ago

the job of a letter carrier was a full-time profession. In the wake of the liberaliza-
tion and privatization of postal services in Europe, the former post monopolies
were looking for new ways to cut costs. One way was the reorganization of the
post delivery system. While the final sorting of mail for particular routes was
previously done by the mail carrier at a local post station, the final sorting is now
carried out in the same highly automated sorting centers where the initial sorting
takes place. The completely sorted mail is delivered to local deposits, where it is
picked up by letter carriers. The carrier then delivers the mail to the addresses on
his or her route.[48]

The relocation of the final sorting has led to a substantial reduction of the
time needed to deliver mail on existing routes. Post companies took advantage
of this reduction and transformed full-time jobs into part-time positions. Companies even invented a new job category for part-time deliverers – assistant or
auxiliary mail deliverers. In the Netherlands 80 percent of staff at the former
national post company are employed on part-time contracts, whereas at German
Post it is slightly below 40 percent (in the letter market segment). However, the
new competitors in the German postal market have part-time rates of more than
80 percent, including almost 60 percent of workers on marginal part-time.[49]

Interestingly, as Lehndorff has pointed out, the fragmentation of work in the
industrial sector was widely accompanied by a standardization of work hours. In
the service sector this is not the case. On the contrary: here the fragmentation of
work is followed by a destandardization of work time. "Basic service work is
often *fragmented* into small employment and work time units in order to achieve
optimal adjustment of staffing levels to daily, weekly, yearly fluctuations in
staffing requirements."[50] Lehndorff argues that the nature of service work does
not explain the high percentage of part-time jobs – there are notable country-
specific differences in part-time rates and part-time hours. Instead it is cut-throat
competition that forces service providers to lower labor costs, and the most
effective way to do so is the use of part-time contracts. However, the same competition not only facilitates the spread of part-time work in services, it also
increases the proportion of surplus labor claimed by capitalists. It is no accident
that large retail chains such Walmart, Carrefour, or Tesco are among the most
profitable companies in post-industrial capitalism.[51]

New economy

By the mid-1990s the media discovered the emergence of a new economy based
on the widespread use of information and communication technologies, especially the Internet. Soon after, academics followed with "scientific" accounts of
the new quality of internet-based commerce and businesses.[52] The discovery of
the new economy, in several regards, is a prolongation and acceleration of the
service sector narrative: companies, which were not present on the Internet, or
were not heavily engaged in new information and communication technologies,
were considered part of the "old economy" and doomed to fail – just as goods-
producing companies were believed to be outdated by the end of the 1970s. The

most successful companies in the new economy were considered to be the ones processing and manipulating knowledge, making knowledge the most valuable asset in the digital economy (the measurement of their success, however, was their soaring stock market quotations rather than actual profits, which in several cases were rather moderate). And while the post-industrial society was thought to promote highly skilled white-collar staff, the new economy was expected to create a new breed of highly skilled, innovative, and flexible knowledge workers. Even post-Marxists such as André Gorz and Toni Negri were thrilled by the idea of a knowledge-based economy and the possibilities for worker empowerment that would come with the fact that the success of capitalism increasingly depends on what is in the heads of workers.[53]

More critical researchers have questioned the "myth of the new economy" and criticized the very broad application of the concept of knowledge work.[54] Empirical studies have shown that although information and communication technology has spread throughout the economy, and many workers are, in one form or another, confronted with ICT in their workplaces, the proportion of highly skilled and innovative information workers has remained marginal in the digital economy – not least because the same information and communication technologies that are driving the new economy were used to deskill workers and routinize tasks (see, for example, the aforementioned call center agents).[55] While the notion of knowledge work is highly contested a common characteristic of workers laboring in areas such as software development, design, advertising, and new media is that they tend to work rather long hours.

In a study on IT work in several European countries, Janneke Plantenga and Chantal Remery have found that by the end of the 1990s IT workers were more frequently putting in longer work weeks than average workers. In France and Germany, for example, IT workers worked weeks of 48 hours or longer twice as often as average employees.[56] And even though work hours of 60 hours and more may be an exception since the bursting of the dot-com bubble, overtime is still fairly common in the sector.[57] Jouko Nätti and his colleagues revealed in a study on the work time of knowledge workers and managers in Finland that about half of respondents reported regular work weeks of more than 40 hours and many had problems actually gauging how much time they spent at work. They noted that, furthermore "high time pressure, a long work hour culture, work time autonomy and high work commitment increased the likelihood of working long hours."[58] Marie-Josée Legault also found that 49 percent of software developers she interviewed in Canada worked more than 40 hours a week and 13.6 percent more than 50 hours.[59] Furthermore, "these overtime hours were rarely paid or compensated by time off and, when they were, they were not compensated in proportion to the hours worked."

Knowledge workers share a tendency to work long hours with other professional and managerial workers. Jerry Jacobs and Kathleen Gerson report that in the US long work hours are most common among professionals and managers: "Over one in three men (34.5 per cent) who work in professional, technical, or managerial occupations work fifty hours and more per week, compared to one in five (20 per cent) of men in other occupations."[60] Many of these professions are exempted from collective work time regulations and their salaries already include compensation for overtime. In Germany, highly skilled white-collar employees (*höhere Angestellte*) are covered by collective work time regulations, but still tend to work longer hours than less skilled or blue-collar workers. Even more striking is that the work time of highly skilled white-collar workers has grown from the mid-1980s to the mid-1990s, while the work time of average workers in Germany was still decreasing.[61] France has introduced collective work time regulations for parts of the French *cadres* (managers) – with the shift to the 35-hour week in 2000 – after thousands of managers had protested they be included in the new legislation. However, for many managers work time was not limited by a specific number of hours. Instead the limitation refers to a specific number of work days to be worked per working year (see Chapter 9).

Knowledge workers and other highly skilled staff not only share the tendency to put in long hours, they also share the fact that their work is difficult to control. To the extent that the success of their work depends on their ability to deal with new and unforeseen situations, the tasks of highly qualified workers are resistant to bureaucratization and Taylorization. As Andrew Friedman has pointed out, while blue-collar workers were increasingly subjected to direct control at the end of the nineteenth and the start of the twentieth century, white-collar employees often enjoyed what he calls "responsible autonomy." According to Friedman the objective of responsible autonomy is to "harness the adaptability of labor power by giving workers leeway and encouraging them to adapt to changing situations in a manner beneficial to the firm."[62] In exchange for using their autonomy in a responsible manner, highly qualified white-collar workers were granted responsible working conditions. They could even vary their work hours in specifically developed flexitime schemes, as long as they met a weekly or monthly average and were available during core business hours.

Friedman wrote in the late 1970s, well before the information technology revolution took off. Of course, a large part of white-collar work today has been Taylorized with the help of ICT, but knowledge workers still enjoy a fair degree of autonomy. The lack of control and the innovative character of work processes make it difficult to compress knowledge work. Management deploys work incentives such as performance-based salaries or wage components to encourage workers to give their best (as practiced in pre-Taylorist times with all workers). More recently, managers have also started to experiment with specific target agreements.[63] Yet while such measures can increase pressure on workers, management can still not determine what exactly they have to do to produce the expected output.

Various commentators have emphasized the importance of mobilizing workers' knowledge and creativity in the digital economy. Post-Marxists such as Gorz and Negri have even abandoned Marxist value theory because of its insistence that value has something to do with work time (according to these thinkers, the measure of value in the digital economy is no longer work time, but knowledge).[64] A popular form of mobilizing the knowledge and creativity of highly skilled workers is to organize work in projects rather than in traditional functional and line structures. Projects are temporary cooperations between staff members, sometimes complemented by external experts, set up to accomplish a specific task. The difference from traditional forms of work organization is that rather than completing one task after another, usually by different specialists, project members with different skills work together simultaneously on a range of tasks.[65] Project work, as a result, stands out for its pronounced cooperative character and for flat hierarchies, which makes it popular among workers despite the negative effects on work hours and work intensity.[66]

Projects are typically used for the development of new products (for the replication of existing products traditional forms of organization such as line production are generally more efficient). Because they deal with new challenges, it is inherently difficult to calculate a project's cost.[67] The common way to calculate costs is to split the requested product into a number of separate tasks and to calculate the time needed to fulfil each individual task. Estimates are based on previous work experiences. The individual estimates are then added up and multiplied with a factor for wage costs. Together with overheads and a profit margin they make up the project's budget. The task is then to fulfil the contract while remaining within the projected cost range.

In the case of strong competition, companies are tempted to make lower estimates in order to improve their chances of winning the contract. Especially since the dot-com crisis, IT companies have drastically cut time budgets. As one manager noted in interview, the company now produces the same amount of output but with half the staff.[68] At the start of the project the budget is reconverted into time, and the time broken down into individual tasks. Each task receives a specific time value (the maximum time allowed to complete the task), as well as a deadline (the last date the task has to be completed). Both are critical variables, which are carefully watched by project members. Project workers, thus, are exposed to even stronger time constraints than regular workers (questioning the post-Marxist assumption that time has been replaced by knowledge as the main source of value).[69] While watching deadlines for delivering their work, project members also have to make sure that they do not spend too much time on the requested tasks. As noted by Sirpa Kolehmainen,

> time is a contradictory factor related to control and autonomy in IS [information systems] expert work. On the one hand, knowledge work has been said to be independent of time and place. On the other hand, projects are bound to more or less rigid timetables for everybody involved to follow.[70]

Deadlines and time budgets become critical tools in governing the work of knowledge workers.[71] As in lean production systems, management limits time with cuts in staff numbers, and ever-tighter deadlines, in order to reduce the proportion of labor time expended per unit of output.[72] As Dorothea Voss-Dahm points out, the fewer human and material resources a project uses, the greater the profit it generates. A project's profit margin increases the fewer discussions are arranged, the fewer people are employed in support functions (e.g., secretaries), the less time is spent on training and the less overtime is recompensed monetarily.[73]

Pressures are further accelerated through frequent customer contact. In larger projects, customers have to sign off completed parts in order to make sure that the final outcome meets their expectations. The final outcome, hence, is the result of a continuous negotiation process. Yet because the production process is relatively flexible and open, customers are tempted to change specifications, increasing pressure on workers to remain in the range of existing resources to meet new demands. While previously it would have been the task of management to negotiate with customers, now workers have to cope with contradictory constraints – such as producing the best output while using minimal resources, including spending as little time as possible.

As a result of the various constraints inherent in project work, project workers tend to suffer from long hours and high work intensity.[74] As Steffen Lehndorff and Dorothea Voss-Dahm note,

> work intensification and longer work hours are most likely to occur under conditions where only specific targets are defined (e.g., project deadlines, financial targets, goals agreed among individuals or groups) and where practical implications for meeting those targets within the contractual work hours become a matter to be resolved by employees themselves.[75]

A comparison between IT specialists who work on projects, and others whose work is organized according to the traditional line principle, has revealed that the latter group makes significantly faster recovery from work-related exertions.[76] The attractiveness of project work is not only that it gives workers more leeway to carry out their work; the attractiveness is also that more is done by fewer people.[77] A software developer describes the situation as follows:

> You have your freedom. You can sit all day at work and install funny and interesting software and have a nice time surfing on the web. Because it is your responsibility to deliver on time. In November I had two-hundred-ninety hours unpaid overtime to manage to finish my project by the first of December.[78]

Voss-Dahm calls the way a worker deals with pressure "self-organized extension of work time.... Work time increases because workers stay beyond contractual work hours, and contractual work hours are exceeded despite workers' freedom to decide about their own work time."[79] As a Canadian IT worker explains: "Well, sometimes maybe I worked a little slower for an hour or two, maybe not consciously ... I set my own goals for what I should get done in the day.... If I haven't done enough in a day ... I feel bad ... I stay at work longer."[80]

The internalization of time constraints has proven so effective that a number of employers in Germany have abandoned the formal recording of work time and introduced what is called "trust-based work hours" (only workers keep records of their work time).[81] The Fourth European Working Conditions Survey confirms that a greater degree of autonomy tends to induce workers to put in longer hours. More than 65 percent of workers who frequently work more than 48 hours a week enjoy flexible start and finish times, while less than 50 percent do so because they are in the top three income categories, and 30 percent because their jobs offer good career prospects: "Paradoxically, these workers are working long hours not despite but because of their autonomy."[82]

In other words, the freedom to choose one's own work hours becomes the freedom to choose long work hours. Harald Wolf and Nicole Mayer-Ahuja have questioned whether "this way of regulating one's own work can meaningfully be described as 'autonomous', considering that duration, location and distribution of work times are usually not determined by individual employees, but by customers, project teams, and superiors."[83] A survey among work council representatives in more than 200 German IT companies has shown that two-thirds of the businesses frequently use overtime, and that overtime is particularly widespread in work areas with immediate customer contacts. The same survey showed that the main reason for overtime was "pressure to meet deadlines" (mentioned by 70 percent of respondents), followed by "sense of responsibility" (61 percent). Only a minority (42 percent) said workers put in overtime because they were expected to do so by their superiors, and even fewer (12 percent) because of premiums.[84]

Of course the existence of collective work time standards and the adherence to collective regulations, including the obligation to pay overtime, depends on the existence of work council representation and the degree of trade union organization. While there are important differences between countries, both tend to be underdeveloped in the knowledge-intensive industries.[85] Even more disturbing is that where collective norms exist, they can be easily experienced as constraints and are often infringed by workers. Thomas Haipeter report from a number of case studies in knowledge-intensive work settings, that "individuals seeking to cope with the demands of their workloads regard these norms as barriers. They try to surmount these barriers while at the same time avoiding sanctions."[86] According to the aforementioned survey among work council representatives in German IT companies, the major part of overtime is carried out unofficially; that is, without the consent of the work council – often by workers who "secretly" continue to work in the evenings and at weekends.[87] In companies without elected work councils the situation is presumably even worse. In interviews with workers at five software development companies in Scotland Jeff Hyman and his colleagues found that 52 percent of respondents worked up to ten unpaid overtime hours per week, and 15 percent more than ten hours.[88]

Some authors have misunderstood coping with contradictory time constraints in the knowledge economy as a general hostility towards collective regulations and a desire for more individuality. Of course knowledge workers want as much freedom as possible to choose their own work hours, but this has not set them apart from other laborers. However, the infringement of formal work time regulations means that knowledge workers not only work particularly long hours, some of these hours are also unpaid. The high proportion of overtime should not come as a surprise: in a situation where capital lacks control over work processes and work time cannot be compressed, long hours are the only way capital can increase surplus labor. And the most convenient way to enhance surplus labor is to make workers put in unpaid overtime.

The freedom to choose one's own work hours excludes the possibility to choose part-time work. Part-time work is particularly rare in knowledge-intensive professions. For the few women who attempt to make a career in branches such as IT services, this means that they usually leave the sector when they become pregnant – even though parents with young children, more than anybody else, would need the flexibility to come and go as they choose. However, as Jill Rubery and Damian Grimshaw point out, the fact that full-timers put in between 60 and 70 hours a week raises interesting questions for part-time workers: "Should a part-timer work thirty-five hours, or should she/he work say twenty hours for half the salary of a full-timer?"[89]

Summary

The very success in reducing work time per unit of output meant that less and less labor was needed for industrial production. In the 1960s a number of scholars heralded the arrival of the post-industrial society, and later the emergence of the service economy. The idea was that more and more jobs would shift from the production to the service sector, and that services would make up a growing share of GDP. In the 1980s British researchers invented the model of the flexible firm. Here the idea was that companies use different forms of flexibility to cope with increasingly volatile markets. An interesting finding, although hardly noted by the researchers, was that service sector companies mainly relied on part-time work to adjust staff capacity to fluctuations in demand (while production firms used other forms of flexibility such as overtime, averaging periods, or temporary workers). Large-scale studies by the OECD and others confirmed the widespread use of part-time jobs in service industries such as retailing. There were two main reasons for this: in services, labor costs make up a large part of total costs. A small increase can therefore threaten corporate profitability. This makes overtime highly unattractive. At the same time, demand for services tends to fluctuate during the day and week rather than month or year. Part-time is an ideal solution that provides short-term flexibility without increasing labor costs. On the contrary: since most part-time workers are women, hourly wages tend to be lower than those of full-time staff.

In the 1990s several commentators announced the arrival of a "New Economy" based on use of the Internet and other information and communication technologies. Internet start-ups and other knowledge-intensive firms stood out because of their flat hierarchies and informal working cultures, leaving workers almost unlimited freedom in carrying out their work. Even post-Marxists such as Gorz and Negri were blinded by the new work environment and assumed that work time was no longer the source of value in the knowledge economy. Interestingly, knowledge workers and other highly qualified staff tend to put in longer hours than other workers. The reason is that knowledge workers and other highly qualified staff are difficult to control. To the extent that workers deal with new objectives and unforeseen problems it is hard to tell if they do what they can in order to achieve the requested tasks. In order to be on the safe side, knowledge workers are persuaded to put in particularly long work hours, some of it unpaid overtime. Hence, in the knowledge economy the freedom to choose one's own work time becomes the freedom to choose long hours.

Notes

1 See Bell (1973) and Touraine (1971). See also Block (1990: 5–20).
2 Fuchs (1968).
3 OECD (2000: 19–20).
4 Jean Gadrey (2003: 5). See also Huws (2003: 130–1).
5 See Sayer and Walker (1992: 64–5), and Gadrey (2003b: 51–61).
6 Gershuny (1978: 72–4).
7 See Baumol and Oates (1997: 87):

> In an economy in which one sector of the economy persistently lags behind the rest in terms of the rate of productivity growth, the produce of that sector must invariably rise in cost relative to cost levels in the rest of the economy.

8 Lehndorff (2002: 418).
9 See Atkinson (1988), and Atkinson and Meager (1986).
10 The other two sources of flexibility are *pay flexibility* and *distancing strategies*. Pay flexibility is intended to reflect the ability to reward core workers with higher wages, while distancing strategies were an early attempt at describing a practice that later became widely known as outsourcing. See Atkinson (1984).
11 Ibid.
12 See Pollert (1988: 72). See also Pollert (1988).
13 See Streeck (1987). See also Boyer (1999: 101–14).
14 Flecker (1998), 211.
15 Hartz (1996).
16 See OECD (2001: 91). See also Smith (2005).
17 Bosch and Wagner (2005: 91).
18 Maruani (2000: 80–1).
19 Walsh (1990: 520–1).
20 Beechey (1987: 157).
21 Beechey and Perkins (1987: 31–4).
22 Ibid.: 39.
23 Kalleberg (2000: 344).
24 See Peck (1996, Chapter 3, "Structuring the labor market").
25 Tilly (1996: 21).
26 Gadrey (2003: 49).
27 Smith *et al.* (1998: 44).
28 Kalleberg (2000: 344–5).
29 See Jany-Catrice and Lehndorff (2005: 216). See also Gadrey *et al.* (2000: 143), and Baret *et al.* (1999).
30 Tilly (1996: 25).

31 Smith *et al.* (1998: 39).
32 Jany-Catrice and Lehndorff (2005: 216).
33 Ibid.: 224.
34 Greenbaum (2004: 112).
35 Gadrey *et al.* (2000: 159).
36 Zeytinoglu *et al.* (2004: 537).
37 Kirsch *et al.* (2000: 69).
38 Ibid., 71.
39 Weinkopf (2002).
40 Holtgrewe (2007: 257).
41 Weinkopf (2002: 461).
42 Durbin (2007: 237).
43 Russell (2009: 74–5).
44 Holtgrewe (2007: 256).
45 Ibid.
46 Russell (2009: 87).
47 Hyman and Marks (2008: 202).
48 Hermann *et al.* (2008: 47–50).
49 Ibid.
50 Lehndorff (2002: 418).
51 Lichtenstein (2009).
52 See Gadrey (2003: 3–38).
53 Hermann (2009: 275–6).
54 Gadrey (2003a: 1–15). See also Thompson (2004) and Huws (2003: Chapter 9, "Material World. The Myth of the Weigthless Economy").
55 Huws, ibid. See also Greenbaum (2004: 72–80) and Warhurst and Thompson (2006).
56 Plantenga and Remery (2004: 193–4).
57 Abel (2007: 110).
58 Nätti *et al.* (2006: 310).
59 Legault (2013: 79).
60 Jacobs and Gerson (2000: 92) write: "Nearly two in five American men with four of more years of college education work 50 hours per week or more, compared to less than one in eight men with less than a high school degree." See also Golden, (2006: 227).
61 See Wagner (2001a: 367). See also Wagner (2001b). The longer hours may be the result of individualization introduced with the 35-hour week in the metals and engineering industry (see Chapter 3).
62 Friedman (1977: 96–7).
63 Target agreements are concluded between management and individual employees and fix certain goals which the respective employee is expected to achieve within a certain time period. See Hermann (2009: 278).
64 Ibid.: 275–6.
65 Ibid.: 283. See also Andrews *et al.* (2005: 45–75), and Boltanski and Chiapello (2005).
66 See Greenbaum (2004: 84–5). See also Kolehmainen (2004: 86).
67 Plantenga and Remery (2004: 198).
68 Mayer-Ahuja and Wolf (2007: 92).
69 Hermann (2009: 284–5).
70 Kolehmainen (2004: 97).
71 Brinkman and Dörre (2006).
72 Hermann (2009: 284).
73 Voss-Dahm (2005: 133).
74 Chasserio and Legaul (2009: 1120).
75 Lehndorff and Voss-Dahm (2005: 308).

76 Gerlmaier (2005: 74).
77 Greenbaum (2004: 85).
78 Cited in Rasmussen and Johansen (2005: 113).
79 Voss-Dahm (2005: 136, 144).
80 Cited in Chasserio and Legaul (2009: 1125).
81 Haipeter *et al.* (2002).
82 See Parent-Thrion *et al.* (2007: 19, Figure 2.7). See also Lehndorff and Voss-Dahm (2005: 309).
83 Mayer-Ahuja and Wolf (2007: 93).
84 Trauwein-Kalms and Ahlers (2003: 270–1).
85 Berrebi-Hoffmann *et al.* (2010).
86 See Haipeter (2006: 333).
87 Trauwein-Kalms and Ahlers (2003: 270).
88 Hyman *et al.* (2003: 227).
89 Rubery and Grimshaw (2001: 177).

7 Gender persistence in domestic work

Introduction

While the previous chapters have analyzed changes in paid work hours, this chapter deals with the nature and development of domestic work. As described in Chapter 3, feminists have argued that the time women spend in paid employment is closely related to the unpaid hours they work in the family household. At the same time feminists have also noted that the major part of housework is carried out by female household members, most notably mothers who frequently leave their paid job when they have small children or at least reduce the number of hours they spend in their paid job. This chapter first explores the emergence of unpaid domestic work as something different from paid labor, with the latter increasingly being carried out by men outside the household. The second part then summarizes the development of domestic work time of women based on time-use studies from as far back as 1900 to the mid-2000s. The following section tracks changes in female and male hours spent on domestic work since the 1960s, followed by an analysis of the current gender-based distribution of household work. The chapter proceeds with a discussion of changes in combined household work hours of men and women and the role of childcare as an increasingly time-consuming part of domestic labor.

The household division of labor

The reproduction of workers and their families not only involves paid work, but also a number of activities that are not leisure and not paid. These activities include, among others, the care of children and other dependent family members, cooking, cleaning, laundry, and in some cases subsistence household production. In feminist debates such activities are subsumed under the label of domestic or household work; in economics they are sometimes also referred to as non-market labor. In pre-industrial times, they were part of a wider household-based production complex in which different family members carried out different tasks which all contributed to the material and social reproduction of the family. In seventeenth century Britain, domestic production covered a wider range of activities including brewing, dairy-work, the care of poultry and pigs, the production of vegetables and fruit, spinning flax and wool, nursing, and doctoring.[1] "Men and women," as Rosemary Crompton notes, "have always worked to generate the resources needed in order to sustain and reproduce themselves."[2]

Tasks were separated between male and female family members – women, for example, were specialized in spinning while weaving was a man's job – but the separation was fluid and the distinction between paid and unpaid work was far from clear.[3] Even when married, women were expected to carry on with productive work – whether in agriculture, in textiles, or in some particular trade. As Ann Oakley notes, "there was no idea of the woman's economic dependence on the man in marriage; it was not the duty of the husband to support the wife, nor was it the duty of the husband to support the children."[4]

With the arrival of industrialization the household division of labor started to change. Initially, however, paid work was still integrated into household production through the putting out system. Women and children worked at home alongside men on the production of garments and other items commissioned by a putting out agent who would provide the raw materials and collect the finished products for a fixed price. Hence "the laboring family in the eighteenth and early nineteenth centuries had been a unit of co-producers to which all who were able made their contribution."[5] It was only through the invention of the factory system and the introduction of increasingly capital-intensive machinery, that paid and unpaid work were gradually carried out at separate locations, which, in turn, opened the way for an intensification of paid work and a marginalization of domestic labor.[6] However, in the early phase of the Industrial Revolution until the mid-nineteenth century women and children were still toiling in factories, supplementing the wages of the family patriarchs, which because of frequent phases of unemployment was rarely sufficient to provide for all the family's needs.[7] As Wally Seccombe notes, "the poorer a family was, the greater this ancillary portion was likely to be."[8] Hence the initial response of proletarians to women working for wages was overwhelmingly positive. According to one estimate approximately a third of the industrial labor force was female in mid-nineteenth century Britain.[9] It was only in the second half of the nineteenth century that women were increasingly expelled from factories and confined to unpaid domestic work.[10]

Several developments contributed to the confinement: first, the shift of production into larger, more technologically advanced factory units, together with the decline of sub-contracting and domestic industries, increased the number of relatively skilled jobs, largely reserved for men, while reducing the demand for female and child labor.[11] Second, middle, and upper class ideas of separate spheres for men and women increasingly diffused to the working class, ideas partly promoted by social reformers who were not only concerned with material wealth, but also with moral standards.[12] Third, as the ten-hour day initially only applied to women and children they created an additional incentive for employers to replace women with male workers.[13]

Interestingly, industrialization also reversed the role of married and unmarried women: while in pre-industrial British society, household work such as cooking, cleaning, mending, and childcare was mainly carried out by unmarried girls, partly under the supervision of married women who worked in the family industry, with industrialization domestic labor increasingly became the responsibility of married women, while girls could work in the factory and at other workplaces for a wage until marriage.[14]

The combined result of the economic and cultural changes was the emergence and consolidation of the breadwinner wage norm in the second half of the nineteenth century. As Seccombe notes, "the male-breadwinner ideal is the notion that the wage earned by a husband ought to be sufficient to support his family without his wife and young children having to work for pay."[15] As mentioned before, however, in the early nineteenth century only a small minority of workers were able to gain high enough wages and find steady year-round employment that was sufficient to support their families.[16] However, the notion of the family wage also implied that women were responsible for maintaining the household while men went out to work.[17]

With the establishment of the breadwinner norm, women were increasingly seen as suppliers of cheap labor, and as such as a threat to male wages, further adding to the desire to ban women, especially those who were married and had children, from factory work (at the same time trade unions up until the 1960s accepted that employers paid women lower wages than men for the same job based on the assumption that they would be provided for by their husbands). The exclusion of women from paid employment, supported by many trade unions acting to protect the interests of their (mostly male) members, further fortified the division of household labor.

> Men's identification as sole breadwinners was accompanied by an increasing emphasis on the household as a woman's sphere – indeed, it was widely seen as improper for men to undertake domestic work. A man's contribution to the family was seen as having been fulfilled once a sufficient proportion of income had been handed over to his wife. Women had always taken the major responsibility for domestic work, but with the consolidation of the breadwinner ideal, the division of labor between men (market work) and women (caring and domestic work) became increasingly rigid.[18]

This does not mean that women were no longer engaged in paid work. Young girls, until marriage or the birth of their first child, were still employed in various occupations and women of various ages and family status filled shopfloors and other workplaces when there was a need for additional workers. As such, women always presented a reserve army of labor that could be called upon during times of labor scarcity but turned away during times of labor abundance.[19] Hence, while women were drafted into occupations that had previously been reserved for men during the two world wars, married women in particular were forced out of paid work during the Great Depression in order to make space for male workers who were expected to provide for their families.[20] As Sylvia Walby notes, the practice of sacking women workers when they became married has a long tradition in the United Kingdom.[21] However, the depression led to an increase in such practices in "an attempt to deal with unemployment at the expense of women."[22] Furthermore, while women drifted in and out of the paid workforce, domestic work remained the sole responsibility of female family members.

The development of domestic work

The breadwinner norm spread in line with a change in the composition of families. Along with other factors such as rising living standards, the dependence on one income to cover all the family expenses encouraged a concentration process. Wider family networks, encompassing two or more generations of family members as well as unmarried relatives, were increasingly replaced by nuclear families, made up of two parents and typically between two and four children. As such, the nuclear family also implied the increasing isolation of women as the only worker, and, for a large part of the day, the only adult in the family household. However, during the postwar decades the nuclear family became the dominant form of working class life and the basis for newly emerging mass consumption patterns.[23] Consumption not only included ownership of a family home and car, but also the purchase of household appliances such as washing machines, vacuum cleaners, and various kitchen applicances. These appliances were supposed to increase the productivity of household labor and thereby reduce housewives' domestic toil. However, a comparison of women's household work found that American full-time housewives actually spent more time on domestic work in the 1960s than they did in the 1920s, their average weekly hours increasing from 52 to 56 hours in this period.[24]

Joanne Vanek, the author of the study, assumed that the labor-saving potential of new household equipment was more than made up by time devoted to shopping, increasing standards of cleanliness, and higher childcare expectations.[25] According to Vanek, few aspects of housework have been relieved as much by technological changes as laundry. While in the 1920s a great many houses lacked hot and cold running water, the following decades saw the invention of washing machines and electric dryers along with the introduction of a large variety of soaps and detergents as well as wash-and-wear clothes. Nonetheless, the amount of time spent on laundry increased rather than declined between 1925 and 1965. "Presumably people have more clothes now than they did in the past and they wash them more often."[26]

A comparison of British data from the 1930s and 1960s shows a similar picture: here the increase of housewives' time spent on domestic work was even steeper.[27] However, Jonathan Gershuny, who analyzed the British data, argues that while middle class housewives spent almost twice as much time on domestic labor in the mid-1970s than they did in the early 1950s, the domestic work time of working class housewives declined considerably over the same period. Gershuny explains the increase in domestic work time among the middle classes as being related to the declining use of domestic servants.[28] It is not clear how Gershuny distinguishes between middle class and working class families; he certainly assumes that many middle class families still had domestic servants in the 1940s and 1950s.

A more recent Australian study that compared households with and without household appliances confirmed the earlier assumption that "owning domestic technology rarely reduces unpaid household work." Instead, "in some cases owning appliances marginally increases the time spent on the relevant task."[29] According to the authors, neither a microwave nor an electric dishwasher has a significant effect on the time women spend on food or drink preparation and cleaning up – even though these appliances significantly reduce the time needed to complete the same tasks using traditional methods.[30] The availability of a tumble dryer actually increases a woman's time spent on laundry.[31] Michael Bittman, James Mahmud Rice and Judy Wajcman conclude from their findings that "domestic appliances ... tend to reinforce rather than undermine the obdurate sex segregation of domestic tasks."[32] The authors also found that higher family income only marginally reduces the time spent on domestic work, even though high-income families own the latest appliances. Confirming the earlier assumption that time devoted to domestic work tends to increase as living standards grow, the authors assume that "higher income households do use their appliances (and paid auxiliary workers) to produce a higher output of goods and services – maintaining larger, more refined and more pleasant homes."[33]

Interestingly, Ursula Huws explains the increase or stagnation of domestic work during the postwar period with reference to a phenomenon that Gershuny has described as self-servicing economy.[34] The basic idea is that technological innovation in the service economy is frequently used to shift tasks that were previously carried out by workers, on to consumers. And in a society in which unpaid work is mainly carried out by female household members (see below), self-servicing means that more and more work is foisted on to women.[35] "Since the beginning of the twentieth century," Huws notes,

> a whole new range of self-service tasks has been added to the traditional responsibilities of the housewife.... The housewife is now expected to transport herself to the nearest supermarket, find the goods she wants, take them down from the shelves, transport them to the checkout, wait, and transport them home – nearly all tasks that used to be somebody's paid job.[36]

Huws's theory is confirmed by Vanek's findings, which show a more than fourfold increase in time spent on shopping and household management tasks between 1930 and 1965.[37]

In a more recent study Valerie Ramey found that time spent by women on household production fell by more than 40 percent between 1900 and 2005 (from 46.8 to 29.3 hours). However, domestic work time only fell by six hours per week between 1900 and 1965, while falling by more than 12 hours between 1965 and 1985 – a time when female labor market participation started to grow while most households were already equipped with advanced household technology.[38] In 1951 about one-third of all women of working age were engaged in paid employment in Britain.[39] The female employment rate subsequently increased to 53 percent in 1973, 63 percent in 1992 and 67 percent in 2013. Other countries followed a similar pattern.[40] A consistent finding in various housework studies is that employed women spend less time on domestic work than full-time housewives.[41] Vanek found in the 1970s that employed women only devoted about half the time to housework as unemployed women.[42] According to Ramey, employed women spent about 40 percent less time on housework in 2005 than non-employed women.[43] Hence, the evidence suggests that growing female labor market participation is the main factor behind the reduction of time spent on housework since the 1960s.

In an analysis of the development of housework in nine countries, Liana Sayer found that the time women devote to housework has declined across all countries.[44] Between the 1970s and early 2000s reductions range from about 40 minutes a day (UK, France, and Norway) to 70 minutes (US, Canada, Germany, the Netherlands, and Sweden).[45] However, in the United States the major part of the reduction took place before the mid-1980s when female housework fell by 80 minutes a day; whereas since the mid-1980s it decreased only by 27 minutes. In the United Kingdom, the time women spent on housework decreased by 40 minutes a day between 1975 and mid-1985 and increased slightly between 1985 and 2000. A similar pattern can be found in Canada, whereas in the Netherlands the reduction of women's domestic work time evolved more evenly.[46] It is not only the fact that women have a job that impacts on the time they devote to domestic chores, it is also how many hours they spend working outside the household. As Tanja van der Lippe notes, "full-time work has a large negative effect on the number of housework hours compared with the nonworking wives, but part-time work also has a negative effect on their domestic hours."[47]

While women reduced the time spent on domestic labor, men increased their share of household work. In the United States, men's participation in domestic work almost doubled between 1965 and 2003, increasing from 42 to 81 minutes a day. In the United Kingdom and Canada the increase amounted to 50 percent. In the Netherlands the growth of men's time devoted to housework was considerably lower, amounting to 13 percent (or ten minutes a day) between 1975 and 2000. In Sweden, furthermore, men's contribution to housework decreased by almost 30 percent between 1981 and 2001.[48]

The increase in men's domestic work time has leveled off in most countries for which data is available. In the United Kingdom, Canada, and the Netherlands it has largely stagnated since the 1980s with current levels at about 80 minutes a day. In the United States, men's time spent on domestic work fell to 81 minutes a day in 2003 after topping at 94 minutes in 1998.[49] And while women's paid work hours seem to have little impact on the hours men spend on domestic work, the more hours men spend at their paid jobs the less time they devote to domestic work.[50] Although other factors such as the reinforcement of gender norms following the heyday of the women's movement of the 1970s certainly play a role, the stagnation of men's domestic work hours may also have to do with the fact that men's paid hours have largely stagnated or increased since the 1980s (see Chapter 10). One of the few exceptions to this trend is France, where the 35-hour week was introduced in the late 1990s and early 2000s. According to a survey among French workers after the introduction of the 35-hour week, men on average have used 21 percent of the additional free time for doing housework (compared to 50 percent used by women).[51]

The persistence of inequality in the distribution of housework

Another consistent finding of various studies is that in spite of the increase in men's domestic work time, women still do the majority of the housework. In the late 1990s and early 2000s women devoted between one-and-a-half and twice as much time on domestic tasks than men – compared to three-and-a-half times in the 1970s.[52] Hence, as Janeen Baxter notes, "women still perform the bulk of household labor."[53] Based on an analysis of the distribution of housework in 26 countries, van der Lippe also finds that "the most striking resemblance between all countries is the fact that regardless of women's position in the labor market, women remain responsible for the family."[54] Even when women have full-time jobs, their domestic workload still tends to be heavier than that of men.[55] Crompton summarizes the development as follows:

> As women have increased their hours spent in employment, so their hours of domestic work have declined and men's hours have increased somewhat. However, gender continues to explain more of the variance in domestic hours of work than any other factor, and women still carry out considerably more domestic work than men.[56]

However, housework is not only unevenly distributed in terms of the time spent on domestic labor, but also with regard to the different tasks involved in household maintenance. While women are mainly responsible for routine tasks such as cooking and cleaning, men are more often engaged in non-routine tasks such as house repairs and lawn mowing.[57]

Taken together, the total domestic work time of men and women decreased by 68 minutes a day in the United States (1965–2003), 61 minutes in the Netherlands (1975–2000), 33 minutes in Canada (1971–98) and 13 minutes in the United Kingdom (1971–2000). However, while the combined time devoted to domestic work has decreased since the mid-1980s in the Netherlands (65 minutes) and in the United States (22 minutes), these levels remained stagnant in the United Kingdom and increased in Canada.[58] Behind the stagnation of domestic work stands a substantial change in the time devoted to different tasks. Comparing the work of full-time housewives in the 1920s and 1960s, Vanek had already noted that an increasing amount of time was spent shopping and on childcare.[59] According to data gathered by Suzanne Binachi, mothers' time spent with children increased slightly from 5.3 hours a day in 1965 to 5.5 hours in 1998 – despite a substantial increase in women's labor market participation over the same period. A father's time spent with his children increased by an hour – from 2.8 to 3.8 hours.[60] Hence "the puzzling thing about the reallocation of mothers' time to market work outside the home is that it appears to have been accomplished with little effect on children's well-being."[61]

Australian data also suggests that the time parents spend in activities with their pre-school aged children has risen from 21 to 30 hours per week between 1947 and 1997. Australian fathers have even doubled the average time they spend with their pre-school children over the same period.[62] An analysis of more recent changes in the United States has found that both working and non-working parents spent more time with their children in the mid-2000s than in the mid-1970s. Liana Fox and colleagues note that "interestingly, employed married mothers during 2003–08 spent almost as many hours in primary childcare as did their nonworking peers in 1975, and employed fathers spent more time caring for children in the later period, whatever their employment status."[63] A broader analysis covering 16 countries also reached the conclusion that "the increase in female labor force participation [since the 1960s] has not led to an overall decrease in parental time."[64] Some authors even argue that these numbers under-estimate the full attention parents pay to their children because time-use studies usually focus on the analysis of primary activities – yet mothers frequently look after their children while at the same time carrying out other tasks.[65]

Part of the increase in time parents spend with their children can be explained by changing social and cultural standards. While children previously presented an economic asset, contributing to the family wage and constituting a safety net for parents when they became too old and too worn out to work, under the bread-winner model they became a source of joy and a major reason for accepting the downsides of modern working and living arrangements. "As child-mortality fell, parents increasingly revalued their children. Worthless in a productive sense, their emotional value became inestimable. Children were priceless assets; without them, family life was inevitably barren."[66] The fact that emotional work cannot be rationalized also added to the increasing importance of childcare in relation to other domestic tasks.

Given the persistence of gender inequality in the division of housework and the limited impact of technological innovation on domestic work time, Maria-rosa Dalla Costa and Selma James were extremely foresighted when they made the following statement in the early 1970s:

> If technological innovation can lower the limit of necessary work, and if the working class struggles in industry use that innovation for gaining free hours, the same cannot be said of housework; to the extent that she must in isolation procreate, raise and be responsible for children, a high mechanization of domestic chores doesn't free any time for the woman. She is always on duty, for the machine doesn't exist that makes and minds children. A higher productivity of domestic work though mechanization, then, can be related only to specific services, for example, cooking, washing, cleaning. Her workday is unending not because she has no machines, but because she is isolated.[67]

Summary

This chapter analyzed the distribution and the development of unpaid domestic work. Although domestic work has always been carried out by women, in preindustrial times it was intertwined with a number of other activities which all contributed to the reproduction of the household. It was only with the arrival of the factory system that unpaid domestic work became distinguishable from paid employment carried out outside the household in specifically designed workplaces. The gender division of household labor, according to which women are responsible for unpaid domestic work whereas men have a paid job outside the home, was subsequently fortified through the proliferation of the male breadwinner model. While time devoted to housework hardly decreased at all in the postwar years – in spite of the spread of household technologies such as washing machines – women started to cut back on domestic work time after they entered paid labor markets in the 1960s and 1970s. While women reduced domestic work time, men increased their time spent on household work. However, growing male participation in domestic labor started to level off in the 1980s and has stagnated ever since. As a result, the bulk of unpaid housework is still carried out by women. Total time devoted to domestic work also fell, but not as much as one might expect from increasing female labor market participation and the invention of new household technology. Some of the time saved on cleaning and other routine household tasks has been invested in the care of children.

Notes

1 Clark (1919: 5).
2 Crompton (2006: 33).
3 Oakley (1993: 49).
4 Ibid.: 21.
5 Crompton (2006: 36).
6 The separation of residence and workplace made it much more difficult to combine paid work with the care of infants and young children.
7 Seccombe (1993: 111).
8 Ibid.
9 Ibid.: 32.
10 Beechey (1987: 57).
11 Crompton (2006: 35).
12 Ibid.
13 Ibid.
14 Oakely (1993: 26).
15 Seccombe (1993: 111).
16 Ibid.
17 Himmelweit (1995: 7).
18 Crompton (2006: 37).
19 Beechy (1987: 66–9).
20 Crompton (2006: 39).
21 Walby (1986: 171).
22 Ibid.
23 Hirsch and Roth (1986: 56–60).

24 Vanek (1974: 16).
25 Ibid.: 17.
26 Ibid.
27 Gershuny (2000: 54).
28 Ibid. 66.
29 Bittman *et al*. (2004: 412).
30 Ibid.: 409.
31 Ibid.: 410.
32 Ibid. 414.
33 Ibid.: 413.
34 Jonathan Gershuny (1978).
35 Huws (2003: 38).
36 Ibid.: 37–8.
37 Vanek (1974: 119).
38 Ramey (2008: 55, Table 6).
39 Crompton (2006: 40).
40 Office of National Statistics (2013).
41 Crompton (2006: 141).
42 Vanek (1974: 118).
43 Ramey (2008: 55, Table 6).
44 Sayer (2010: 27).
45 Ibid.
46 Ibid.: 28, Table 2.1.
47 van der Lippe (2010: 5).
48 Sayer (2010: 28, Table 2.1).
49 Ibid.
50 van der Lippe (2010: 54).
51 Ministère de l'emploi et de la solidarité [Ministry of Employment and Solidarity] (1999: 51).
52 Sayer (2010: 31).
53 Baxter (1997: 220).
54 van der Lippe (2010: 45).
55 Ibid.
56 Crompton (2006: 142).
57 Sayer (2010: 30).
58 Ibid.: 28, Table 2.1.
59 Vanek (1974: 117).
60 Bianchi (2000: 405, Figure 1; and 411, Figure 7).
61 Ibid.: 401.
62 Bittman (2004: 160).
63 Fox *et al*. (2013).
64 Gauthier (2004: 656).
65 Folbre *et al*. (2004: 21).
66 Seccombe (1993: 204).
67 Dalla Costa and James (1972: 29).

Part III
Work time struggles

8 The establishment of a normal work day and week

Introduction

According to Marx, workers as individuals have little impact on the length of the work day and the distribution of work time – unless, one could add, they have special skills which make them unique and therefore not easily replaceable by capital. In general, work time is determined by production requirements and the desire of capital to increase surplus labor time. It is only through collective struggles that workers can confront the power of capital and establish what Marx has called a normal work day. This chapter looks at the collective struggles that led to successive work time reductions between 1830 and 1970. The research covers Britain, Canada, France, Germany, Sweden, and the United States as leading capitalist countries and representatives of distinctive work time regimes. The chapter starts with the struggle for the ten-hour day, followed by the international campaign for the eight-hour day. The next section describes the confrontations that led to the introduction of the 40-hour week after the Great Depression and in the postwar decades. The struggle for shorter work hours was only one way to increase free time; workers have also fought for paid vacation. The fourth part of the chapter deals with the introduction and development of paid vacation during and after the Second World War.

The ten-hour day

From a Marxist perspective one can expect an increase in work hours as a result of the extension of the capitalist mode of production, as long as there is no organized resistance from the simultaneously growing working classes. In fact there is evidence that work hours increased during the First Industrial Revolution at the end of the eighteenth and the beginning of the nineteenth century. Edward P. Thompson, for example, assumes that there was an increase in work hours as a result of growing work discipline exerted by the factory owners, which made it increasingly difficult to stay away from work during work days.[1] Oksar Negt believes that annual hours have increased as a result of the abolition of "Saint Monday" and religious holidays.[2] More recent research shows that the increase in work hours in Britain amounted to approximately 20 percent between

1760 and 1830.[3] This means that despite technological advancements, "a very substantial part of the increase of output was the result of extra-toil."[4] This extra toil, or what Marxists call surplus labor, caused growing dissatisfaction among the new class of proletarians. While previously individuals may have turned away and looked for other sources of income, the lack of alternative means of subsistence demanded a collective response of the dispossessed workers to put a limit to the work day. Britain was in a pioneering position. Large parts of the peasantry were already eliminated from the countryside before the Industrial Revolution got under way at the end of the eighteenth century. The early and radical proletarization, as John Saville notes, "gave British society certain special characteristics much earlier than anywhere else in the world."[5]

At the first stage it was only children suffering severe physical harm from 16-hour work days who benefited from the emerging struggle for shorter work hours.[6] In 1819 the British government introduced a 12-hour work day for children in cotton textile factories, but since the law was hardly enforced it had a very marginal effect or none at all. In 1847 the government took another approach and imposed a ten-hour work day for children and women as part of the so-called Factory Acts. After this, the authorities actually put the legislation into practice – see Marx's extensive quotes from factory inspector reports in *Capital* – which resulted in the establishment of a "normal work day."

The initial restriction on children and women's work hours has tempted some scholars to portray the introduction of the ten-hour day more as an act of humanity by the ruling classes rather than the result of a "protracted civil war" as described by Marx. According to Garry Cross, the emphasis on elites obscures the political objectives of the shorter hour movement.[7] Rather than emerging out of growing middle class humanitarianism, the British Factory Movement was an "affirmation of human rights by the workers."[8] Social reformers, progressive employers, and conservative agrarians, for individual reasons, may have joined the struggle for shorter work hours at certain times, but it was the workers' shorter hours committees which "appeared [in] every period of legislative debate over work hours from 1819 through 1847."[9] Most importantly, the Factory Movement was a *collective* response to overlong work hours, confirming Marx's assumption that workers can only collectively confront capital. The introduction of the ten-hour work day, which gradually covered male workers from the 1850s, subsequently became a landmark in the history of the British labor movement. As such it also offered a blueprint for the emerging class struggles on the European continent. As Wolfgang Abendroth points out, "through their success the English workers have provided concrete evidence for the possibility that immediate trade union action could force public powers to make sociopolitical interventions."[10]

While in the first half of the nineteenth century the fight for shorter work hours was driven by spontaneously formed shorter hour committees, the very success of these committees prompted the development and growth of the trade union movement after 1850, and especially after the adoption of the Trade Union Act in 1871.[11] According to M. A. Bienefeld, "the demand for shorter hours was a very important rallying point around which many new unions were established." According to accounts from several trade union leaders from the 1850s, shorter work hours – more than any other issue – provoked workers to support trade union action and encouraged them to join the union.[12] Colin Crouch records in a comparative study on the development of industrial relations in Europe that local collective bargaining was already fairly developed in Britain in 1870. In the late 1860s British trade unions had founded the Trade Union Congress (TUC) as a nationwide umbrella organization, whereas in other countries trade union organization, if it existed, was still very localized and fragile.[13] The growth of the trade union movement, in turn, reinforced the struggle for shorter work hours in the second half of the nineteenth century. The mutual dependence between trade union growth and the fight for shorter work hours is typical of early attempts to limit the work day and such mutual dependence is found outside Britain. Mike Davis, for example, calls the American Federation of Labor "the child of the historic agitation for the eight-hour day."[14]

Soon the British trade unions no longer relied on the state to mediate their work time demands and instead negotiated work hours directly with the employers. From the 1870s onwards, statutory regulations increasingly gave way to voluntary collective bargaining between employers and trade unions as the principal mechanism of regulating work time.[15] Bienefeld shows in his study on the development of work hours in nineteenth century Britain that not only were work hours frequently reduced as a result of strikes, but also that the actual length of the work day reflected the particular strength of the union in a certain trade or workplace. Reductions first happened in trades with relatively powerful unions, and they happened at times when these unions were particularly strong. As the unions' bargaining positions were rather favorable during times of high growth and low unemployment, it was during these periods that work time reductions were achieved. And it was during the same periods that employers were rather receptive to wage demands.[16] There is thus a connection between shorter work hours and higher wages – but both depend on trade union strength and/or a relative shortage of labor. The latter had some impact in the US and Canada. However, it was the early development of trade unions in Britain that made sure that the United Kingdom was the first country to introduce a ten-hour work day in the mid-nineteenth century, whereas the absence of strong unions or the ban on working class organizations explains the delay of work time reductions in France, Germany, and other countries.[17]

France and Germany followed the British example with a delay of almost 50 years. Both countries experienced major waves of social unrest in the 1830s, 1848, and the 1870s. Following a series of workers' riots the French government introduced a statutory work day for children in 1841. The legislation established a maximum workday of eight hours for children under 12 years old and of 12 hours for children aged between 12 and 16. The law was limited to factories with 20 and more employees. But more importantly it lacked an effective inspection system and was therefore "ineffective and inapplicable."[18] The government of the largest German state, Prussia, enacted legislation establishing a maximum ten-hour work day for children and minors under 17 years old in 1839. The provision also imposed a one-hour break around noon, as well as two 15-minute breaks – one in the morning and one in the afternoon. Children were furthermore not allowed to work on Sundays and religious holidays between 9 p.m. and 5 a.m.[19] Other provinces adopted similar provisions in the 1850s and 1860s and the law became universally applied in 1869.[20] Germany also lacked an effective inspection system before 1878, but the law seemed to have some impact as the number of children in factories decreased after 1840.[21]

The next critical juncture evolved in 1848. In this year a number of revolutions erupted across Europe. In France, a mass uprising ousted the monarchy and replaced it with popular government. The new government immediately introduced a ten-hour workday in Paris and an 11-hour day in the provinces.[22] However, the reduction lasted only for a few months. The conservative forces, which soon dominated the Second Republic, not only cracked down on a workers' rebellion in Paris, but also extended the work day to 12 hours before lifting all restrictions in 1851.[23] In both countries unions achieved some important victories in the 1860s and 1870s but gained little with respect to shorter work hours. In France, work time in many sectors and companies decreased between one and two hours between 1864 and 1871.[24] In Germany, the particularly powerful bookmakers' guild achieved the introduction of a nine-and-a-half-hour day in 1873. But most unions were struggling to defend existing standards against growing pressure from employers to expand work hours.[25] In roughly two-thirds of all strikes that took place between 1875 and 1879 workers demanded protection from longer work hours.[26] In fact it took another 20 years, until 1892, before France introduced an 11-hour work day for children and women, after Germany in 1891 had imposed an 11-hour day during week days and ten hours on Saturdays and those days preceding religious holidays.[27]

In both countries, the delay in work time reduction was due to legal obstacles to trade union organization. In France, the le Chapelier Law since 1791 had prohibited industrial association based on the assumption that there was no need for mediation between the interests of the individual and the interests of the public.[28] In 1810, the Napoleonic penal code specified sentences of one to three month and two to five years for attendance or organization of workers' meetings.[29] Strikes were illegal until 1864 and trade unions until 1884. In Germany, the ban

Table 8.1 Work time around 1870

	Hours per day	*Hours per year*
Canada	10	3,050
France	12	3,186
Germany	12	n/a
Sweden	13	3,965
United Kingdom	10	2,990
United States	10.5	3,244.5

Source: Huberman (2002).

on workers' combinations was lifted in 1861, but the social democratic party organization was declared illegal between 1878 and 1889.[30] After unions were legalized in France, French workers founded the Confédération Générale du Travail (CGT) in 1895. The consolidation of the union movement was followed by a wave of strikes in 1899–1900 and 1904–06.[31] In 1900 the government agreed to a reduction of half an hour every year until the establishment of the ten-hour workday in 1904.[32] In 1905 the miners' union gained an eight-hour workday. And while in 1906 a general strike for an eight-hour day was defeated, the government introduced a new law making Sunday a general day of rest.[33] In Germany, the ten-hour day became almost universally applied in the manufacturing industry in the 1890s. In Berlin and Charlottenburg, 90 percent of male workers worked ten hours per day or less in 1894. A new wave of strikes broke out in 1905–06 during which the miners in Prussia gained a nine-hour day.[34]

The eight-hour day

While many British trade unions had already won a nine-hour day by the 1870s, work time on the European continent and in North America still stood at ten or 11 hours in the 1880s.[35] However, at the end of the 1880s French, German, and other European labor organizations, together with the American Federation of Labor (AFL), joined British workers in an international struggle for the introduction of the eight-hour work day. In Britain a number of progressive intellectuals produced a series of pamphlets in support of the eight-hour day. Sydney Webb, for example, predicted that the eight-hour day would be the "inevitable result of an age of democracy."[36] The eight-hour day was already part of the program adopted by the First International Workingmen's Association in 1866, but it was the Second Socialist International, founded in 1889, which made the eight-hour day the most important demand of the international labor movement.[37] The 400 delegates from 20 countries who took part in the inaugural meeting in Paris agreed unanimously to hold eight-hour manifestations on the first of May of the following year.

On May 1, 1890, mass rallies and one-day strikes were held in many urban centers and mining towns in Europe and North America.[38] In Britain, protests were postponed to the first Sunday in May in order to avoid a conflict with employers about the resulting walkouts. In London alone some 250,000 workers rushed to the streets to show their support for the eight-hour day, among them an aged Friedrich Engels who cheered that "the English proletariat, newly awakened from a forty years' winter sleep, again enter[s] the movement of its class."[39] In sum, the campaign was an impressive demonstration of working class power. It was not only an outstanding example of international solidarity; it also showed the close link between the fight for shorter work hours and the consolidation of the labor movement. Karl Kautsky, the leader of the German social democrats, stated in a pamphlet issued for the May Day celebrations in Germany that the demand for the eight-hour work day was a "powerful tool to inspire workers and to unite the working class."[40] The limitation of the work day not only facilitated the physical and mental recovery of workers, it also created room for meetings, education, and political agitation, as well as the development of distinctive working class culture, which were all pivotal for the development and strengthening of the still nascent labor movement.

Despite the impressive turnout none of the national labor movements participating in the first May Day demonstrations reached the introduction of the eight-hour day in the following decade. In the United States the labor movement was already in retreat in the second half of the 1880s. The demand for the eight-hour work day had emerged during the American Civil War and spread rapidly in the wake of the postwar republican euphoria. As in Britain 20 years earlier, eight-hour leagues were organized across the country in the second half of the 1860s, in the wake of a still-embryonic trade union movement. For some time it even looked as if the demand would be met. In 1869, eight states passed eight-hour legislation and the federal government introduced an eight-hour day for federal employees. Yet as in the case of earlier work time legislation in France and Germany, it turned out that the laws were flawed because they lacked provisions for enforcement, contained loopholes, or allowed for conflicting interpretation. Despite the setback, the eight-hour demand continued to loom in a series of strikes and protests in the 1870s – including a local strike in 1872 that led to the introduction of the eight-hour day in New York City.

In order to take the struggle to the next level, the leadership of the newly founded American Federation of Labor called for a nationwide strike on May 1, 1886. Several hundred thousand workers answered the call and took part in the protests. In Chicago the demonstration spilled over in support of a lockout at a local plant. On May 3, two workers were killed outside the factory. The next day about 1,000 workers gathered at Chicago's Haymarket Square to protest against the lockout and oppression by the police. As the meeting was dispersing, a bomb was tossed into the police ranks. The police responded by firing into the crowd, killing at least one protester and injuring 70 more. The incident was followed by further killings and a wave of arrests and repression against trade union leaders across the United States.[41] David Roediger and Philip Foner argue that the Haymarket events had a devastating effect on the American eight-hour movement. Within a few weeks the campaign had lost its drive and in the wake of continuing police repression, Samuel Gompers and the rest of the AFL leadership abandoned mass rallies and strikes in favor of smaller and more moderate campaigns.[42] This was perhaps not the first time that union leadership cautioned its membership to be more patient when it came to the demand for shorter work hours – and it was certainly not the last. In the case of the AFL the move was part of a larger shift to the right, which ultimately resulted in the adoption of a strictly member-oriented American business unionism.[43] Still, in 1888, the AFL leadership proclaimed that no American worker should work longer than eight hours a day after May 1, 1890 – a date which was happily endorsed by the Second International to become the date for its international May Day demonstrations.

Without constant and vigorous pressure the eight-hour day did not make significant progress in America before the First World War. During the war some unions won the eight-hour day with the support of President Woodrow Wilson.[44] The railway workers gained a special law introducing the eight-hour day to the railway sector in 1916. In addition, the government made the awarding of war contracts dependent on the condition that workers engaged in them would work only eight hours a day. Legislation, furthermore, introduced an eight-hour day for children aged between 14 and 16, and several states adopted eight-hour laws for women. But Wilson declined to adopt a general eight-hour law. Not only were workers in favor of such a measure, Henry Ford, who had voluntarily reduced work time in his factory in 1914 (see Chapter 5), also supported the introduction of a general eight-hour day.[45] The War Labor Policies Board estimated that more than 925,000 workers gained the eight-hour day during 1917 and early 1918, though this still left a large part of the American workforce outside the new work time standard.[46]

In most countries the eight-hour work day was introduced after the end of the First World War. In large parts of Europe the years after the war were a period of exceptional social unrest and insurgency. In Russia the eight-hour day had been introduced during the Bolshevik Revolution. Smaller revolutions followed after the war in Hungary and parts of Germany. Mass demonstrations and strikes occurred all over Europe.[47] Capital was on the defensive because it was partly held responsible for the war and its horrors. In this situation resistance against the hastily drafted eight-hour bills was only moderate. In France an eight-hour law was adopted in anticipation of the May Day demonstrations in April 1919. The French Parliament unanimously voted for the legislation and even the French *patronat*, not exactly a friend of shorter work hours, welcomed the eight-hour day.[48] In Germany, the eight-hour day was established in 1919. As Michael Schneider notes, employers were happy to accept the work time reduction if it would prevent them from being expropriated.[49] In Britain, expropriation was not on the immediate agenda and while Parliament discussed a new work time bill – drafted by a joint committee with representatives from the trade union and employer camp – many trade unions achieved the introduction of the eight-hour day in a series of strikes in 1919–21. In 1924 three-quarters of the total trade union membership was covered by a 48-hour agreement.[50] Obviously the British trade union movement at this point felt so strong that it thought it would not need a legal back-up.[51]

The years after the First World War were an exceptional period in work time history. The majority of developed countries temporarily shared the same work time standard (the only other time this was the case was in the late 1960s and early 1970s when most countries had a 40-hour week – see further below). As Garry Cross notes, the

> radical demand for a reduction from a nine-, ten-, or even twelve-hour workday [to an eight-hour day] challenged, as could no wage increase, the economic and cultural status quo. Not only had the eight-hour day been a symbol of the Second International, but it had been a transnational goal of labor and reformers in a developing world economy where competition blocked improvements in the labor standard at the national level.[52]

The newly formed International Labor Organization (ILO) seized the opportunity and adopted an international work time convention in 1919. Most of the 85 member states signed the convention, declaring that they would introduce an eight-hour day and 48-hour week within the next three years. Among the few countries that initially declined to sign the agreement was Canada.[53]

The Canadian labor movement also pressed for the introduction of the eight-hour day after the war. As Greg Heron notes with respect to the strike wave that erupted the country in 1919, including a six-week general strike in Winnipeg, "the single demand that probably rolled up most of the aspirations of the workers' movements in this period was for a shorter workday."[54] In 1919 about a quarter of all strikes were about shorter work hours, "far more than ever before or since."[55] Some unions won shorter work hours on the local level, but the strike wave did not translate into a nationwide work time reduction. While Canada hesitated to sign, mainly because it feared the competition of American companies not restricted by an eight-hour law, a number of countries, which initially had supported the convention, did not ratify the agreement in the following years.[56] In fact, among the larger Western European nations, only France, Spain, and Italy ratified the agreement.[57]

From 1920 onwards, employers in several countries fought for modifications and exceptions to undermine the eight-hour standard they had agreed to only a few years earlier. In Germany, employers attacked the existing regulation for being "too schematic."[58] Deviations required special permits which the authorities issued only very reluctantly until 1920. The government responded to such criticism by amending existing legislation in 1923. The new regulations not only allowed for two overtime hours per day without special permission; they also opened the possibility for the social partners to negotiate longer hours on an industry level (several unions negotiated such agreements). As a result of the changes the eight-hour day effectively "disappeared," as one official trade union publication noted. Weekly work hours immediately increased to 50.4 hours in 1924.[59] The erosion of established work hours, especially when introduced by law, is a recurrent feature of the struggle for shorter work hours. The work time Emergency Act of 1927 reduced the number of exemptions, but at the same time made it easier for companies to deviate from the eight- and 48-hour standard if workers were rewarded with overtime bonuses for additional hours (previously overtime hours were paid at the same rate as regular hours).[60] The French government also introduced the possibility of working overtime in the 1920s, but in France the conflict was far from resolved. The overtime issue resurfaced in the struggles over the introduction of the 40-hour week in the 1930s (see below).[61]

The 40-hour week

While in Europe most labor movements had gained in strength by end of the First World War, the US trade unions suffered a major defeat as a result of a deliberate attack by employers. Estimates suggest that the "open shop crusade" cost the American trade union movement about 30 percent of its membership.[62]

The eight-hour day had partially been introduced during the war, but work hours did not decrease further in the wake of deteriorating union power. In the midst of a period of weakness, the AFL decided to launch a national campaign for the introduction of a 40-hour week in 1926, perhaps hoping to rebuild the membership base by reactivating the struggle for shorter work hours. The campaign was a complete failure. While AFL leaders celebrated a doubling in the number of members enjoying a 40-hour week at the 1928 national convention, most of these belonged to five particularly well-organized unions in the building trades, and even there the majority were painters.[63] On the eve of the Great Depression the National Industrial Conference Board registered 270 companies with a 40-hour week, employing some 418,700 workers – a large number of them working for Ford, who had voluntarily introduced the 40-hour week in 1926.[64]

The situation changed dramatically with the onset of the Great Depression. In 1928–29 sales started to fall, factories cut their output, and unemployment increased.[65] In response to the crisis employers not only laid off workers, they also cut work hours in order to adjust production to rapidly vanishing demand. Average weekly work hours fell below 35 hours during the depression years as several major industrial companies reduced work time first to 40 and then to 30 hours a week. In 1932, more than half of all workers and 63 percent of those in manufacturing worked part-time.[66] Chris Nyland estimates that the depression caused an "aggregate permanent reduction of basic work time ... of approximately twenty per cent."[67] At the peak of the crisis one in three Americans was without a job. In this situation trade unions no longer pressed for shorter work hours to have more time to rest, but instead moved to share the shrinking amount of work among a larger number of workers – a powerful motive for work time reductions, which repeatedly played a decisive role in the struggle for shorter work hours. As Benjamin Hunnicut notes, under these circumstances "even businessmen, industrialists and conservative politicians, the traditional champions of long hours, seemed to have come around to support the cause, albeit reluctantly and with conditions."[68]

While many enterprises reduced work time in the wake of the crisis, others actually increased work hours because they no longer held inventories and instead produced on demand – increasing pressure to finish products as fast as possible to ship them to customers.[69] Because of the highly fragile economic situation the unions were unable to gain shorter work hours in negotiations with individual employers. As a result the AFL, traditionally favoring collective bargaining over employment legislation, called for the adoption of a work time law. The AFL leadership assumed that a reduction of the work week to 30 hours at current wages would solve the unemployment problem in the United States. Union leaders like AFL president William Green insisted that the introduction of the moving assembly line and other mass production methods were partly responsible for the job losses. By continuing the payment of existing wages for shorter hours, employers would merely share some of the gains they had achieved in the preceding decade.[70]

Democratic senator Hugo Black also saw the reduction of work time as the best way to solve the unemployment problem. He introduced a bill to Congress in 1932 that would have imposed a work week of no more than 30 hours.[71] Surprisingly, the bill passed the Senate and for some time it looked as if it could become law. However, while the bill was debated in the House, American employers intensified the fight against the 30-hour week. The struggle was spearheaded by the National Association of Manufactures (NAM) which denounced the bill as communist-inspired. They found support from numerous business people "who were fully content to support a voluntary and temporary share-the-work movement, [but] were horrified by the prospect that the workweek might never recover from the depression."[72] President Franklin D. Roosevelt supported the idea of shorter hours to fight unemployment, but was skeptical about the bill. As his labor secretary Frances Perkins recalls, "there were no provisions for emergency variation or for appropriate modifications in different industries dependent upon different natural resources and conditions."[73] The administration feared that an inflexible 30-hour week could harm slowly recovering businesses, and urged the installment of boards with the power to permit overtime of up to ten hours per week. The AFL leadership objected to the concession.[74] While the bill narrowly missed passage in the House, the Roosevelt administration came up with an alternative plan to regulate hours, wages, and other issues.

The result was the adoption of the National Industrial Recovery Act (NIRA or NRA) in 1933. The NRA was widely seen as a trade-off for the defeat of the 30-hour bill, although the trade unions continued to demand the adoption of a statutory 30-hour week.[75] The NRA introduced procedures to adopt so-called industry codes. The main task was to regulate prices, but the industry codes also included provisions for work hours and wages. As Nelson Lichtenstein notes, "the NRA repudiated laissez-faire economics and, in its place, sought to codify American capitalism by promulgating scores of industry 'codes' that would put a floor under wages and prices and a ceiling on hours and efforts."[76] Over the two-year lifespan of the legislation, 487 codes were adopted covering 13 million workers. Some 57 percent of the codes introduced a 40-hour week as recommended by the Department of Labor; 43 percent provided for a shorter and 49 percent for a longer work week. The length of the work week could vary from 36 to 60 hours.[77] Following the demands of trade union leaders, most of the codes imposed a strict limit for daily and weekly work hours – which, as described below, later legislation in America failed to do. Yet at the same time they addressed the employers' wish for flexibility by granting a large number of exemptions. Exemptions were made for certain professions (managers, engineers, electricians, mechanics, etc.), for emergency situations, and for production subject to seasonal fluctuations (so-called "tolerance" or "peak-period" provisions). But only a few codes provided for the possibility of overtime working.[78]

After the Supreme Court repealed the NRA in 1935, Roosevelt urged Congress to pass new legislation to "end starvation wages and intolerable hours."[79] But negotiations on the Fair Labor Standards Act only progressed slowly. In terms of work hours the initial bill foresaw the establishment of boards authorized to introduce maximum work hours for each individual industry. The law only stipulated that weekly work time could not exceed 48 hours.[80] Union leaders rejected the 48-hour week and supported an amendment that "would have made it unlawful to employ anyone for more than eight hours a day or forty hours a week, but would have permitted 'emergency work.' "[81] The compromise reached between the government and the unions imposed a regular 40-hour work week with the obligation to pay overtime premiums for hours exceeding the 40-hour threshold. Overtime rates would be one-and-a-half the value of regular rates.[82]

The overtime premium did the trick: the prospect of allocating more money for its members induced union leaders to give up their opposition to flexible work hours and even accept a stepwise reduction of weekly work hours to 44 hours in 1938, 42 hours in 1939, and 40 hours from 1940 onwards.[83] The payment of wage supplements for work time flexibility became the basis for the Fordist work time compromise of the postwar decades. As Perkins notes, "the fact that excess hours are penalized by overtime costs has proved sufficient to keep hours at reasonable levels and yet flexible enough to make it possible to work more than forty hours when necessary."[84] While this may have been true for the years following the adoption of the law, the absence of an absolute maximum work time provision ultimately allowed American employers to require their workers to put in vast amounts of overtime hours, resulting in substantially longer work hours than in other countries from the 1970s onwards.

Initially the FLSA covered only 20 percent of the labor force and even though its scope was gradually extended in the following years, it was only through the simultaneous expansion of collective bargaining that a general 40-hour week could be reached in the United States in the early 1950s.[85] The NRA had not only established maximum hours and minimum wages, but also a provision that required employers to negotiate with trade unions who met certain criteria.[86] The Roosevelt administration took the subsequent repeal of the NRA as an opportunity to fix some of the shortcomings of the previous regulation, including, most importantly, the possibility to set up company unions to circumvent negotiations with independent unions (which employers had frequently used during the NRA). The result was the adoption of the National Labor Relations Act – better known as the Wagner Act.[87] The Wagner Act established the principle that unions had the right to represent their respective workers in negotiations with their employers if they could show sufficient support among workers in a specific company or plant.[88] Despite the company-based fragmentation of industrial relations, the Wagner Act gave unions a tool to push into new areas which were previously thought out of reach for union organizers. The main force behind the following unionization drive was the Congress of Industrial Organizations (CIO), founded as an alternative to the more craft-based AFL in 1935 (the AFL and CIO merged to become the AFL-CIO two decades later). The CIO deliberately targeted the masses of unskilled or semi-skilled laborers working in the rapidly growing mass production industries.[89]

A decisive confrontation in this regard took place at a General Motors plant in Flint. Among other things, the union's strike demands included a 30-hour week with double pay for weekend and holiday work. If the demands tabled by the union in December 1936 are read as a priority list, "shorter hours ranked just after recognition and the establishment of a secure seniority system."[90] After GM declined to meet the demands, workers shut down production. They did so by using a new strike technique: rather than picketing the company from outside, they occupied the production facilities in what became known as a sit-down strike. GM asked the state of Michigan to bring in the National Guard to remove strikers from the company's premises, but the Democrat governor refused. Left on its own, GM gave in and started negotiations with the United Auto Workers (UAW) to end the six-week strike in early 1937.[91] While GM subsequently acknowledged the right of the union to represent GM workers, the company nonetheless succeeded in turning down the 30-hour week. As Ronald Edsforth notes,

> General Motors' ability to resist the initial UAW effort to shorten the work week in 1936–37 had enormous significance as a historical precedent within the industry as whole. Having agreed to a five-day, forty-hour week for GM workers, UAW leaders found it impossible to reduce work time standards at other major companies when they subsequently recognized the union.[92]

However, the Flint sit-down strike was still a major breakthrough for the union movement. With similar successes in other companies, UAW membership soared by more than ten times between 1936 and 1937.[93] Overall, American unions won five million new members between 1933 and 1937, at least half of them during just a few months in 1937. And another four million workers joined the trade union movement during the Second World War.[94] The war in several regards helped to consolidate the still fragile system of industrial relations: the War Labor Board (WLB) encouraged employers to bargain with unions, partly by offering them large government contracts. Such a contract, no doubt, played an important role in convincing Ford to accept the striking UAW as a bargaining partner in 1941. At the same time, the WLB pressed unions to accept management prerogatives – including the right to order overtime – which they had challenged in the violent struggles of the 1930s.

The Great Depression arrived in France later than in other countries. By 1931, however, the economy had dropped into severe recession. Before long the dire economic situation turned into a political upheaval. In the wake of a series of bankruptcies and plant closures, anger and frustration resulted in mass factory occupations, strikes, and mass rallies. The protest movement led to the election of a left wing government in 1936. The head of the Front Populaire, Léon Blum, had promised to "solve the crisis of unemployment by judiciously redistributing the available work among all the workers."[95] The new government kept its promise and reduced work time to 40 hours a week in 1936. At the same time the new legislation also introduced two weeks of paid vacation.[96] Steve Jefferys argues that while reflecting the temporary weakness of French employers, the 40-hour law was "essentially politically driven rather than the outcome of workers' demands." Work time, according to Jefferys, was "no major rallying [issue] for French workers devastated by the loss of 1.3 million industrial jobs between 1931 and 1936."[97] But politicians and trade union leaders such as the president of the CGT, Léon Johaux, promoted the 40-hour week precisely as a remedy for mounting unemployment. The law mentioned the struggle against unemployment and the necessity that workers profit from technological progress; it also made reference to the international 40-hour convention of 1935, and concluded that "this law is claimed by the world of workers."[98]

Work time fell quickly in light of the new regulation. In early 1937, 3.5 million industrial workers had already reduced their work time to 40 hours per week; and by September 1938, "it was in theory nearly universal."[99] Employment in establishments with more than 100 workers immediately increased by more than 10 percent, while average yearly work hours fell by 400 hours between 1935 and 1937.[100] The law was implemented through a series of decrees adopted for each industry through detailed timetables, "ruling out any variation in the schedule and any individual arrangement."[101] The approach is reminiscent of the industry codes adopted during the NRA in the United States. The French codes, however, provided for much less flexibility. Opponents, accordingly, argued not so much against the reduction of work time as against the rigid application and the lack of flexibility, including the impossibility of working overtime – which was also thought responsible for the simultaneous drop in industrial output. Temporary exceptions were possible, but only in very specific cases such as emergencies, national defense interests, or an extraordinary increase in labor demand.[102] Overtime working, too, was handled very restrictively, limited to some special professions, and to a maximum of two hours per day.[103] According to Francois Guedj and Gerad Vindt, unions strictly opposed overtime working because they still remembered how the eight-hour day had been undermined by widespread overtime working after the First World War.[104]

Roosevelt's secretary of labor, Frances Perkins, later argued that the rigidity of the legislation contributed to the collapse of the French Republic. In a speech delivered in 1940, she emphasized the difference between the French and American approaches. The American 40-hour law was

> very carefully framed to avoid this rigidity, and any employer in the land can legally and automatically ask his employees to work as many hours beyond forty as he cares without permission of the government as long as he pays the overtime rate of time and one-half.[105]

What Perkins forgot to mention was that after the disintegration of the popular front government in 1938, and the installment of Edouard Daladier as prime minister, the French government amended the legislation, loosening overtime restrictions – initially granting up to eight (and later up to ten) overtime hours per week without government permission – and allowing for a large number of exemptions.[106] Thus, the French labor movement eventually won the 40-hour work week, but only with far-reaching concessions with regard to work time flexibility. As such the process showed striking parallels to the US experience.

Canada closely followed the example of the United States in the postwar period. As Jane Jenson *et al*. have pointed out, Canada imported the Fordist mass production model and the productivity wage bargaining formula via branch plants of American auto companies, which had been established to avoid tariffs and quotas.[107] Plants were preferably located near Detroit and the US border, making southern Ontario the center of the growing Canadian auto industry. This does not mean that the Canadian unions got around fighting "long and bitter strikes to extract the benefits of a Fordist wage relation" – including the 40-hour week.[108] With the exception of Ford workers, who enjoyed a 40-hour week after the company voluntarily reduced work time in the 1920s, Canadian autoworkers worked substantially longer hours than their counterparts south of the border. Following the six-week work stoppage in Flint, GM workers in Oshawa also went on strike in 1937. They failed to win union recognition, but they gained a 44-hour week and a substantial wage increase. This was significant progress in the Ontario context, where 60 percent of men and 50 percent of women still worked between 49 and 60 hours a week in 1942–43.[109] Even more importantly, the Oshawa strike brought the United Auto Workers to Canada. Other American unions followed so that by 1949, 70 percent of Canadian union members were organized in local chapters of international unions headquartered in the United States.[110]

Labor unrest continued from the 1930s to the Second World War. During the war the unions profited from an increasing shortage of labor. Despite a general ban on strikes, the number of protests did not decline. In 1943 one out of every three trade union members was on strike.[111] Repeated disruptions threatened war production and the repressive response by the government drove voters to the Cooperative Commonwealth Federation (CCF), which had emerged from a radical farmer association mainly based in the western provinces, to a nationwide working class party.[112] Confronted with a new competitor on the left, the governing Liberal Party was suddenly willing to make concessions.[113] The most important concession was the passage of Privy Council Order 1003 in 1944. Similar to the Wagner Act, the order granted unions the exclusive right to represent workers at the company level if they could prove sufficient support.[114] The provision was continued after the war as part of the Industrial Relations and Dispute Investigations Act. As a result, union membership increased from 15 percent in 1935 to more than 24 percent by the end of the war.[115]

In the wake of continuous pressure from organized labor – 1946 and 1947 were particularly intense years, with 6.9 million days lost in 461 strikes – average work hours in manufacturing fell from 48 hours in 1944 to 43 hours in 1950 and further to 41 hours in 1960.[116] The leading companies already had collective agreements providing for a 40-hour week by 1953, and 90 percent of Canadian autoworkers enjoyed a 40-hour week by the mid-1950s.[117] As Deborah Sunter and René Morisette have pointed out, the average work week only fell about 1.5 hours in the 25 years prior to 1946, while decreasing a further nine hours over the next 11 years.[118]

While Canada had imported the 40-hour week as part of collective bargaining, the adoption of a 40-hour law was complicated by the federal structure of the Canadian state according to which the provinces enjoy considerable auto-nomy. In 1930 the federal government had established the obligation of an eight-hour day for work performed under government contracts, but the provinces, which were attributed the legal power to regulate work hours at provincial level by a 1925 Supreme Court decision, did not show much enthusiasm for reducing work time. During the war both federal and provincial governments were con-fronted with mounting pressure from workers. In Ontario, where existing legis-lation set the maximum work time at 60 hours per week, the conservative government adopted a 48-hour law in 1944 – not least as a measure to regain some of the working class vote it had lost in the previous election.[119] Although the Ontario work week was considerably longer than the 40-hour week intro-duced in the US, the Canadian law established a maximum work time limit, whereas American work time legislation only imposed a threshold after which employers had to pay overtime supplements. Other provinces followed after the war. While Alberta and Saskatchewan also introduced a 48-hour week, British Columbia and Manitoba reduced weekly work time to 40 hours.[120] In 1965 the federal government introduced the obligation to pay overtime supplements after 44 hours of work per week for federal employees.[121] Ontario followed with the introduction of a 44-hour overtime threshold in 1968.[122] In the following years the rest of the provinces also reduced work hours so that by the early 1980s, federal and provincial work time legislation established a standard work time of between 40 and 44 hours per week.[123]

In Britain, Germany, and Sweden the 40-hour week was introduced in the postwar period. The British Amalgamated Engineering Union (AEU) had won a 44-hour week in 1927, but more ambitious plans to reduce work hours to 40 hours per week to redistribute employment among the increasing number of unemployed workers had failed. After the war, British trade unions started a new attempt to win the 40-hour week. Employers, not surprisingly, rejected the trade union plan. But the Labor government, elected in 1923, was also hesitant on the grounds that shorter hours would limit the desperately needed output.[124] As a result, collective agreed work hours only decreased to 45 and 44 hours by the end of the 1940s.[125] Work hours fell slowly despite a rapid expansion of the trade union movement. By 1950 more than 45 percent of dependent employees were union members, and that proportion had increased to almost 50 percent by the mid-1960s.[126] With growing output and living standards, British workers increased the pressure for shorter work hours. The engineering workers con-tinued to set the pace: their union won a 40-hour week in 1960.[127] Three years later a million industrial workers (7 percent of the workforce) covered by col-lective agreements had gained a 40-hour week. The proportion had increased to 50 percent by 1966, and more than 80 percent by the end of the decade.[128]

The German trade unions, too, called for the introduction of a 40-hour week in 1930–31 to redistribute shrinking employment among a larger number of workers.[129] Although the government supported the idea of work sharing, the emergency decree that was passed in June 1931 only included a recommendation – not an obligation – to reduce work time to 40 hours a week. Average work hours in manufacturing fell from about 50 hours in 1927 to 42 hours in 1932 but still 17 percent of German workers put in more than 48 hours per week in 1930.[131] During the war work time limitations were suspended. After the war the economy slowly recovered and weekly work hours reached the prewar levels of 47 and 50 hours in 1948.[132] In 1952, the Federal Trade Union Organization (DGB) raised the work time issue at the May Day demonstrations and made it a major objective in its 1955 "action program."[133] The campaign reached its peak with the popular slogan "Saturday Daddy belongs to me" cheered at the May Day parades in 1956.[134]

The German metalworkers' union IG Metall spearheaded the fight for shorter work hours in the postwar decades. In 1965, IG Metall went on strike for 16 weeks in Schleswig-Holstein in support of a 45-hour week. A reduction to 44 hours followed in 1959, and the union reached an agreement for a stepwise introduction of the 40-hour week starting in 1960. According to this agreement work hours were to be reduced to 42.5 hours in 1962, 41.25 hours in 1964, and 40 hours in 1965.[135] The reduction did not happen as smoothly as anticipated. In 1963, IG Metall called a strike in Baden-Württemberg after the employers unilaterally terminated the agreement. The government intervened and successfully pressured employers to continue with the work time reductions, but the introduction of the 40-hour week was effectively postponed to 1967.[136] Other unions followed and also negotiated for a stepwise introduction of the 40-hour week in the 1960s and 1970s. Between 1960 and 1974 collectively agreed weekly work hours fell by about 10 percent to an average of 40.3 hours.[137] In 1971, the 40-hour week applied to 77 percent of blue-collar workers and 52 percent of white-collar staff.[138]

Sweden also experienced massive social disruptions in the 1930s, but the conflicts did not lead to an open political confrontation or an overthrow of the parliamentary system as in other European countries. Instead, the government successfully pressured the two conflicting parties, the Trade Union Confederation (LO) and the Employers' Federation (SAF), to reach an agreement about the unions' right for collective representation and the employers' right to manage companies. The Saltsjöbaden Agreement not only assured industrial peace; it also laid the foundation for a highly centralized bargaining system.[139] The government introduced two weeks of paid vacation in 1938, but the social partners did not cut work hours in response to the crisis. In fact it was the Swedish government which took the first cautious steps towards a reduction in work hours in the mid-1950s. The government appointed a special commission to investigate the feasibility of shorter work hours. The commission recommended a gradual reduction of weekly work time for blue-collar workers to 45 hours between 1957 and 1960, which the government then put into practice.[140] The process was repeated in 1963. However, while the commission was still working, the social partners agreed to a reduction of the work week to 42.5 hours in 1966.[141] The next impulse came from the government – after the work time commission had recommended the introduction of a 40-hour week in the late 1960s, the government adopted legislation in 1970 reducing the work week in several steps to 40

Table 8.2 Phases of work time reductions

Phase 1	*Ten-hour day*	1850–1900	UK 1847; Germany 1891; France 1892; Sweden 1905
Phase 2	*Eight-hour day*	1890–1920	Austria 1919; Belgium 1921; France 1919; Germany 1919; UK 1919–21; Netherlands 1919; Sweden 1920; Italy 1923
Phase 3	*40-hour week*	(a) 1930–50	France 1936; US 1950; Canada 1955
		(b) 1960–80	Germany 1970; Finland 1970; UK 1970; Italy 1973; Austria 1975; Belgium 1975; Norway 1976
Phase 4	*35-hour week*	1995–2000	Germany 1995; France 2000

Source: Own compilation from various sources.

hours between 1971 and 1973. As a result average weekly work hours in manufacturing fell from 41 hours in the early 1960s to 38 hours in the early 1980s.[142] The 1970 legislation, for the first time, also covered the work time of white-collar workers whose work hours had previously been negotiated at the firm or industry level.[143]

Paid vacation

Shorter work hours is only one way of increasing free time; paid vacation and the length of retirement are also limiting the time workers have to spend at their jobs. The struggle for paid vacation took off at the turn of the nineteenth century and ran through to the twentieth century. In the nineteenth century, days off were mostly unpaid and granted by employers on a voluntary base, often to reward particular employees. In Germany, paid vacation was first introduced for civil servants, and around the turn of the century extended to clerks – partly to widen the division between white- and blue-collar workers in the German working class. In 1901, almost 51 percent of white-collar workers in the banking and insurance sector, and more than 40 percent in manufacturing sector, enjoyed two weeks of paid holidays per year, while paid vacation for blue-collar workers was extremely rare.[144]

In Britain, a government inquiry disclosed that in 1906 workers on average had 11 or 12 authorized days off per year, and that paid holidays ranged from 8.5 days in chemicals, paper printing, and food, drink, and tobacco, to nine days in the building trades, ten in textiles and 13 in engineering and iron and steel.[145] In a few trades, including certain sections of the railway and newspaper industries and in the road, sanitary, and maintenance departments of local authorities, entitlement to paid vacation was included in collective agreements before the First World War.[146] In the early twentieth century, paid holidays slowly became part of the general wage-work bargain. As Alice Russell notes, "they were no longer a 'gift' arbitrarily bestowed on the 'deserving', but a component of income earned by workers."[147] A few more agreements were concluded during the war, but it was during the strike years of 1919 and 1920 that two million workers won the right to paid holidays.[148] However, despite the rapid growth of holiday entitlement after the First World War a large part of the British workforce remained excluded. Many of the early agreements were reached in fast-growing sectors, or in relatively sheltered industries unaffected by foreign competition. They were absent in industries such as textiles, iron and steel, engineering, shipbuilding, coalmining, building, and construction.[149] As in the case of the shorter work week, competition got in the way of social progress. The several attempts between the mid-1920s and the mid-1930s by union-friendly members of the British Parliament to introduce legislation guaranteeing a general entitlement to paid vacation, ultimately failed.[150] In 1938 a special committee found that slightly more than 40 percent of the workforce received holidays with pay.[151] Nevertheless, the 1938 Holidays with Pay Act, which was adopted in response to the findings, did not provide for a general entitlement to paid vacation. Instead, it only gave the authority to introduce paid holidays to industry boards and other statutory bodies installed to mediate wage disputes in sectors with weak organization.[152]

In France the popular government not only introduced the 40-hour week in 1936, but also a general entitlement to two weeks of paid vacation.[153] And while the 40-hour week was highly controversial, the right to vacation was "the product of a far broader consensus, supported by the Catholic Right with its promise of family leisure."[154] Thus, while the successor of the Popular Front allowed companies to use overtime to exceed the 40-hour standard, the entitlement to two weeks of vacation remained firmly in place. Furthermore, while weekly work hours remained unchanged until the early 1980s, holiday entitlements increased repeatedly during the postwar decades. French workers received the right to three weeks of vacation in 1956, four weeks in 1963, and five weeks in 1981. While following quite distinctive trajectories in the history of shorter work hours, France and Sweden show remarkable similarities in the development of paid vacation: Sweden, too, introduced two weeks of paid vacation in 1938. Statutory holidays were subsequently extended to three weeks in 1951 and four weeks in 1963. Since 1977 Swedish workers have had a right to a minimum of five weeks of paid holidays per year.[155] In 1990 the government introduced two more days as a first step towards a sixth week of vacation, but the law was later repealed, leaving vacation entitlement at five weeks per year.[156]

The British government introduced a statutory right to four weeks of paid vacation with the adoption of the European Work Time Directive in 1998. Yet for most parts of the postwar period British workers relied on collective bargaining to win and extend paid holidays. In 1951 nearly three-fifths of manual workers were entitled to 12 days, and about a third enjoyed 18 days off, including public holidays.[157] The unions subsequently increased the pressure to extend holidays, partly at the expense of shorter weekly hours. As a result, 97 percent of manual workers had two full weeks of paid holidays by 1960.[158] Additional days off were reserved for workers with particular seniority. In 1962, 10 percent of employees profited from additional seniority-based holidays, and the proportion increased to 30 percent by the end of the decade. General vacation entitlements picked up again in the second half of the 1960s. The proportion of manual workers entitled to three and more weeks of paid vacation increased from 3 percent in 1965 to 15 percent in 1969 and 63 percent in 1971. In 1975, only 1 percent of manual workers in Britain had holidays of two weeks or less. Five years later, 74 percent had four weeks of paid vacation.[159] In Germany, too, the expansion of paid vacation in the post-Second World War period was mainly driven by collective bargaining. Most German workers had two weeks of paid holidays per year in the first half of the 1950s. In 1960, the number increased to an average of three weeks.[160] In 1963 the government adopted the Federal Holiday Act, granting a three week minimum entitlement for all workers. But the law was quickly outdated by further progress in collective negotiations. By the end of the 1960s average collectively agreed paid holidays accounted for four weeks per year and reached an average of five weeks in 1975.[161]

Canada established the right to paid vacation during the Second World War. In Ontario the Hours of Work and Vacations with Pay Act introduced one week of paid holidays in 1944. This was a remarkable achievement compared to the US, where the Fair Labor Standard failed to establish the right to a paid vacation. In the early 1960s, Manitoba, Saskatchewan, Alberta, and British Columbia increased vacation entitlement to two weeks, as did the federal government with respect to federal employees. In 1968 Ontario closed the gap and also introduced a second week of paid holidays.[162] While statutory vacations remained short by international standards, Canadian unions were more successful in expanding vacation time via collective bargaining. In 1946, Chrysler workers at Windsor went on a 126-day strike for higher wages and more vacation. In the end they won three more days off.[163] More holidays were added in the postwar decades. In manufacturing the average paid vacation reached 2.7 weeks in 1959 and 3.6 weeks in 1979.[164]

The United States established a temporary right to a vacation during the Second World War. The National War Labor Board granted one week of paid holiday after a year of service, and two weeks after five years.[165] Vacation entitlements were subsequently incorporated in most collective agreements after 1945, but the right was never established by law. The lack of a general vacation law created vast inequalities in the consumption of holidays, especially between unionized and non-unionized workers. Workers in highly productive and unionized sectors such as the auto industry enjoyed two weeks of paid vacation in 1947, four weeks in 1958, and six weeks in 1968.[166] Outside the unionized sectors, paid vacation grew much more slowly. On average, paid holidays increased from 1.3 weeks per year in 1960 to 1.9 weeks in 1968 and two weeks in 1979. Since the early 1980s average holidays have remained more-or-less stagnant. In 2007 the average private sector worker enjoyed nine days of paid leave and six paid public holidays per year. Yet the focus on average duration

Table 8.3 Development of paid vacation

1 week	US 1942–45; Ontario 1944; UK 1950
2 weeks	France 1936; Sweden 1938; Germany 1950–55; UK 1960; US auto industry 1968; Ontario 1968
3 weeks	France 1956; Sweden 1951, Germany 1963; UK 1975
4 weeks	US auto industry 1958; France 1963; Sweden 1963; Germany 1970; UK 1980
5 weeks	Germany 1975; Sweden 1977; France 1981

Source: Own compilation from various sources.

obscures the fact that almost one in four American workers has no paid leave at all (paid public holidays are reserved for government workers and workers in similar positions).[167] The shorter paid vacation explains a substantial part of the work time gap between the United States and Europe as well as between the US and Britain.

Summary

Rather than falling automatically with growing productivity and living standards, the reduction of work time was the result of a persistent struggle waged by trade unions. These struggles resulted in the establishment of a ten-hour work day between the 1830s and 1870s, an eight-hour day after the First World War, and the 40-hour week in the 1930s and after the Second World War. The fight for shorter working hours, in turn, not only "freed" time for the development of worker associations and a working class culture, but also boosted (international) working class solidarity. The acceptance of overtime when paid at a higher rate than regular work hours also demonstrated the temptation of more consumption and the limits of working class solidarity. However, the compromise also showed the importance of work time flexibility for capital. Increasing productivity also played a role in the struggle for shorter work hours: on the one hand it encouraged trade unions to demand shorter hours in order to avoid technological unemployment; on the other hand trade unions accepted longer hours if it allowed their industries to compete with the technologically advanced nations. The 40-hour week, plus overtime payments, became a cornerstone of the Fordist standard employment relationship in the postwar years. However, the early move to the 40-hour standard meant that US workers enjoyed considerably shorter work hours than their European counterparts in the postwar decades. Germany, the UK, and Sweden closed the gap in the late 1960s and early 1970s. While the US forged ahead in terms of shorter work hours, it lagged behind in terms of paid vacation. Outside the strongly organized industrial sectors, American workers have considerably shorter vacations than their counterparts in Europe. In Europe the reduction of work hours was accompanied by a continuous expansion of vacation entitlements in the postwar decades.

Notes

1   Thompson (1967).
2   Negt (2001: 150–1).
3   Voth (2000: 168–9).
4   Ibid.: 271–2.
5   Saville (1988: 7).
6   Protection of children was partly introduced after military authorities in several countries complained of problems conscripting enough healthy young men for the army.
7   Agrarians supported the ten-hour legislation as payback for the industrialist's attack on the Corn Laws, which had imposed special tariffs on imported corn. The Corn Laws protected British farmers but resulted in comparably high food prices. They were repealed in 1846. See Cross (1989: 26).
8   Thompson (1964: 340).
9   Cross (1989: 27).
10   Abendroth (1965: 22–3).
11   Hyman (2003: 29).
12   Bienefeld (1972: 143).
13   Crouch (1993: 70–1).
14   Davis (1986: 34).
15   Barnard *et al.* (2003: 227).
16   Bienefeld (1972: 134).
17   Crouch (1993: 71–5).
18   Fridenson (2004: 30–2).
19   Scharf (1987: 105–6).
20   Ibid.: 107.
21   Ibid.
22   Guedj and Vindt (1997: 33).
23   See Jefferys (2002: 243); and Rigaudiat (1993: 25).
24   Fridenson (2004: 64).
25   Scharf (1987: 158–60).
26   Ibid.: 149.
27   Guedj and Vindt (1997: 212).
28   This indicates the early suppression of workers' demands after the victory of the French Revolution. See Lorwin (1954: 4).
29   In principle the ban on association also applied to employers, but with much lower penalties. See Shorter and Tilly (1974: 21–2).
30   Ibid.: 121.
31   Ibid. See also Jefferys (2002: 244); and Rigaudiat (1993: 27).
32   See Cette and Taddei (1994: 38); and Husson (1998: 181).
33   See Jefferys (2004: 349). See also Rigaudiat (1993: 28).
34   Schneider (1984: 82).
35   In France only 40 percent worked 11 hours, while the rest labored 12 or more hours in the 1880s. See Cross (1989: 56–7).
36   Cited in ibid.: 57.
37   Ibid.
38   There were 100,000 protesters in Vienna and Barcelona, 60,000 in Budapest, between 40,000 and 50,000 in Marseille and Lyon, 35,000 in Prague, between 20,000 and 30,000 in Roubaix, Lille, Stockholm and many other cities, and 20,000 in Warsaw.
39   Cross (1989: 73).
40   Scharf (1987: 198).
41   Avrich (1984).

42 Roediger and Foner (1989: 142–5).
43 This was part of a general reorientation towards the business-union model in which unions pursue narrow workplace-oriented tasks rather than broader social and economic goals.
44 Roediger and Foner (1989: 194–5).
45 Ibid.
46 Ibid.: 203.
47 Sassoon (1996: 55).
48 Guedj and Vindt (1997: 73–4).
49 Schneider (1984: 98).
50 Russell (2000: 69).
51 Cross (1989: 139).
52 Ibid.: 129.
53 Thomas (2009: 40). Canada ended up ratifying the agreement in 1935.
54 Heron (1998: 279–80).
55 Ibid.
56 Thomas (2009: 40–1). In fact Canada had a problem adopting the convention because according to a 1925 Supreme Court decision the federal government lacked the authority to regulate work hours, except for its own workers.
57 Italy signed only conditionally.
58 Hinrichs (1988: 71). See also Schmiede (1984: 372–3).
59 Schneider (1984: 155). See also Hinrichs (1988: 4).
60 Schneider, ibid.: 130–2.
61 Guedj and Vindt (1997: 75–6).
62 Goldfield (1987: 8); Nelson (1997: 98–9).
63 Roediger and Foner (1989: 241).
64 Ibid.: 238. However, Ronald Edsforth (1995: 156) reports that workers had to pay for the shorter hours with a pay cut – from $36 to $32 or $20 a week – and that Ford required workers to come in and work on Saturdays when demand for the new Model A increased. In any case, the 40-hour week was abandoned in 1929.
65 Lichtenstein (2002: 22).
66 Hunnicutt (1988: 1, 48).
67 Nyland (1989: 147).
68 Hunnicutt (1988: 147–8).
69 "There was much testimony that hours were being lengthened rather than shortened in many plants, because no one dared to produce without an order an anyone receiving an order worked long hours to fill it as fast as possible" (Brandeis 1957: 202).
70 Roediger and Foner (1989: 247).
71 Hunnicutt (1988: 149–54).
72 Ibid.: 157.
73 Perkins (1946: 193).
74 Brandeis (1957: 203).
75 Roediger and Foner (1989: 249).
76 Lichtenstein (2002: 25).
77 Political influence also played a role. After the unions had protested against the 40-hour week prescribed by the Cotton Textile Code, Roosevelt intervened and the hours were reduced to 36. See Edelman (1957: 169). In the case of the Automobile Code it was the other way round: here the code initially established a 35-hour week, but after Roosevelt had intervened on behalf of the auto manufacturers, the work week was extended to 36 hours. See Edsforth (1995: 157–8).
78 Brandeis (1957: 219).
79 Cited in Samuel (2000: 36).
80 Perkins (1946: 254).

81 Linder (2002: 251). Another proposition suggested making the work week depend on the rate of unemployment. When unemployment was higher than eight million workers, the work week should fall to 30 hours; when unemployment was lower, it should rise to 40 hours. See ibid.

82 Hunnicutt (1988: 246). Roediger and Foner (1989: 255). Similar provisions existed in some union contracts and in a few NRA codes, but the main example for a legal entitlement to overtime pay in the US was the statutory eight-hour day won by railway workers in 1919.

83 Hunnicutt (1988: 246). Roediger and Foner (1989: 255).

84 Perkins (1946: 266).

85 Excluded from such coverage were supervisors, public employees, seasonal workers, retail sales persons, and some additional groups in private services. See Rosenberg (1991: 297).

86 Kochan *et al.* (1986: 22–3).

87 Brody (1980: 103). *See also* Lichtenstein (2002: 36–7) and Nelson (1997: 117–88).

88 Kochan *et al.* (1986: 26–7).

89 Davis (1986: 55–65). See also Gordon *et al.* (1987: 177).

90 Edsforth (1995: 159).

91 Lichtenstein (2002: 50–1).

92 Edsforth (1995: 160).

93 Lichtenstein (1982: 12.)

94 Lichtenstein (2002: 52–3). See also Kochan *et al.* (1986: 30–1).

95 Guedj and Vindt (1997: 83).

96 There were also provisions which compelled employers to bargain with trade unions. These provisions are known as the Accords de Matignon.

97 Jefferys (2002: 245).

98 Chatriot *et al.* (2003: 12). See also Chatriot (2004: 89).

99 Cross (1989: 221).

100 Jefferys (2002: 244).

101 Freyssinet (1998: 642).

102 Rigaudiat (1993: 30).

103 Ibid.

104 Guedj and Vindt (1997: 84).

105 Cited in Linder (2002: 246).

106 Rigaudiat (1993: 30–1). See also Freyssinet (1998: 643) and Chatriot *et al.* (2003: 18–20).

107 Jenson (1989).

108 Ibid.: 79. See also Jenson and Mahon (1993).

109 Kinley (1988).

110 Jenson and Mahon (1993: 74).

111 Yates (1993).

112 The CCF was founded as loose alliance of farmers, workers, and urban intellectuals in 1932. It was reorganized and renamed the New Democratic Party (NDP) in 1961. The NDP is the traditional social democratic party in much of English-speaking Canada, but not in Québéc.

113 Phillips (1997: 64).

114 Jamieson (1957: 109–10). See also Thomas (2009: 50).

115 Jenson and Mahon (1993: 75).

116 Dymond and Saunders (1965).

117 Canada Department of Labour (January 1956).

118 Sunter and Morissette (1994).

119 Thomas (2009: 51).

120 Although Saskatchewan and Manitoba adopted this as the limit not of maximum work time, but of obligation for overtime payments. See Advisory Group on

Working Time and the Distribution of Work (1994: 40–5). See also Dymond and Saunders (1965: 55–60).

121 Evans (1975: 22–3).
122 Thomas (2009: 67–8).
123 With the exception of two smaller provinces – in Nova Scotia and Prince Edward Island – overtime premiums are obligatory only after 48 hours a week. Maximum work hours are 12 hours a day in Alberta, 16 hours a day in Newfoundland, 60 hours a week in the Northwest Territories, 48 hours in Ontario and 44 hours in Saskatchewan. See Advisory Group on Working Time and the Distribution of Work (1994: 80).
124 Russell (2000: 109).
125 Ibid.: 112.
126 Crouch (1993: 197, 224).
127 Barnard *et al.* (2003: 227).
128 Coates (1989: 161).
129 Schmiede (1984: 377).
130 Schneider (1984: 142–3).
131 Ibid.: 144.
132 Ibid.: 154. See also Hinrichs (1991: 29).
133 Hinrichs (1991). See also Scharf (1987: 616–17).
134 Schneider (1984: 155).
135 Ibid.: 162.
136 Ibid.: 162–3, 166.
137 Schudlich (1984: 382).
138 Deutschmann (1982: 32).
139 Visser (1996: 177).
140 Weigelt (1989: 206).
141 Ibid.
142 Anxo (1995: 130).
143 Ibid.
144 Schneider (1984: 84).
145 Russell (2000: 69–70).
146 Ibid.: 71.
147 Ibid.
148 Ibid.
149 Ibid.: 72.
150 Ibid.: 74–80.
151 Ibid.: 86–7.
152 Cross (1989: 225).
153 Ibid.: 226.
154 Ibid.
155 Weigelt (1989: 206–7).
156 Anxo (2009: 68).
157 Russell (2000: 176–7).
158 Ibid.
159 Ibid.: 180.
160 Schneider (1984: 169).
161 Thomas (2009: 51).
162 Ibid.: 192.
163 Yates (1993: 61–2).
164 Sunter and Morissette (1994: 10).
165 Greis (1984: 31).
166 Ibid.: 34–7.
167 Ray and Schmitt (2007: 1).

9 Work time reduction and flexibilization

Introduction

Collective work time reductions largely came to a halt after the introduction of the 40-hour week. This chapter explores two examples, where the struggles continued and trade unions and other social forces reached the introduction of the 35-hour week. However, while in Germany the 35-hour week was introduced through collective negotiations, in France it was a newly elected government that took the initiative and cut work hours, as promised in the election campaign. In both cases the reduction in work hours was a reaction to spiraling unemployment. While the 35-hour week has remained an exception, and more radical plans to move to a 30-hour week were abandoned, many countries experienced a rise in part-time work. In addition, some countries introduced extended leave schemes as an alternative to shorter daily and weekly work hours. The chapter starts with an analysis of the introduction of the 35-hour week in Germany and France. The next section deals with the rise of part-time employment, followed by a description of the leave systems in Sweden and Denmark.

The 35-hour week in Germany

The majority of German workers enjoyed a 40-hour week in the early 1970s, but the drive for shorter work hours came to a halt in the mid-1970s. The pace of work time reduction decreased markedly in the second half of the 1970s.[1] During the same period, postwar growth slowed down markedly while unemployment increased. Most trade unions in Germany favored a reduction of the retirement age to cope with growing unemployment, resembling the preferences of their older male members – as opposed to the interests of younger male workers who would have favored more vacation, and female members who preferred shorter weekly work hours that would make it easier to combine paid and unpaid work.[2] An exception was the printers' and paper workers' union which early on fought for the introduction of the 35-hour work week because the introduction of new technology in the printing industry had radically diminished employment.[3] In the late 1970s, IG Druck and Papier was joined by IG Metall, at the time with 2.7

million members the largest union in Western Europe and a pacemaker for shorter work hours in the postwar decades.[4]

IG Metall, to the surprise of many in the field, made the move to the 35-hour week a major bargaining demand in negotiations about a new steel industry agreement in 1978.[5] The metal and engineering sector employer organization categorically rejected a departure from the 40-hour standard, which it had approved only a few years before. After five rounds of bargaining passed without progress, IG Metall organized a strike vote in November. Some 87 percent of its members supported strike action. Since the employer side still refused to talk about shorter hours 37,000 workers walked away from their jobs in nine steel plants in North Rhine-Westphalia by the end of November. At the beginning of 1979, three more plants, with some 20,000 employees, went on strike. The strike met vicious criticism in the conservative press, while employers responded with lockouts and personal intimidation. After six weeks of strike activity the two parties finally found consensus. The following agreement confirmed the 40-hour week but established an entitlement to six weeks of vacation and provided for six additional days off for workers on nightshifts, and three additional days off for workers aged 50-plus. In exchange the union agreed to accept the 40-hour week for the next five years. Even though a majority of workers accepted the compromise, it was widely considered as defeat for the union.[6]

Even though IG Metall had lost the confrontation, the union did not abandon the goal of shorter work hours. The union delegates unanimously agreed in 1983 on a union convention that the 35-hour week should remain on the top of the priority list of future achievements (while the Federal Trade Union Association was to lobby the government for a reduction of the legal retirement age). Disagreement emerged about variation of work hours and the problem of expected work intensification. One delegate demanded the introduction of a rigid seven-hour work day. Another proposed the development of a detailed performance catalog to make sure that employers would not increase the pace of work to make up for time lost through the cut in work hours. This was a remarkable departure from the long-standing union position that shorter hours were beneficial because they induced employers to increase productivity. Both motions, however, were rejected. The union leadership argued that for the time being the 35-hour week would be enough to swallow for the employers' side.[7]

It was not long before IG Metall raised the 35-hour issue in negotiations for a new metal and engineering industry framework agreement in the same year. The demand for shorter hours was also a response to the fact that German workers were still putting in 90 overtime hours per year in the midst of the crisis. According to trade union calculations, overtime accounted for an equivalent of approximately 1.2 million jobs.[8] The employers' side responded with the slogan "no minute less than forty hours," and instead offered early retirement schemes. However, the employer's association departed from the established path by raising their own demands – usually employers merely rejected (or accepted) union demands. The employers' side had a strong interest in more work time flexibility – to adjust work hours in line with volatile demand and to extend operating times of increasingly costly equipment.[9] Up to this point averaging periods were limited to a few weeks.[10] As both sides showed little willingness to compromise, observers described the situation as "two locomotives careering towards each other at full speed."[11]

The union was again portrayed as irresponsible by the conservative media, but this time it was also publicly criticized by the conservative government, which had replaced the social democrats in the 1982 election. While the employers unleashed a public campaign denouncing the trade union plan for shorter work hours, IG Metall organized a series of warning strikes. In a next step the union held strike ballots in the bargaining districts of Baden-Württemberg and Hesse (sector bargaining in Germany takes place on a regional level). In both cases more than 80 percent of members approved strike action. IG Metall was not the only union on the brink of striking in pursuit of the 35-hour week. Like IG Metall, the printing and paper workers went on strike for a 35-hour week in 1978 – and like their colleagues from the metal industry they lost. Now they joined the struggle again. As was the case with their counterpart in the metal and engineering sector, employers in the printing and paper industry responded with outright rejection. As so many times before (and after) in the struggle for shorter work hours, employers argued that a reduction in work hours would increase production costs and consequently price them out of business.

With negotiations still making no progress by early 1984, the printing and paper workers' union decided to call a strike in mid-April – a month before the metalworkers walked away from their jobs. What followed was one of the longest and most intensive industrial actions in postwar Germany. IG Metall went on strike for seven weeks in Baden-Württemberg and Hesse, while the printers and paper workers' union went out on strike nationwide for 12 weeks.[12] Although the metalworkers union sought to limit its strike action to the shutdown of strategic enterprises – in fact it was employers who locked out thousands of workers to increase strike pay costs for the union – several hundred thousand workers took part in demonstrations, walked away from their jobs, or were locked out of them.[13] Substantial parts of production, including parts of the German automobile industry, came to a halt during the strike.[14] Surprised by the unions' strength and determination – the assumption was that the strike would be over within three weeks – the metal and engineering sector employers' organization called for external mediation. The strike was brought to an end in July by the so-called Leber compromise (the mediator was Georg Leber, a former trade union leader and federal minister).[15] In a nutshell, the compromise combined a reduction of weekly work hours with the flexibilization of work time. The exchange of shorter work hours for flexible work time arrangements became the recipe for further work time reductions in Germany during the 1980s and 1990s.[16] After the end of the strike in the metal and engineering sector, employers in the printing and paper industries also gave in and accepted external mediation (which they had rejected twice before during preceding negotiations). The agreement that followed was modeled after the Leber compromise. Yet the printing and paper workers' union only signed after the employers agreed to waive some of the flexibilization measures.[17]

While weekly work hours were reduced to 38.5 hours per week, the actual hours could exceed 38.5 hours in a single week as long as the average over a two-month period remained 38.5 hours. In a similar way, work hours of individual employees in the metal and engineering industries (but not in the paper and printing sectors) could vary between 37 and 38.5 hours as long as the average hours of all employees did not exceed 40 hours. This allowed employers to continue to employ particularly important staff for 40 hours a week.[18] A third major concession in terms of flexibility was the shift of the bargaining area: the implementation of the averaging procedures and individual differentiation was to be negotiated at the company level.[19] Decentralization became an important element in the flexibilization of work time in Germany and other countries (see Chapter 10). Furthermore, although the 38.5-hour week was introduced without a wage cut, workers accepted moderate wage increases in return for shorter work hours.[20] Initially companies made only limited use of their new freedom to vary work hours. Smaller companies may have lacked the technical means to exploit averaging periods and other flexibility schemes.[21] But even large employers rarely took advantage of the possibility to vary the work hours of staff members. An analysis of 3,300 plant agreements in 1985 revealed that only 13 percent included individual differentiation.[22] The same analysis also revealed that large companies took the greatest interest in flexible work hours.[23]

Some researchers have argued that the initial phase was a trial-and-error period in which companies experimented with flexible work time models. Flexibilization took off after a near ten-year "incubation phase" in the mid-1990s.[24] In any case, German employers developed a growing interest in flexible work hours. In 1987 the employers' association in the metal and engineering industries agreed to a further reduction in weekly work hours in exchange for more work time flexibility. Weekly work hours were reduced to 37.5 hours in 1988 and to 37 hours in 1989. In exchange, the averaging period was extended to six months, while individual hours could vary between 36.5 and 39 hours. The agreement at the same time was exceptional, as it had been enacted for a three-year period and collective agreements in Germany usually last for only one year. Obviously employers had a strong interest in avoiding another work stoppage.

Retrospectively the three-year period meant that workers had to pay for shorter work hours through significant wage moderation. Growth picked up in the late 1980s, while wages remained frozen. However, 12 years after the first 35-hour strike took place, IG Metall finally won its battle in support of the 35-hour week in 1990. The agreement with the metal and engineering sector employer organization anticipated a stepwise reduction of the work week to 36 hours in 1993 and 35 hours in 1995 – and excluded further working reductions until 1998. While the averaging period for weekly work hours remained six months, the union conceded that up to 13 percent of a plant's workforce could voluntarily work up to 40 hours per week and could be compensated either in the form of higher wages (but without overtime supplements) or more free time (in the form of sabbaticals). The proportion was later increased to 18 percent, and in exceptional circumstances even up to 50 percent (see Chapter 4).[25] Given the unfavorable experience of the 1987 agreement, the union insisted that wages would be negotiated on an annual basis.

The 35-hour week was subsequently extended to the paper and printing industry, the steel sector, and the electronics industry. However, after the mid-1990s the drive for shorter work hours came to a halt, and the 35-hour week remained an exception limited to the most efficient and successful parts of the German economy. Thus, as Steffen Lehndorff notes, "the thirty-five-hour week got stuck halfway through."[26] While the reduction of industry-wide work hours came to halt, some employers still experimented with combinations of shorter hours and more flexibility. Probably the best known example is the introduction of the four-day work week at Volkswagen in 1993. VW struggled with a severe slump in demand after the wane of the post-unification boom. The management estimated that the company could dispense with as many as 3,000 workers (30 percent of its current staff). Instead of laying off workers, management and IG Metall negotiated an agreement that sought to protect employment through a substantial reduction in work time. The fact that the federal state of Niedersachsen was a major shareholder in the company certainly helped in striking the deal. According to the agreement weekly hours were cut from 36 to 28.8 hours, but weekly work hours could last up to 38.8 hours without the need to pay overtime supplements as long as average hours were no longer than 28.8 hours per week over a one-year averaging period (initially the weekly maximum was 35 hours). In addition, workers also accepted a reduction in overtime rates and a cut in basic wages. Given the scope of work time flexibility, human resources director Peter Hartz described VW as a "breathing company". It gave the car manufacturer unprecedented room for adjusting work hours to suit fluctuations in demand. However, despite the advanced degree of flexibility, VW terminated the four-day week and increased work hours to 33 hours for production workers, and 34 hours for administrative staff, in 2006.

The 35-hour week in France

In contrast to the United States, the United Kingdom, and Germany, France moved to the left in the early 1980s. François Mitterand was elected as the first social democratic president in decades, and the government was formed by a left wing coalition that included the French Communist Party.[27] The government initially sought to confront the economic crisis that had erupted in the 1970s and that was continuing to hamper economic growth in the early 1980s, with the implementation of a left-wing program that included economic stimulus by deficit spending and the nationalization of troubled enterprises. In addition, until the mid-1980s, the government fought spiraling unemployment through a significant reduction to the statutory retirement age (from 65 to 60 years old), and with a plan to reduce work hours from 40 to 35 hours per week.[28] However, since the government also wanted to improve collective bargaining so as to bolster stability in an increasingly turbulent economic environment, it did not adopt new legislation to reduce shorter work hours, as is usually the practice in France. Instead it encouraged social partners to negotiate shorter hour agreements.

Although the peak organizations of capital and labor actually agreed on a common protocol for the introduction of a 39-hour week in 1981, the following sector-level negotiations proved to be much more difficult and time consuming than anticipated. By the end of the year only 18 sector agreements had been signed, covering only two million workers.[29] Disappointed by the meager result, the government returned to the traditional method of French work time regulation and introduced new legislation imposing the 39-hour week from 1982 onwards. While establishing an overtime limit of 130 hours per worker per year, the new legislation introduced some flexibility by allowing for sector-level negotiations on the averaging of work hours.[30] The government, furthermore, made a new attempt to revive social partner negotiations by adopting a series of new measures known as the Aroux laws.[31] These laws strengthened firm-level bargaining by extending the rights of work councils (which had existed since 1945 but until now had played only a minor role).[32] As we will show below, the growth of company agreements became a major component in the flexibilization of work time in the 1990s and after 2000.

Faced with a mounting deficit and growing international pressure, the Mitterand government took a political U-turn in 1983, abandoning Keynesianism and adopting neoliberal austerity measures in order to boost French competitiveness (a policy advocated as *la rigeur*). As a result of the policy shift the reduction of the work week was no longer on the government's agenda.[33] As Jean-Yves Boulin and his colleagues note,

> from 1984 the tone of the discourse altered. In a context of continuously increasing unemployment, any improvement in the employment situation was seen to depend on an improvement in the competitiveness of companies, which could only be acquired through greater flexibility.[34]

Some of Mitterand's advisers still promoted the idea of work time reduction as a measure to reduce unemployment. Yet in the spirit of what some commentators have called "left realism" they acknowledged that companies should be compensated for granting shorter work hours.[35] Like German companies, French employers were looking for more flexibility to better cope with market fluctuations. The Conseil National du Patronat Français (CNPF) had tried to negotiate for more flexibility, but with little success. The combination of shorter hours and greater work time flexibility, hence, looked like a win-win situation that would fit the interests of both sides.[36] But whereas in Germany the same formula was used to solve one of the most intense labor conflicts in postwar history, France only introduced a voluntary version as part of the 1986 Delebarre Law. The legislation gave employers the possibility to increase work hours to 41 and 44 hours per week without paying overtime premiums, if average work hours in turn were reduced from 39 to 38 hours in the first case and to 37.5 hours in the second case.[37] In both cases, maximum overtime was limited to 80 instead of 130 hours per year per employee.[38]

While the Delebarre Law linked flexbilization to a reduction in work hours, the following work time reforms (launched by conservative governments after the social democrats had lost the 1986 parliamentary election) promoted work time flexibility without the need to cut hours. The Séguin Law, adopted in 1987, eliminated the need to reduce work hours and the special limitation of overtime when work hours were averaged. At the same time it expanded the maximum work time to 48 hours per week. And whereas the 48-hour limit still depended on sector-level approval by trade unions, union delegates in smaller companies were empowered so sign company agreements up to a maximum limit of 44 hours.[39] The scope of flexibilization was further widened with the so-called Five-Year Law in 1993. The new averaging amplitude was set at ten hours per day, 48 hours per week and 46 hours over 12 consecutive weeks, while the averaging period was extended to one year.[40] The Five-Year Law also revived the idea of shorter work hours as a method of work sharing. But instead of forcing companies seeking greater flexibility to reduce work time, the new legislation offered financial incentives to companies which voluntarily reduced work hours and created employment.

Accordingly, companies which reduced work time by at least 15 percent and created at least 10 percent more employment benefited from a 60 percent reduction in social security contributions in the first, and 70 percent in the second and third years (additional employment had to be maintained for a minimum of three years). Although few companies took advantage of the measure it was a remarkable step because with the adoption of the law the conservative members of the French Parliament implicitly acknowledged that work time reductions could create jobs. According to several observers, support for the Five-Year Law was crucial in shifting the once controversial debate into a pragmatic discussion. The Robien Law, adopted in 1996, extended the social security rebates to seven years and reduced contributions by 50 percent in the first year and 40 percent in the following years when new employment amounted to 15 percent.[41] The changes made the new scheme more popular: between 1996 and 1998 about 3,000 Robien agreements were signed, covering some 280,000 employees. However, the impact on the unemployment rate remained marginal.[42]

Unemployment became a highly controversial issue. In 1992, Agir Ensemble Contre le Chômage organized a series of protests against growing unemployment and massive cuts in unemployment benefits. Three years later the situation further escalated after the government disclosed a plan for a radical reform of the social security system, which would put additional pressure on unemployed workers.[43] Workers responded to the so-called Juppé plan with a massive strike and protest movement that paralyzed France for several weeks in December 1995. According to Stephen Jefferys, "more workers came on to the streets to demonstrate than had done in 1968."[44] Strike activities were concentrated in the public sector with a 25-day strike by railway workers and a 23-day strike by local transport workers. But even though private sector workers did not directly participate in strike action, they showed their support by taking part in a series of mass demonstrations. As a result, "not only did this workers' mobilization postpone any serious attempt to reform the pension system, but it also led directly to the 1997 parliamentary election."[45] The election was dominated by the unemployment problem. Unemployment had reached 12.6 percent in the election year and was one of the highest in Western Europe. The opposition parties attacked the conservative government for being unable to solve the unemployment problem. After flexibilization of the labor market and other measures to improve the competitiveness of French companies had seemingly failed to reduce unemployment, the social democrats returned to a more traditional leftist program of measures that included the reduction of work time. Prime Minister Lionel Jospin promised to introduce the 35-hour week as part of his election campaign.[46]

However, the government was anxious to make sure that the 35-hour week would not substantially raise labor costs.[47] First, it was expected that productivity gains would limit increases in labor costs. Second, work time flexibilization would help employers to save overtime supplements and thereby reduce labor costs. Third, the government would offer subsidies to those companies that shifted to the 35-hour schedule. And fourth, the government suggested that trade unions should moderate their wage demands in upcoming collective negotiations.[48] Despite this pragmatic approach, the government failed to convince the French *patronat*. The newly founded Mouvement des Entreprises de France (MEDEF) welcomed the subsidies, and accepted voluntary work time reductions, but categorically rejected a compulsory shortening of the work week.[49]

The actual introduction of the 35-hour week took place in a two-stage process: the First Aubry Law of June 1998 established the objective as well as the procedure of work time reduction and determined access to transitory subsidies granted to companies which created additional employment.[50] The Second Aubry Law of January 2000 laid out details for the implementation of the 35-hour week, including averaging amplitudes and periods, overtime regulations, and the work time of managers. The second law also regulated the allocation of permanent subsidies for companies with a 35-hour agreement – but without the requirement to create additional employment. Accordingly, private sector companies with more than 20 employees were required to introduce the 35-hour week from June 2000 onwards, while companies with 20 employees or fewer were granted an additional two-year extension period (as discussed in Chapter 10, however, many companies with twenty workers or fewer never switched to the 35-hour standard). A particularly controversial issue was the work hours of managers. In 1999 thousands of *cadres* took to the streets to demonstrate in support of their demand for a 35-hour week. The legislation introduced three categories of managers. First, it specified managers who worked according to a collective working schedule, and for these the work week was reduced to 35 hours, just like regular employees. For managers with individual work hours, work time was limited to 217 work days per year. Executive managers, as a third category, were excluded from work time regulation.[51]

Given the possibility to average work hours over 12 months, the new work time standard amounted to the introduction of a 1,600-hour working year rather than a 35-hour week. The reduction could take the form of shorter weekly work hours or additional days off. In reality, many companies took advantage of the latter possibility. In addition, the legislation introduced the possibility to save up to 22 days per employee per year on a time account.[52] Maximum overtime remained 130 hours per worker per year, with hours between the 36th and 39th hour gradually getting counted as overtime. For overtime between the 36th and 43rd hour per week, overtime premiums amounted to 25 percent, and beyond that 50 percent. As discussed in Chapter 10, overtime limits were taken back by the following conservative government.[53]

To fully exploit the scope of flexibilization provided by the law, employers had to negotiate 35-hour agreements with the unions. In companies without union delegates, employees mandated by one of the five officially recognized unions were enabled to negotiate agreements.[54] Companies with fewer than 50 employees could qualify for benefits by simply adopting one of the agreements negotiated on the sector level. While the employer side vigorously opposed the 35-hour legislation, trade unions were divided. Some unions enthusiastically supported the government plan for shorter work hours; others criticized it "for not laying down the conditions of bargaining in more precise detail, especially for negotiations on compensatory pay and the greater flexibility of work time."[55] One hotly debated issue was the definition of work time. Although the law stated that work time was "the time during which the worker is at the employer's disposal and must conform to his order without being able to take care of personal matters," employers took the opportunity to redefine work time by excluding paid breaks previously granted as part of regular work hours.[56]

At PSA Peugeot Citroën, for example, workers were entitled to a 1.75-hour break as part of the company's 38.5-hour week. With the shift to the 35-hour week the break was excluded from work time. This move immediately reduced the work week to 36.75 hours, although workers put in the exact same number of hours as before. To meet the 35-hour standard, the car manufacturer effectively reduced work time only by 1.75 hours.[57] Given the flexibility and financial compensation granted by the Aubry Laws, it is no wonder that the CEO of PSA was "relatively satisfied" with the 35-hour week.[58] A similar approach was taken in the retail trade. Before the introduction of the 35-hour week cashiers in supermarkets enjoyed a three-minute break every hour. With the move to the 35-hour week these breaks were excluded from work time. As a result food retailers cut work time only by 2.25 hours per week, instead of the four hour difference between 39 and 35 hours.[59] As Philippe Askenazy notes, "for cashiers who are paid at the minimum wage, this mechanism also reduced labor costs and remuneration."[60]

In sum, nearly two-thirds of those who moved to the 35-hour week in 2000 were confronted with a new calculation of their work time.[61] Not all *cadres* were satisfied with the new regulation either. While many benefited from the fact that their work time was, for the first time, subject to meaningful regulation, some complained about an actual increase in work hours as employers were trying to assign as many managers as possible to the group with individual work hours. In fact, about 12 percent of all private sector employees belong to this category.[62] Since the legal maximum was limited to 217 days per year, their work hours can amount to as many as 2,800 per year.

Officially the Aubry legislation only applied to private sector companies. However, the majority of public sector workers were also affected in one way or another by the 35-hour reform.[63] That said, public sector employers could choose from a larger variety of measures to reduce work time. Most benefited from additional days of vacation. Judges, for example, received an additional eight days per year – saved on a work time account with the prospect that additional vacation could be used as part of a sabbatical taken at some point in the future.[64] Because the government rarely hired additional workers to compensate for shorter hours, the main effect of the shift to the 35-hour week is the piling up of "saved" work hours in work time accounts. This has already created problems in the hospital sector. By the end of 2007 approximately 3.5 million days were saved on public sector work time accounts.[65]

While employers officially rejected the 35-hour week, they engaged heavily in 35-hour negotiations – to secure government aid and maximum flexibility. Shortly before the adoption of the Second Law, 30,000 companies, employing two million workers, had adopted the 35-hour week.[66] In 2003, 60 percent of the French workforce enjoyed a 35-hour week. Some 85 percent of workers in companies with more than 200 employees had shifted to the 35 hour norm, compared to 50 percent of workers in companies with 20 to 50 employees and 25 percent in those with 20 and fewer workers.[67] The overall effect of the work time reduction is estimated to account for between 8 and 12 percent of previous work hours.[68] The vast majority of 35-hour agreements signed in the production sector contained measures to average work hours over the course of a year.[69] Wage moderation was also widespread: about half of those who moved to the 35-hour week before 2000 were affected by a temporary "wage freeze," and another 22 percent by lower wage increases; the numbers fell to a third and 14 percent, respectively, for those who saw their work time cut after 2000.[70]

In sum, the pragmatic approach to the 35-hour week meant that not all workers were happy with the changes. Many complained about increasing flexibility of work hours and greater work intensity. As Pierre Durand notes, "most employees found they had to complete in thirty-five hours the same amount of work they had previously done in thirty-nine." As a result, "the reduction of work hours did not go down well with a section of manual workers, who found that their buying power was stagnating, if not actually decreasing, while overtime was abolished almost completely."[71] In a survey published in 2001, 28 percent of respondents experienced the introduction of the 35-hour week as a deterioration of working conditions, while 63.7 percent stated that work had become more stressful. The number of those dissatisfied may have increased still further with changes to the 35-hour week introduced since 2002.[72] Yet the fact that subsequent conservative governments did not change the 35-hour norm is reason to believe that a majority of French workers still see the move to the 35-hour week as an improvement. Despite, or perhaps because of, the substantial concessions granted to companies, the 35-hour week created significantly less employment than anticipated. Instead of the 700,000 additional jobs hoped for by the government, most studies assume that shortening of the work week created 350,000 additional jobs.[73]

Part-time work

Only a few years after Sweden had introduced the statutory 40-hour week, some groups started to demand for a 30-hour week. The main mover behind the 30-hour campaign was the social democratic women's organization, which saw the six-hour day as an important step in attaining gender equality.[74] The six-hour day, so the general assumption went, would allow men and women to equally share paid and unpaid work, whereas part-time work was seen as an individualized solution which would reproduce rather than solve gender differences.[75]

Initially the idea of a 30-hour week found considerable support. The social democratic party included the 30-hour week in its 1975 party program, while the blue-collar and white-collar trade unions both passed motions in favor of the six-hour day at their trade union congresses in 1976.[76] However, the social democratic government was not entirely convinced. Following earlier practices, the government appointed a committee to study the effects of previous work time reductions in order to clarify the possible effects of the new work time standard. As a result, the government supported the long-term objective of establishing a 30-hour week, but was in favor of an extended transition period with several rounds of work time reductions to be negotiated by the social partners.[77] However, concrete measures were never adopted after the social democrats were defeated in the 1976 general election, and support for the 30-hour week subsequently faded in the emerging economic crisis – as noted in Chapter 3, Swedish social democrats never considered shorter work hours as a useful measure to fight unemployment. The debate on the 30-hour week briefly resurfaced in the early 1980s, but by this time Gösta Rehn's idea of freely chosen work hours had gained considerable influence among social democratic party leaders (see below).[78]

While the demand for collective work time reductions vanished, Sweden experienced a rapid growth in part-time employment. The proportion of part-time workers increased from 17 percent in 1970 to 25.6 percent in 1982, along with an even more impressive growth in female employment.[79] Both female and part-time employment benefited from the expansion of the Swedish welfare state, as many of the women who entered the labor market found part-time jobs in social services, education, and healthcare.[80] Part-time work became increasingly popular because it allowed women to combine paid work with childcare and other household responsibilities. To support such arrangements the government introduced legislation in 1979 that granted parents with children up to the age of 12 a right to reduce their work time to six hours per day.[81] Such regulations institutionalized part-time work as a transitional form of work, with parents returning to full-time employment when their children grow older.[82] After an initial surge in part-time work, the proportion of part-time employment in

Sweden has been fairly constant, or decreased slightly – while the average length of part-time hours has increased significantly. However, part-time work in Sweden is still predominately female, and the concentration of part-time employment in healthcare and social services has also been remarkably stable.[83]

In other countries, too, part-time employment mainly spread as a way of reconciling female labor market participation and motherhood. In Britain the long work hours and the lack of childcare facilities has left working mothers with young children little choice other than to switch to a part-time job.[84] However, the absence of a Scandinavian-style welfare state has meant that a large share of part-time work is concentrated in private services, including, most notably, the wholesale and retail sector.[85] As described in Chapter 6, part-time work here is mainly used to adjust the labor force to shifting demand and to cover unsocial hours in the evenings and at weekends. Accordingly, the range of part-time hours in Britain is much wider than it is in Sweden, and includes a substantial share of very short part-time employment. In 1995, 25 percent of British women with a part-time job worked fewer than ten hours a week, compared to 11 percent in Sweden.[86] The expansion of part-time work in private services also meant that part-time jobs were replacing full-time positions.[87] The reason was not only the greater flexibility of part-time workers, but also lower hourly part-time wages. This served to further aggravate the gender pay gap.[88]

In France, part-time work developed somewhat later than in Sweden and the United Kingdom, and in contrast to Sweden and the United Kingdom part-time employment did not play a decisive role in boosting female employment. French women, too, increasingly entered labor markets in the 1960s and 1970s, but they did so mainly on full-time contracts.[89] In 1980 the French female employment rate reached 40 percent of total employment, whereas part-time work accounted for a mere 8 percent of all jobs (which was considerably lower than in Sweden and the UK). French mothers could work full-time because there were sufficient childcare facilities and mothers with children were not expected to leave their jobs (these two factors still play a role as the French part-time rate is still lower than in Sweden and in the UK).[90] Part-time work took off in the 1980s and 1990s against a background of an accelerating labor market crisis and growing unemployment. According to Margaret Maruani, French employers used part-time mainly as a measure to reduce labor costs and to exploit female labor market flexibility.[91] As a result, part-time work in France is typically associated with segregation, feminization, and deskilling. In the 1990s one in two women who worked part-time worked for a cleaning firm.[92]

Germany is also a latecomer with respect to part-time work. As such it shares the experience of France in that part-time work took off in the 1980s against the background of a severe labor market crisis which in Germany deepened in the 1990s as a result of German unification.[93] At the same time it also shares a characteristic feature with Sweden and the United Kingdom in that part-time work is mainly used as an instrument to reconcile motherhood and paid employment.[94] However, the German government also created a strong incentive for part-time work in 2003 by exempting so-called "mini jobs" – i.e., jobs that pay less than €450 per month – from social security obligations, as part of the Hartz reforms (named after former VW manager Peter Hartz, who also invented the concept of the "breathing company" discussed in Chapter 9). The number of mini job holders subsequently increased from 4.83 million in March 2003 to 7.1 million in December 2007. More than 15 percent of all jobs in Germany are mini jobs, and in some sectors – such as cleaning – mini jobs account for almost 50 percent of employment.[95] The German part-time rate, as a result, surpassed the Swedish and British rates in 2008.[96]

Hence, as predicted by Swedish feminists, the shift from collective to individual work time reductions has fortified gender-specific labor market segmentations and in a number of countries facilitated the casualization of female employment.[97] Even in the Netherlands, where part-time work accounts for more than 45 percent of total employment and where more than 20 percent of men work part-time hours, part-time work comes with a number of disadvantages, including lower incomes, less job training, and less promising career development prospects.[98]

As Maruani sums up,

> during the 60s, [part-time work] ... was set up as a remedy for the scarcity of labor, as way of attracting women into the labor market. In the 70s, it was thought of as an instrument of family policy, a means of influencing the birth rate while allowing professional and family life to be reconciled more effectively. With the 80s, the family went out: Under cover of chosen hours, part-time work took its place in the increasing growth of flexible employment.

However, there are important differences between countries. The comparably longer part-time hours work available in Sweden is clearly less discriminatory than the shorter part-time work hours offered in Germany, France, or the UK. Across Europe women tend to prefer part-time employment of between 20 and 30 hours in preference to the shorter hour part-time jobs promoted in Germany and elsewhere.[99]

Individual leave schemes

Swedish economist Gösta Rehn published an influential report in the early 1970s proposing a society of free choice based on freely chosen work hours.[100] Rehn notes that in the past standardized work time reductions were useful in the fight for shorter work hours because standard hours benefited everyone and they could easily be enforced. Given past experience, trade unions today are still hostile towards deviations from the standard work week or day, including part-time hours.[101] However, in a society where major work time reductions have already been achieved, Rehn argues there is more room and more need for individual variations in work hours.[102] "People are different and they have different needs and capabilities in different periods of their life."[103] And given the diversity of

Table 9.1 Development of part-time employment (percent)

	1980			1985			1990			1995			2000			2005			2008		
	*	**	***	*	**	***	*	**	***	*	**	***	*	**	***	*	**	***	*	**	***
Canada	14	26	70	17	28	60	17	27	66	19	28	62	19	27	56	18	27	62	18	26	54
France	8	17	82	11	22	83	12	24	84	16	29	82	17	31	82	17	30	82	17	29	82
Germany	n/a	n/a	n/a	13	30	90	15	34	90	16	34	87	19	38	86	24	44	83	26	46	80
Sweden	24	46	87	24	44	87	23	40	83	24	35	80	22	36	78	23	36	74	24	36	72
UK	n/a	n/a	n/a	22	45	88	22	43	86	24	44	82	15	44	81	26	43	78	25	42	76
US	17	27	67	17	27	68	17	25	68	19	27	68	17	25	68	17	25	67	17	25	66

Source: OECD.

Notes

* Part-time work as a share of total employment.

** Part-time work as a share of total female employment.

*** Female part-time work as share of total part-time employment.

individual preferences work time reductions can no longer be based on standard rules. "Since the differences are too manifold to be fixed by differentiated laws, the only practical solution is free choice."[104] Rehn's preferred method of free choice is the introduction of "freely chosen and temporary periods of non-working."[105]

In the academic world, Rehn's ideas inspired a series of studies on life course analysis. The goal of these studies is, on the one hand, to explore different time needs during different periods of a person's life such as time in education, early working careers, parenthood, mature working careers, and retirement; on the other hand the goal is also to define work time policies that are responsive to changing needs, and welfare policies that support families during the transition from one life phase to another.[106] In political terms, Rehn's freely chosen work hours hypothesis led to the introduction of extended leave periods in countries such as Sweden and Denmark – in the Swedish case partly as an alternative to the thirty-hour week which had been discussed in the early 1970s.[107]

The Swedish government introduced the first leave schemes in 1974.[108] Parental leave initially lasted for a maximum of six months. The duration was gradually extended to 16 months in the 1990s. During the first 390 days the parent who goes on leave receives 80 percent of their gross earnings. In the remaining 90 days parents are entitled to a flat rate compensation of 60 Swedish krona per day.[109] Since 1993, parents have had to share the leave period if they want to take advantage of the maximum duration. Initially a minimum of one, and later of two months, must be taken by the second parent otherwise they expire and the total amount of parental leave is limited to 14 months. Since more than 80 percent of parental leave is claimed by women, the two extra months are also known as "daddy months."[110]

In addition to parental leave the Swedish government also introduced the possibility to take time off from work for educational reasons. The rules for educational leave are more flexible – there are no limitations with regard to the length of leave or the nature of the training – but in contrast to parental leave workers on educational leave are not entitled to financial compensation. However, participants can apply for funding from a scheme that provides public loans with highly subsidized interest rates.[111] Furthermore, there is no need to request employer consent – at best, employers can postpone the start of training by six months – and workers have the right to return to their job after completing their training.[112]

Participation in the education scheme reached its height in the early 1980s, with 50,000 workers on education leave. Between 1990 and 2004 the average yearly number of participants decreased from 45,300 to 22,500.[113] The number may have increased in the 2008–09 crisis, but only a very small fraction of the Swedish workforce takes the opportunity to leave work for an extended time to improve their education. According to a survey from the 1980s, more than two-thirds took educational leave to improve their general career prospects, while 15 percent acquired firm-specific skills which they could use in their current jobs. Only a minority (18 percent) studied simply out of a general interest.[114]

According to another survey three-fourths of participants were between 25 and 44 years old, while only 9 percent were older than 55 years of age. The fact that educational leave is rarely taken advantage of by older workers underlines its role as labor market instrument rather than as a simple time-out from work.[115]

Denmark followed the Swedish path and introduced an even more comprehensive leave program in the 1990s.[116] The Danish leave system contained not only parental and educational leave, but also sabbatical leave. And while a legal entitlement only existed with regard to parental leave – in the other two cases participants depended on employer approval – all participants could apply for financial compensation amounting to between 60 and 100 percent of the applicant's unemployment benefit entitlement. The leave period varied between 13 and 52 weeks. For educational and sabbatical leave, participants had to be older than 25 and employed for more than three years. In the case of sabbatical leave, the employer was required to take on an unemployed person as a substitute for the staff member on leave (as a measure of work sharing). Furthermore, unemployed workers could also apply for training leave.[117]

Initially the Danish program was immensely popular. In 1995, a year after its introduction, a total of 150,000 people took advantage of one of the three schemes. On average, 82,000 workers were on leave at any time during the year, including 42,135 on parental, 32,502 on educational, and 7,480 on sabbatical leave (sabbaticals were less popular because many employers were not prepared to hire an unemployed person as a substitute worker). More than 80 percent of leave days were taken by women, including more than 90 percent of parental and more than 70 percent of educational leave.[118] Average leave periods were 258 days for parental leave, 222 days for sabbaticals, and 184 days for educational leave.[119] Some 60 percent of all leave days were taken by public sector workers.[120] The government responded to the unexpected popularity of the leave scheme – the participation of nurses caused a shortage of labor in the health services sector – by reducing compensatory pay, and restricting access. Total year-round participation subsequently declined from 82,116 people in 1995 to 34,201 in 1999 (including 107 persons on sabbatical).[121]

According to some observers, falling participation was not only due to increasing restrictions and barriers, but also to decreasing unemployment levels.[122] It seems that workers, at least in part, took advantage of leave schemes as an alternative to being unemployed. In 1999, with unemployment reaching a new low, the government abolished sabbatical leave; in 2001 unemployed people were banned from access to educational leave, and in 2002 education leave was abandoned altogether.[123] What remains from the celebrated Danish leave system is a year-long parental leave.[124]

While several observers put great hope in the introduction of paid leave – referring to the Danish case, Gorz argued that "the principles of this system contain in embryo the outlines of a different society and economy" because paid leaves recognizes the "right to work discontinuously, while also recognizing the right to a continuous income" – existing schemes hardly promote a society of freely chosen work hours as envisaged by Rehn.[125] Instead, existing leave schemes are either a measure to reconcile paid work and parenthood, or an instrument to increase labor market opportunities.

Summary

In many countries work time reduction came to halt in the 1980s and 1990s, and in some countries full-time hours even increased – partly to compensate for a decline in real wages (see Chapter 10). Among the few exceptions, where social actors still successfully pressed for shorter hours, are Germany and France. Both countries experienced a partial shift to the 35-hour week. However, in both cases the main argument for shorter work hours was not to gain more free time but to reduce unemployment via work sharing. Furthermore, in both countries shorter hours could only be achieved at the expense of more flexible work time schedules. In Germany, the exchange of shorter work hours for more flexibility not only solved a stalemate between the trade union and the employer organization in the metal industry in the 1980s, but also became a formula for further work time reductions in the 1990s. In France, the government also introduced far-reaching work time flexibilization in order to limit the growth in labor costs caused by the introduction of the 35-hour week. As a result the 35-hour week is really is a 1,600-hour year with varying daily and weekly work hours and with flexible vacation time. However, increased flexibility, together with an intensification of work, has also meant that not all workers have welcomed the shift to a 35-hour schedule.

While collective work time reductions came largely to a halt, individual work hours decreased still further through the spread of part-time work. Many of the women who were increasingly entering the labor markets of the 1970s and 1980s took up a part-time job in order to combine paid work with domestic labor. Yet while the availability of part-time work helped increase female labor market participation rates, it did little to overcome gender inequality. With the exception of the Netherlands, part-time employment is overwhelmingly female, and in all countries part-time workers suffer from lower hourly wages, limited career prospects, and lower income-dependent benefits. Part-time work also contributed to a gender-specific polarization of work time, and income inequality.

In some countries, governments introduced extended leave periods as an alternative to shorter daily and weekly work hours. The idea was that workers should be able to adjust work hours to changing needs over their life course. The most popular form of this has been parental leave. However, parental leave is not so much an expression of free choice as a reproductive necessity. It enables women to maintain a foothold in the labor market while taking time off to have children. Educational and training leave, too, are rarely used to further personal interests; usually participants want to improve their labor market situation or their career prospects. In sum, existing leave schemes are far from presenting the nucleus of an alternative society. Instead they are instruments to cope with work-related challenges such as the reconciliation of family and work, and life-long learning.

Notes

1 Whereas between 1960 and 1975 the average agreed annual reduction of work hours amounted to 1 percent, between 1975 and 1983 agreed work hours decreased only by 0.3 percent annually. See Bosch (1990: 614).

2 Surveys showed that in 1981 most respondents (44 percent) preferred early retirement to longer vacation (36 percent) or shorter weekly work hours (20 percent). In 1989 the picture has changed, with more respondents preferring shorter weekly hours (35 percent) to early retirement (30 percent) or longer vacations (25 percent). The later survey also revealed that only 10 percent of respondents were opposed to a reduction of work time. See ibid. See also Bahnmüller (1985: 36–7).

3 Ferlemann (1984: 674).

4 Mayr (1984: 662).

5 Bahnmüller (1985: 38–9.) Bosch (1990: 614).

6 Bahnmüller (1985).

7 Ibid.: 42–3.

8 Ibid.: 48–9. See also Ferlemann (1985: 67).

9 Bahnmüller (1985: 54–5). See also Kurz-Scherf (1985: 100–4). Flexible work hours were not only seen as a possibility to respond to short-term changes in demand; they were also seen as a way to extend operating hours of increasingly complex and costly machinery (which because of rapid technological progress could soon be outdated). See Herrmann *et al.* (1999: 33).

10 The limit was only two to three weeks in the metal industry in Nordwüttemberg and Nordbaden. Kurz-Scherf (1985: 99).

11 Ibid.

12 Bosch (1990: 616).

13 Bahnmüller (1985: 110–32). Bosch (1986: 279).

14 Bosch (1986).

15 Bahnmüller (1985: 133–45).

16 Bosch (1990: 617).

17 Ferlemann (1984: 680).

18 Bosch (1990: 616).

19 Schmidt and Trinczek (1988: 88).

20 Ferlemann (1985: 63).

21 Schmidt and Trinczek (1988: 85–6).

22 Bosch (1990: 623).

23 Ibid. Siemens, for example, negotiated varying individual hours for most of its plants, and introduced variable hours to maintain existing operating times despite shorter work hours.

24 Herrmann *et al.* (1999: 35–6).

25 The agreement, furthermore, included two benefits for parents: parents with small children were granted the right to work flexitime, while in companies with more than 500 workers parents could take unpaid parental leave of up to five years.

26 Lehndorff (2001: 119).

27 The PCF left the government in 1984.

28 Freyssinet (1997: 124–5); See also Askenazy (2013: 324).

29 Ibid.: 134.

30 Ibid.: 134–5.

31 Named after labor minister, Jean Aroux.

32 Howell (1992: 176–8).

33 Askenazy (2013: 324).

34 Boulin *et al.* (2003: 174).

35 Compston (1997: 59).

36 Freyssinet (1997: 164–6).

37 Compston (1997: 59).
38 Freyssinet (1997: 173).
39 Ibid.: 177–8).
40 At the same time, financial incentives for compensatory time off were introduced and the social partners were encouraged, but not required, to negotiate work time reductions. See ibid.: 209–12.
41 Ibid.: 227. The new provision included two different forms of work sharing – an *offensive version* with the objective to create additional employment, and a *defensive version* to avoid redundancies. If the work time reduction accounted for 10 percent, and 10 percent additional employment was created, the employer's social security contributions were reduced by 40 percent in the first year and 30 percent in the following six years. In the case of a 15 percent reduction in work time, and a 15 percent extension of employment, employer contributions were cut by 50 percent in the first year and 40 percent in the following six years. For defensive agreements rebates were granted for three years (with the possibility to renew them for another four years), while employers were obliged to maintain the employment level for a minimum of two years.
42 The most optimistic estimates assume that the Robien Law created or safeguarded between 20,000 and 30,000 jobs. See Freyssinet (1998: 651).
43 Alain Juppé had announced plans to reduce the public social security debt by increasing employee social security taxes and by extending the period that public employees were required to make payments into the pension fund (from 37.5 to 40 years), while at the same time amending the constitution of the funds to limit the influence of trade unions. See Dufour (1999: 88).
44 Jefferys (2000: 158).
45 Ibid.
46 Askenazy (2013: 325–6).
47 Ibid.: 326.
48 Ibid.: 328; see also Hermann (2000: 563–4).
49 Ibid.
50 To receive subsidies the companies had to meet certain conditions. In an *offensive version*, work time was expected to be reduced by at least 10 percent of previous work hours, and additional employment created for at least 6 percent more workers. For a 15 percent work time reduction and a 9 percent increase in employment, employers were offered higher rates. In the *defensive version*, work time reductions also had to account for 10 percent, but employment only had to be maintained at existing levels.
51 The regulations amounted to an additional eight days off on top of the mandatory five weeks of vacation and 11 public holidays. Askenazy *et al.* (2004: 159–60).
52 Saved days had to be spent as compensatory time off within five years; in special cases the period could be extended to ten years.
53 Overtime hours between the 36th and 39th hour were gradually becoming overtime hours, and thus subjected to full overtime compensation over a period of several years.
54 Confédération Française Démocratique du Travail (CFDT), Confédération Française des Travailleurs Chrétiens (CFTC), Force Ouvrière (FO), Confédération Générale du Travail (CGT), Confédération Française de l'Encadrement – Confédération Générale des Cadres (CFE-CGC).
55 Dufour (2006: 95).
56 Askenazy *et al.* (2004: 158–9).
57 Hayden (2006: 512).
58 Ibid.: 525.
59 Askenazy (2007: 7).
60 Askenazy (2013: 330).

61 Ibid.: 8.
62 Ibid.: 330.
63 About a quarter of the public sector workforce, including teachers from primary school right through to university level, was exempted from the 35-hour week. Ibid.: 332.
64 Ibid.: 332–333.
65 Ibid.
66 Ibid.: 330.
67 Ibid.: 335.
68 Ibid.
69 Bloch-London (2000: 39–40).
70 Hayden (2006: 518).
71 Durand (2007: 148).
72 Ibid.: 149.
73 Askenazy (2013: 339).
74 Weigelt (1989: 218).
75 Ibid.: 219.
76 Ibid.: 218.
77 Ibid.
78 Ibid.: 227.
79 Ibid.: 207.
80 Mörtvik and Regnér (1997: 187).
81 Ibid.
82 Daune-Richard (1998: 224–5).
83 Mörtvik and Regnér (2004: 102).
84 Rubery and Fagan (1997: 213).
85 Ibid.: 219; Bergman *et al.* (2004: 102).
86 Daune-Richard (1998: 220).
87 Rubery and Fagan (1997: 213).
88 Ibid.: 221.
89 Maruani (1997: 70).
90 Daune-Richard (1998: 218, 220).
91 Maruani (1997: 70, 73).
92 Ibid.
93 Killmann and Klein (1997: 85).
94 Ibid.: 81.
95 Dribbusch (2010). For the development of "mini jobs" see Brandt (2006).
96 Yerkes and Visser (2006: 245).
97 Rubery (1998: 140–2).
98 Data from EUROSTAT. Yerkes and Visser (2006: 244).
99 Bielenksi *et al.* (2002: 69).
100 Rehn (1973).
101 Ibid.: 332.
102 Ibid.: 329.
103 Ibid.: 327.
104 Ibid.
105 Ibid.: 335.
106 See, for example, Anxo *et al.* (2011).
107 Weigelt (1989: 227).
108 Anxo (2011: 126).
109 Ibid.
110 Ibid.
111 Ibid: 116–17.
112 Gould (1993: 72).

113 According to labor force survey data from Statistics Sweden.
114 Gould (1993: 72).
115 Ibid.
116 Madsen (1998).
117 Ibid.: 696.
118 Jensen (2002: 271).
119 Ibid.
120 Madsen (1998: 696); Jensen (2002: 273).
121 Jensen (2002: 271).
122 Ibid.
123 Andersen (2002).
124 Flecker *et al.* (2010: 24–5).
125 Gorz (1999: 96–7).

Part IV
Conclusions

10 Neoliberalism and the surge in work hours

Introduction

This chapter reviews changes in work hours since the 1980s, during a period of neoliberal economic and political hegemony. During this period there was a significant break with earlier work time trends. The chapter starts with a discussion of the nature and significance of neoliberalism as a social and political project, and its consequences for work time. The next section presents examples of concessions and exemptions from collective work time norms, followed by an analysis of the impact of the erosion and decentralization of collective bargaining for work hours and the consequences of work time flexibilization. This is followed by a section on the individualization of work hours through opting-out schemes and the surge in overtime, as well as the workfarist restructuring of welfare states. The chapter ends with an analysis of the outcome of the changes in terms of the length and distribution of work hours.

Neoliberalism

Neoliberalism is a popular term mainly used to mark a turning point between the postwar era and the decades that followed the economic crisis of the 1970s. As such it bears a range of different meanings, which sometimes leads to confusion and misunderstanding. It competes with other major concepts such as post-Fordism or globalization, which also suggest a profound transformation of capitalism over the last four decades. However, the advantage of the concept of neoliberalism is that it emphasizes the political character of the response to the crisis, whereas post-Fordism and globalization are usually presented as quasi-natural developments, resulting in specific constraints that cannot be escaped. Neoliberalism was foremost a political response to a postwar crisis which was widely understood by the ruling classes to be the result of too many worker rewards having been granted (especially for trade union members), all of which had weighed on private profits.[1] An essential element of the response, thus, was to break working class strength, which had been heightened during the postwar decades thanks to low unemployment, high levels of trade union organization, the granting of substantial labor rights, and the introduction of advanced welfare

states. An essential outcome, accordingly, was a falling share of wages as a proportion of GDP, and a rising share of profits.[2] In short, neoliberalism was a
"ruling-class political program to respond to the challenges from the Left."[3] Yet
precisely because it was a political response, it was only loosely linked to neoliberal theory.[4]

To be sure, neoliberal aversion to the state – and admiration for the market,
individualism, and entrepreneurship – shaped Thatcherism and Reagonomics
and fueled austerity, privatization, and deregulation.[5] But neoliberal politicians
repeatedly departed from neoliberal doctrines if necessary to kickstart growth or
win elections.[6] In addition, social forces and institutions mediated the implementation of neoliberal policies, resulting in a variety of actually existing neoliberal-
isms.[7] Differences also exist with regard to the timing of the neoliberal
counterrevolution: in the United States and Britain the changes started in the
early 1980s; in other countries the systematic restructuring took off more than a
decade later.[8] This does not mean that there are no commonalities. One commonality that stands out is faith in the market as the main, if not the exclusive,
problem-solving instrument – even if the problems were created by markets in
the first place. Another commonality is the refusal to even contemplate
alternatives.[9]

Markets and competition, in several regards, played a crucial role in the neoliberal counterrevolution. As Sam Gindin points out, "neoliberalism emerged as
the corrective, restoring and extending the creative winds of capitalist competition. It was – and this is crucial – a *class* response rather than the result of the
responses of individual capitalists."[10] The introduction of post-Fordist production systems and the spread of production across the world were instrumental
because they facilitated the intensification of worldwide competition. Competition is beneficial from a capitalist point of view, even though individual capitalists may go out of business. Overall, competition strengthens the position of the
capitalist class, while undermining the strength of the working class because the
latter is built on solidarity – the opposite of competition.[11] Competition helped
create a high number of unemployed workers who were critical to weakening the
trade union movement and facilitating the shift from welfare to workfare policies; competition ended national or local growth pacts between employers and
workers, or transformed them into pacts for competitiveness based on substantial
worker concessions; and competition eliminated the weakest elements of the
capitalist class and thereby disciplined not only employers, but even more so
their workforces. In short, competition reinforced capitalist dominance over the
working class, which the latter had challenged at the end of the long postwar
boom. The result was the transformation of established patterns of social reproduction and the development of a "new social rule, specific to neoliberalism."[12]

In terms of work time, the new social rule required more people to sell their
labor power to gain the means of existence and, in sum, put in more work hours.
However, because of the neoliberal promotion of markets and competition, work
time had not increased for all workers; instead the result of the destandardization
and flexibilization of work time had been a growing polarization of work hours,

with some workers working very long days and others very short ones. Regulation theory has argued that with the shift from Fordism to post-Fordism the main accumulation pattern had shifted from a predominantly intensive, to a predominantly extensive, accumulation regime.[13] While intensive accumulation focuses on the maximization of relative surplus value (increasing productivity), extensive accumulation strives for an augmentation of absolute surplus value (extension and multiplication of work days). This picture is only partially accurate: instead, neoliberalism aims for a simultaneous growth in productivity and work hours (hours per worker and/or number of workers in employment), while wages are kept flat. Accordingly, the principal characteristic of the neoliberal work time regime is the widening gap between necessary and actual work time, which in the postwar decades had been kept under *relative* control through work time reductions and (real) wage increases.[14]

With the neoliberal turn, decreasing work hours are no longer seen as a sign of social progress and as a tool to combat unemployment; in a complete reversal of earlier argumentations, longer work hours are, instead, advocated as a measure for safeguarding jobs. With some delay, this argumentation even came to dominate public discourse in Germany and France, although both still cut work hours in the 1990s. In 2003 the Cologne Institute of Economic Research initiated a public debate in Germany by arguing that a one-hour extension of work time would create an additional 60,000 jobs; while in France the conservative government, which took office in 2002, used the slogan "working more, earning more, and creating more jobs" to justify its changes to the 35-hour week (see below).[15] Even trade unions sometimes bought into the idea of competition bargaining and accepted an increase in work hours in the hope that this would protect employment. The abandonment of demands for shorter hours is a sign of the degree to which trade union leaders have internalized a neoliberal ideology in which short-term microeconomic logic prevails over long-term macroeconomic rationality. A similar process has taken place in consideration of the welfare state: while in the postwar decades a decreasing retirement age was seen as a sign of economic wealth and social welfare, even the most developed countries now emphasize the need to extend working careers in order to "save" the retirement system.

The weakening of working class solidarity was key to establishing the new order. In the case of work time, solidarity was undermined through flexibilization and individualization of work hours, rather than an outright prolongation of the work day or week. Workfare programs, activation schemes, and the elimination of early retirement, have similar effects with regard to welfare: such reforms suggest that it is the fault of the individual that he or she cannot find a job, or even worse, that he or she does not want to work and instead exploits the social safety net. On a concrete level four developments have been instrumental in widening the gap between necessary and actual work time: the granting of concessions and exemptions from collectively agreed work hours; the erosion and decentralization of collective bargaining structures; the flexibilization of work hours, especially when allowing for an extension of work time; the promotion of individual employment contracts, possibilities of opting out of collective or statutory norms, as well as the granting of large amounts of overtime. The erosion of collective work time regulations was complemented by a workfarist restructuring of welfare regimes, pushing more workers into paid employment and prolonging the working life of those who have a job.

Concessions and exemptions

Even at the onset of the 1970s crisis, the United Autoworkers in the US still won a reduction of the retirement threshold to 30 years of service, a fourth week of paid vacation, and an additional six days off as part of the Paid Personal Holiday Program (PPH). The UAW leadership planned to gradually increase the amount of personal holidays to 48 days a year, effectively establishing a 36-hour work week (which some union members had already demanded in the 1976 bargaining round).[16] UAW president Douglas Fraser noted in 1978 that "the four-day week is inevitable.... The only question is how fast do we get there."[17] The union managed to increase the amount of personal holidays to nine days in 1979, but the development came to sudden end in 1980. In the wake of a looming economic crisis and a struggling American auto industry – Chrysler was on the verge of bankruptcy and had to be bailed out in 1979 – the UAW agreed to accept cutbacks to help automakers regain profitability. Yet while the concessions were widely advertised as a measure to secure jobs, one of the major "givebacks" was the PPH program. Thus, instead of sharing work through a reduction of work hours – a key demand of trade unions during the Great Depression – the UAW accepted an effective *extension* of work time to safeguard jobs.

The ongoing contract with Chrysler was opened in 1980. The union not only waived the entitlement to existing personal holidays, but also future paid holidays already included in the contract. In terms of work time, the total "giveback" at Chrysler amounted to 17 days per year. Ford and General Motors followed suit and demanded similar concessions. In both cases, the UAW agreed to eliminate about two weeks of paid vacation. At American Motors (which was bought by a recovered Chrysler in the late 1980s) the concessions even amounted to three weeks (in this case, the company was at least supposed to pay back some of the savings earned from implementing longer hours after 1989). The auto industry was not alone. In the rubber industry, the Rubber Workers' Union agreed to an elimination of one week of paid vacation at two major plants between 1981 and 1983. The United Steel Workers union, which was still pressing for a 32-hour-week in the late 1970s, gave up the extended 13-week vacation plan reserved for certain groups of workers in 1983. In addition, workers who were eligible for at least two weeks of vacation temporarily lost one week.[18]

While American workers accepted an effective extension of work time, the German trade unions demanded a reduction of the work week in order to fight spiraling unemployment. As described in Chapter 9, IG Metall went on strike for the 35-hour week in 1978, and again in 1984. Yet after the 35-hour week had been implemented in the metal, steel, and printing industries in the mid-1990s, the collective work time reduction in Germany also came to a standstill. In 2003 IG Metall made an attempt to extend the 35-hour week to eastern Germany, where work time remained at 38 hours per week after German reunification.[19] The east German steel industry accepted adoption of the 35-hour week, but the metal and engineering sector companies refused to cut work hours. Employers such as Volkswagen, which at that time still operated with a 28.8-hour week at Wolfsburg in western Germany, argued that its eastern German production site needed the cost advantages of the longer work week. The following four-week strike turned out disastrously for the union. The leadership had to terminate the campaign without gaining a single significant concession, and with no prospect that the fight would be picked up again in the near future (permanent work time reductions were not an issue in Germany during the 2007–2009 crisis).[20] What made the defeat even more bitter was that work council representatives in major companies publicly denounced the strike after it led to stops in production in western Germany, questioning the union's ability to sustain solidarity across the country.[21] While tactical errors and leadership conflicts may have played a role in the defeat, the inability to extend the 35-hour week was also a sign of vanishing trade union power in Germany.

The defeat was also a signal for companies in western Germany that the 35-hour week was no longer off limits. In 2004, two western German employers, both symbols of Germany's corporate power and the corporatist approach of German capital, gained temporary exemptions from the 35-hour standard after threatening to relocate production to cheaper locations.[22] Siemens was able to extend the work week at its production sides in Kamp-Lintfort and Bocholt from 35 to 40 hours without a raise in wages. In exchange the company promised to maintain production for the two-year duration of the agreement (though regardless of the agreement, production at both locations was sold to Siemens' competitor BenQ in 2005 and the new owner filed for insolvency in 2006).[23] For IG Metall, particularly troublesome was the fact that the company work council agreed to the concessions before even informing trade union headquarters.[24] As Reinhard Bispinck argues

> the unpaid increase in the workweek from 35 to 40 hours at the Siemens plants in Bocholt and Kamp-Linfort was particularly important in sending out the signal that if enough pressure is brought to bear then it is possible to get even IG Metall to accept (unpaid) increases in work time.[25]

In the same year, DaimlerChrysler (now just Daimler) introduced a general 40-hour week for its research and development department staff, as well as a stepwise implementation of the 39-hour week for all service and support workers (catering, security, logistics, etc.).[26] While production workers continued to work 35 hours, they had to swallow a cut in paid breaks. Here the company agreed to maintain production until 2011. Daimler is no exception: other car manufacturers, too, increased the proportion of workers putting in 40 hours a week or more. According to Thomas Haipeter and Steffen Lehndorff, at the development center at Porsche the rate is 32 percent, while at BMW's headquarters in Munich it is well over 21 percent. The agreement on the 35-hour week gave metal sector employers the possibility for continuing to employ parts of their workforce on 40-hour contracts. In exceptional cases up to 50 percent of staff can switch to a 40-hour week.[27] Yet while companies were initially reluctant to exploit this possibility, it became highly popular over time: in 2002, 88 percent of employers in the metal and electronics industry operated with parts of their workforce on the 40 schedule; 62 percent used the limit to the full extent and many employers would have welcomed more leeway in scheduling longer individual hours.[28] As the deviation is based on individual agreements with the respective workers, the extension of work hours is linked to an individualization of the employment contract.[29]

Following considerable pressure from the federal government and in an attempt to better coordinate the growing number of "wildcat" agreements, IG Metall signed the so-called Pforzheimer agreement with the metal sector employer organization in 2004. According to the agreement the union accepts temporary deviations from existing collective standards if the deviations safeguard or create jobs, or improve the competitiveness of the company, its capacity for innovation, and the conditions for new investments.[30] Any deviations must still be confirmed by the company work council and the trade union. By the end of 2006, 850 "opening agreements" had been concluded in the metal and electronics industries.[31] About one-third of the agreements lasted for three and more years, the rest between one and three years. The majority of deviations concerned work hours and wages, but the single most important issue was the extension of work time: 58.8 percent of all agreements included an extension beyond collective agreed work hours. In the vast majority of cases, the increase in work hours was agreed without monetary compensation. Wages also played an important role, but the reduction of basic wages was relatively rare. Instead wage concessions mainly concerned wage increases, special payments, and vacation pay.[32]

The same picture can be found in the chemicals industry: here the signing of opt-out clauses from existing collective agreements has a much longer tradition and goes back to the mid-1990s. However, the number of exemptions has increased constantly and quadrupled between 1994 and 2004. In 2006, 41 of the "opening agreements" in the chemical industry affected work hours, and almost 80 percent of these agreements included an extension of work time from 37.5 to 40 hours per week.[33] The granting of exemptions to companies in economic difficulty is not new, but the systematic extension of work time is a rather new development in Germany. In both sectors about 10 percent of all companies covered by a sector agreement took advantage of an "opening agreement."[34] Some researchers emphasize the fact that 90 percent of the companies still "play by the rules." Yet although the vast majority of companies adhere to collectively agreed work time standards, the extension of the work day and week to safeguard employment still presents a fundamental break with an earlier approach to work time, and, indeed, amounts to a "turning tide in work time policies."[35] After introducing the four-day work week in the 1990s to avoid layoffs, even Volkswagen returned to a 35-hour week in 2006 to "safeguard" jobs.[36]

While in the private sector trade unions have so far only accepted exemptions from standard work hours, the public sector in Germany saw a wave of permanent work time concessions. In 2005, collectively agreed weekly work hours at Deutsche Bahn were extended from 38 to 39 hours without additional compensation. In this case, too, the extension of work time was part of an employment pact to safeguard jobs in the partly privatized national railways company.[37] In 2006, a two-week strike of public employees employed by the federal states (*Länder*) ended with a variable extension of the 38.5-hour week. Even before the negotiations for the new agreement, some governments had unilaterally introduced longer work hours for newly hired employees (between 40 and 42 hours). The strike settlement included an extension to 40 hours in eastern Germany, while in western Germany weekly work time varied from 38.7 to 39.7 hours depending on the state.[38] The policy shift is remarkable: in the postwar decades public sector unions were at the forefront of the struggle for shorter work hours, while governments hired additional workers to mitigate slumps in private sector labor demand. In 2007 the service workers' union, known as verd.i, agreed to a four-hour extension of weekly work hours in departments of German Telekom, the former national telephone service provider which had introduced a 34-hour week to safeguard jobs a few years earlier. The agreement followed a six-week strike by telecom workers.[39] Affected were about 50,000 employees who were transferred to three new service subsidiaries. Their work week increased to 38 hours without wage compensation. Management had argued that the longer work week brought Telekom employees in line with staff of the company's main competitors.[40] Given the austerity measures adopted in response to the widespread public deficits caused by the 2007–2009 crisis, the pressure on public sector unions will increase in the coming years. And because public sector workers have seen very moderate wage increases in the past few years, the "givebacks" will most likely focus on longer work hours.

In sum, German trade unions, like their American counterparts 20 years earlier, made significant work time concessions in the face of mounting pressure from German capital. Thus, as Heiner Dribbusch and Thorsten Schulten note,

> the proactive approach of reducing weekly work time with wage compensation to tackle unemployment, which was prominent among German unions during the 1980s, ended in the early 1990s, and since the mid-1990s employers have succeeded in turning the tide towards longer work hours.[41]

The effect can already be seen in work time statistics: within only three years, work weeks in public services and in the metal and engineering industry in Germany have increased by roughly an hour.[42] Actual weekly work hours in the metal and engineering sector in western Germany reached 39.1 hours in 2006, despite the collectively agreed 35-hour week. In the same year, average work hours in the entire west German economy reached the level of 1988 – before the introduction of the 35-hour week.[43] According to Lehndorff, "these work time extensions were not caused by ups and downs of the economy. They were the outcome of a shift in political power relations".[44]

Erosion and decentralization

While in the United States the unionization rate started to decline by the mid-1950s – in 2010 only 12 percent of American workers still belonged to a union, in the private sector a mere 7 percent – the British trade union movement continued to grow during the postwar decades.[45] In 1980 almost half of all British workers were trade union members and in 64 percent of all workplaces there was at least one recognized union present.[46] Union power could also be seen in the continuous strikes of the 1960s and 1970s, culminating in the "winter of discontent" in 1978–79 when public sector workers challenged the labour government's austerity program. Britain enjoyed a comparably high trade union density, and the British bargaining system was also fairly centralized. In 1970 approximately 60 percent of private sector workers were covered by multi-employer agreements or wage council provisions.[47] But the situation started to change in the early 1980s. In 1979 the Tories won the general election and Margaret Thatcher became prime minister. The conservative government was convinced that trade union power went too far and set out to free businesses from constraints imposed by collective bargaining, including collective work hours.

The government's attack on the trade union movement combined changes in the recognition procedure with restrictions on the scope and depth of industrial action. The latter included a ban of secondary activities, the obligation to hold externally monitored strike ballots, and the possibility to sue unions for damage caused by unlawful protests. In addition, compulsory union membership in so-called "closed shops" was eradicated, and the right to disorganize was strengthened.[48] Linda Dickens and Mark Hall conclude that "deregulation was embraced as a way of freeing employers to take the most effective measures as they saw them."[49] The result was not only the limitation of trade union autonomy and the restriction of the scope of industrial action, but also a move away from collective bargaining and towards individual employment relationships as the preferred method of work regulation.[50] The British trade unions did not simply accept the changes. The 1984 miners' strike was one of the decisive confrontations between the government and organized labor. And the defeat of the miners' union was symptomatic of the defeat of the British trade union movement.

The long-term effect of the changes was threefold: there was a decline in trade union membership, which fell to 16.5 percent in the private and to 58.5 percent in the public sector in 2006; decreasing trade union representation in workplaces, reaching 38 percent in 2004; and an erosion of collective bargaining coverage.[51] The proportion of workers covered by collective bargaining decreased from 70 percent in 1984 to 39 percent in 2004. In the private sector only a quarter of all employees are affected by some sort of collective bargaining.[52] However, collective bargaining has not only become the exception in the private sector. Where bargaining takes place it happens almost exclusively at the company level (through company-wide or workplace-level bargaining). Only 3 percent of private sector workplaces are covered by a multi-employer agreement – compared to 18 percent in 1984. As William Brown, Alex Bryson and John Forth note, the near-disappearance of multi-employer bargaining is the most significant trend in collective bargaining in Britain: "[T]his shrank at a much faster rate than collective bargaining per se."[53] As a result of the changes in the collective bargaining system, only a minority of private sector workers are still covered by collective bargaining, and of those who are covered the vast majority are covered by a company agreement. Industry-wide regulations of work time play almost no role outside the public sector.[54] As described further below, the adoption of the European Working Time Directive, which imposes a 48-hour limit on weekly work hours, hardly served to change this because of the individual opt-out provision.

Germany, once a role model for coordinated capitalism with strong trade unions and sector-wide collective bargaining, has also experienced erosion and decentralization of collective bargaining. In Germany, however, the 1980s were still a period of relative trade union strength with unions such as IG Metall still making progress in collective bargaining – including the stepwise introduction of the 35-hour week in the first half of the 1990s (see Chapter 9). The situation has changed since the mid-1990s, partly fueled by German reunification and the subsequent increase in unemployment. Since then, the trade union movement has been increasingly on the defensive. Union density fell from 36 percent in 1991 to about 20 percent in 2007.[55] With decreasing trade union power, employers started to abandon collective bargaining – by leaving bargaining units, or in the case of new companies by not joining established bargaining systems. The privatization of public services also played a role in fragmenting and weakening existing collective agreements.[56] In contrast with France and other European countries with similar or lower trade union membership rates, state support for collective bargaining in Germany is weak and the number of cases in which agreements have been made binding for all employees by law has actually decreased. While in the early 1990s, 4.5 percent of all collective agreements contained an extension clause, this proportion had decreased to 1.5 percent by 2007.[57] IG Metall and other unions accepted the "opening agreements," described above, not only to maintain production in Germany, but also to prevent employers from leaving the respective bargaining units.

Despite concessions, the proportion of workers covered by a collective agreement in western Germany decreased from 76 percent in 1998 to 63 percent in 2007, while in eastern Germany the proportion fell from 63 to 54 percent over the same period. In sum, 38 percent of workers across Germany were not covered by a collective agreement in 2007. In terms of companies, only 39 percent of all companies still had a collective agreement in western Germany, and only 24 percent in eastern Germany.[58] The differences are not only significant between western and eastern Germany, but also between sectors: at 89 percent, public administration is among the sectors with the highest coverage rate, while business services at 37 percent is among the lowest (in western Germany).[59] Although sector-wide (multi-employer) agreements are still the main pillar of the German system of industrial relations, company agreements have become somewhat more important: 7 percent of workers in western Germany and 13 percent in eastern Germany were covered by a company, as opposed to a sector agreement in 2007.[60]

The erosion of sector bargaining was partly complemented by a decline in work council representation, although here the development is less clear.[61] Some 54 percent of eligible private sector workers (that is, workers in companies with five or more employees) in western Germany, and 61 percent in eastern Germany, worked in companies without work council representation in 2007.[62] Between 1994 and 2007 the proportion has increased by 5 percent in western Germany and 3 percent in eastern Germany.[63] While there is ongoing debate about the significance of the changes, it is clear that a growing number of German workers are neither covered by a collective agreement nor represented by an elected work council. In western Germany the proportion has increased from 21 percent in 1998 to 31 percent in 2007; in eastern Germany it grew from 35 percent to 42 percent over the same period.[64] More importantly, even where companies still have elected work councils, including most of the large companies, these are facing growing pressure from management to agree to more flexible and longer work hours.

The company level has become the main bargaining arena on work time issues in Germany.[65] It took about ten years for companies to take full advantage of the possibilities granted in exchange for the 35-hour week, including the possibility for negotiating variations and deviations in daily and weekly work hours on the company level (see Chapter 9). The result was a slow but persistent bargaining drift from the sector to the company level.[66] In the literature the changes have been described as "regulated" or "controlled" flexibilization, because company negotiations take place within limits imposed by sector agreements, and deviations must still be confirmed by (sector) trade unions. The term "controlled flexibilization," however, is somewhat misleading. What is really at stake is an acceleration of competition, with local workforces making concessions to outperform competing companies. Work hours are negotiated on the company level not so much because of individual adjustment to local production needs; the main reason is that local workforces and their representatives are more susceptible to the forces of competition.[67]

In the wake of accelerating (global) competition and the (real or virtual) threat of relocation, work councils find themselves under growing pressure to accept concessions, including longer and more flexible work hours, in order to prevent production being shifted to another location – even though, as the aforementioned example of Siemens shows, concessions rarely save jobs in the long run. From a work council perspective, as Markus Promberger and his colleagues note, flexible work hours become "an instrument of a world market oriented, competitive production, which guarantees the survival of the production location and therefore of [local] employment."[68] From a supra-company perspective, in contrast, the result is a deregulation and decollectivization of work time, even though trade unions and work councils may still have a say in the process.[69] Of course the changes in Germany are much less dramatic than in Britain, but in both countries the erosion and decentralization of bargaining structures has led to a widening gap between collectively agreed and actually worked work hours. In Britain the difference amounts to five hours per week.[70] In western Germany the difference reached three hours per week in 2006.[71]

The introduction of the 35-hour week in France was accompanied by a boost in company bargaining on work hours. The government deliberately promoted such negotiations by offering considerable leeway for local adaptation of the 35-hour week if the firm-level social partners reached a consensus. The government also promoted company-level negotiations by granting financial incentives to companies with 35-hour agreements. In mid-2003, before the special incentives were eradicated by the following conservative government, 20.6 percent of firms had a 35-hour agreement, covering 50.6 percent of the workforce. In the case of firms with more than 20 employees (which were required to introduce the 35-hour week) 56 percent had reached an agreement, covering 76.3 percent of the respective workforce (see Chapter 9).[72] In the French case, the growth in company bargaining was widely perceived as progress compared to an earlier situation when work time issues were determined by the government, with few social partner consultations. However, the boost of company bargaining can also undermine collective work time regulations when company bargaining is prioritized over sector-level bargaining, and agreements can go beyond statutory limits. With the recent amendments to the 35-hour week social partners on the company level have been empowered to almost freely choose company-based work hours (see below).[73]

Flexbilization and extension

The introduction of the 35-hour week in Germany and France was linked to a far-reaching flexibilization of work hours (see Chapter 9). Flexibilization refers to changing daily, weekly, and monthly work hours, as well as the extension of the work day into the evening, and the work week into the weekend. As noted in Chapter 8, the Fordist work time compromise of the postwar decades provided ample flexibility, but flexibility had to be paid for by overtime premiums. In contrast, the changes introduced over the last three decades enable employers to vary work hours without the need to pay overtime supplements. There are at least three ways employers can vary work hours without extra cost. First, employers in many countries can extend work hours of part-time staff right up to the full-time limit without having to pay overtime premiums. Second, averaging periods of up to one year allow employers to vary work hours within certain limits as long as the average over the averaging period amounts to the standard work week. A third and increasingly popular possibility is the use of work time accounts. Workers can park overtime hours on individual work time accounts for a longer period, often several years, with the prospect that they will be taken as time off in lieu at a later point.

Work time accounts are highly popular in Germany. The spread of such accounts is closely linked to the introduction of the 35-hour week in the first half of the 1990s. To some extent work time accounts are a prolongation and expansion of the flexitime arrangements introduced in the 1980s as a concession to white-collar workers who worked longer hours than their blue-collar colleagues.[74] Yet the work time accounts installed in the 1990s, and after 2000, differ from flexitime arrangements insofar as they reflect the interests of the company at least as much as the interest of the individual worker. As Haipeter and Lehndorff note with respect to the German automobile industry, work time accounts have become "an integral part of companies' flexibility strategies."[75] While in 1999 about a third of all German employees had a work time account, by 2005 the proportion had increased to slightly less than 50 percent.[76]

Work time accounts have two essential limits: the maximum number of hours, and the maximum time period hours can be banked on the account. Problems start when these limits are reached: according to a study from 2000, only in a third of companies were excess hours actually taken as time off.[77] In 29 percent of companies excess hours were paid out, and in another 18 percent they were eradicated; in 9 percent the limits were ignored and the credits extended.[78] Haipeter and Lehndorff give practical examples from an expiry of "surplus" credits at DaimlerChrysler, monetary remuneration at BMW, and a continuation beyond the agreed limit at Opel.[79] According to trade union sources, 750,000 deposited hours expired in a single work year at Daimler headquarters in Stuttgart.[80] When deposits are not taken as time off, the installment of work time accounts fuels a creeping increase in work hours, blurring the distinction between flexibilization and extension.[81] Many work time accounts were emptied during the 2008–09 recession. According to one study, statistically speaking every German worker consumed 8.9 "banked" hours in 2009. This means that more than 358 million hours were deposited on work time accounts before the crisis, or more than 200,000 work years.[82]

France may experience a similar development in the near future. As part of the 35-hour week, companies were granted the possibility to introduce work time accounts. Workers could save up to 22 days on these accounts. Work time savings could not be compensated monetarily and had to be taken as time off in lieu within five years, and in exceptional cases within ten years (see Chapter 9). With the 2005 reform of 35-hour legislation, the cap on saved hours was lifted, and the five-year limit was eliminated. The reform, furthermore, eliminated the need to take work time savings as time off in lieu, while giving companies the possibility of depositing revenues from pay rises and profit-sharing plans into work time accounts.[83]

Individualization and opting out

Another popular form of eroding collective work time regulations and increasing work hours is the individualization of employment contracts through the introduction of opt-out clauses. As described in Chapter 8, the Canadian province of

Ontario introduced a 48-hour week in 1948, replacing the earlier 60-hour week. A 44-hour overtime threshold was introduced in 1968 along with the entitlement to a second week of paid vacation, but the maximum work week has not changed since the Second World War. With respect to other countries and other provinces within Canada, the 48-hour limit was comparably long, and most workers in unionized workplaces enjoyed a 40-hour or shorter work week. In addition, the provincial government also issued exemptions for production sites with longer work weeks. During the 1980s and the first half of the 1990s more than 400 companies operated with these special permits.[84]

Despite the comparably business-friendly regulations, the progressive conservatives, who won the provincial elections in 1995 with a program called the "Common Sense Revolution," made the flexibilization of employment legislation a focus of their re-election campaign in 1999. The regulation of work hours and other employment norms were branded as "red tape," obstructing flexibility and diminishing the province's competitiveness in an increasingly globalized world. Improved competitiveness, according to the party's leaders, would not only safeguard existing jobs, but attract new investments, create new jobs and, hence, lower the unemployment rate – all of which resembled the familiar "longer hours for more jobs" argumentation. After re-election the conservative government presented the work time reform in a document called "Time for Change." At the heart of the reform was the introduction of a 60-hour week based on the individualization of the employment relationship.[85]

While confirming existing work time limits, the amendments adopted in 2000 introduced the possibility that any worker could work up to 60 hours per week based on an individual agreement between the employer and the employee. The legislation specified, furthermore, that the agreement must be in written form and kept in the workplace, where it could be shown to a government inspector on request. Both parties had the right to revoke the agreement, and according to the law no employee without a valid agreement could be forced to work longer than the regular hours provided by the legislation.[86] While the government promised greater flexibility for employers and employees, the new legislation opened the way for a substantial extension of work time. As Mark Thomas notes, the 60-hour provision "shifted the regulation of work time standards back to private relations between employers and employees and implicitly created the means for employers to exert greater control over the scheduling of extra hours."[87] Precisely because employment relations became a private matter negotiated between private parties, workers were deprived of the possibility of collectively withstanding the pressure to put in longer hours (except if they could not be replaced by their employers). In some companies workers had to sign individual 60-hour agreements as part of the hiring process.[88]

In addition to the individual 60-hour week, the daily work time limit was increased from eight to 13 hours and the obligation for a weekly rest period was eliminated in favor of a bi-weekly rest period. But more importantly, weekly work hours could be averaged over a four-week period without the need to pay overtime supplements as long as the average did not exceed 44 hours per week.

While four weeks is a rather short period, given the fact that in Europe averaging periods of up to a year are fairly common, the combination of averaging and a 60-hour work week meant that workers can be made to work far beyond the 44-hour threshold without overtime premiums.[89] While most unionized workers were not immediately affected by the changes – this is perhaps the reason why organized labor condemned the legislation but did not spend much effort organizing resistance – the introduction of the 60-hour week was a signal for employers across the province to demand an extension of collectively agreed work time. In 2001, an employer in Windsor tabled the introduction of a 60-hour week as part of a series of concessions the company wanted from the union in order to cut production costs. The workers had to strike for ten weeks to protect existing work hours and had to give away some vacation days to settle the conflict. In 2002, a truck plant in Chatham also pushed for the introduction of the 60-hour week in order to help the company to regain its competitiveness. Here the workers left their jobs for six weeks to convince their employer that a 60-hour week should not be an option.[90]

In 2003, the consevatives lost the provincial elections and were replaced by the liberals. In the election campaign the liberals had promised to take back the 60-hour week. Yet the subsequent amendments adopted in 2004 did not exactly end the 60-hour provision. Instead the new legislation continued to allow for individual deviations from the 48-hour standard. The difference is that since 2004 the written agreement between employer and employee must be filed with the government and approved by the director of employment standards. The legislation, furthermore, repealed the four-week averaging period, but introduced the possibility for individual averaging agreements between an employer and an individual employee, which, again, must be filed with the government. Thus, as Thomas notes, "the legacy of the 60-hour week legislation remained largely intact, even after the defeat of the government that brought it into effect."[91]

Another example of individualization and opting out is the British adaptation of the European Working Time Directive. The Labour Party, which had won the 1997 election and ended two decades of conservative government, started its first term in office with the promise to promote "fairness at work." Part of the new approach to work and employment issues was the adoption of the European Working Time Directive, which the previous conservative government had delayed and (unsuccessfully) challenged in the European Court of Justice in Luxembourg. As described in Chapter 8, the British work time regime is traditionally based on collectively agreed work time rather than statutory hours. The erosion of the collective bargaining system described above, however, meant that more than 60 percent of workers were no longer covered by a collective agreement in 2004 (75 percent in the private sector).[92] As a result of the changes in the bargaining system, the United Kingdom has the largest proportion of workers putting in long work hours in Europe. Britain, hence, was one of the few countries where the Working Time Directive could have made a real difference –in most other countries in Europe national regulations impose shorter hours than foreseen in the directive.

That the legislation had only limited impact on actual work hours is the result of the way it has been implemented. Officially, New Labour's goal was to ensure "fair treatment of employees within a flexible and efficient labor market." In practice, the government was more inclined to ensure flexibility, and its commitment to fairness went only as far as not obstructing employers' possibility to deploy their workers in a flexible fashion.[93] The Working Time Directive, adopted by the European Council in 1993, included a number of exemptions and two major derogations from its 48-hour cap on weekly work hours (averaged over a 17-week period). Individual employees could opt out from the work time provision and social partners could negotiate deviations, including an extension of the averaging period. The opt-out clause was highly controversial, and limited until 2003 when the law called for a review of the measure. In any case, only a few countries took advantage of the opt-out possibility and transposed it into national law. The labour government included both possibilities in the 1998 regulations that implemented the EC Working Time Directive. While initially the legislation demanded detailed records from employers, a 1999 amendment significantly relaxed the requirements after businesses complained about the administrative burden. Since then workers simply have to sign an opt-out agreement, while employers are expected to keep up-to-date records (workers can revoke opt-out consent at any time but have to give the employer seven days notice before the changes take effect). The labour government also went further than other countries in enabling deviations based on social partner agreements. In Britain, such agreements do not necessarily need to be confirmed by trade unions or shop stewards. In workplaces without trade union representation, which account for 62 percent of all workplaces, agreements can be simply be signed by unelected worker representatives.

However, collective agreements played only a minor role in extending the length of the work week beyond the 48-hour limit. The most common instrument in circumventing the directive's work time provisions is the op-out agreement. Catherine Banard, Simon Deakin, and Richard Hobbs, estimate that at least 10 percent of British workers have signed an opt-out agreement. Yet in some sectors such as manufacturing and financial services the figure is almost 90 percent. The authors estimate that up to three million workers would be affected if opting out was cancelled.[94] Although the legislation emphasizes that the agreement must be voluntary, new employees frequently sign them together with their employment contracts. They may withdraw their consent later on, but refusal to sign is certainly not helpful for career prospects within a company. Another study assumes that at least 17 percent of those working long hours have been pressured to sign away their rights.[95] Despite the fact that opting out meant that the adoption of the Working Time Directive had only a limited impact on Britain's notorious culture of long hours, the labour government refused to drop the opt-out clause when it was up for review in 2003.[96] As Dickens and Hall note, "there was an apparent reluctance to privilege collective bargaining and collective voice over more individualized methods." And they further conclude that "the New Labour legal framework was consequently one that sat well with the individualization of employment relations which took place during the 1990s."[97]

The French government also introduced the possibility of deviations based on individual agreements between employers and employees in 2005, but workers rarely took advantage of what the government calls "chosen work hours" and the measure remained largely ineffective. Yet the government was more successful in promoting overtime working. Overtime is another form of individualization. The conservatives, who replaced the social democrats in the 2002 elections, immediately started modifying the 35-hour legislation. One of the first measures was to stop the extension of the 35-hour week to companies with 20 or fewer workers and to revoke the subsidies for establishments that had shifted to the 35-hour standard (by lowering social security contributions for all companies, regardless of their work hours). Interestingly, however, the government did not alter the 35-hour norm – despite considerable pressure from French employers. Instead the government left the 35-hour week in place but increased the leeway and incentives for overtime working.

The 2003 legislation on "wages, work time and job creation" (also known as the Fillon Law) increased the maximum overtime quota from 130 to 180 hours per year.[98] At the same time, overtime supplements were made the subject of collective bargaining with the obligation that premiums account for at least 10 percent, and at most 25 percent, of regular wages. In the following year the overtime quota was raised to 220 hours.[99] The 2007 "law promoting work, jobs and purchasing power" and the 2008 "law for the renovation of social democracy and the reform of work time" took the matter even further: overtime limits were made the subject of company bargaining, meaning that workers could work in excess of 220 hours per year when a company agreement was reached.[100] At the same time, overtime was made more attractive: employers benefited from reduced social security contributions on overtime hours and (for companies without an overtime agreement) an extension of the reduced 25 percent overtime rate to the first eight instead of the first four overtime hours. Workers lost some overtime supplements but profited from a waiving of income taxes on overtime hours.[101] The changes created an incentive for both workers and employers to declare as many hours as possible as overtime. The number of overtime hours increased by 28 percent in 2008, to reach 185.6 million in the last quarter of the year – after which they decreased somewhat. Some of the hours may have been faked because of tax advantages, but the amount of overtime is certainly remarkable for a recession year.[102] In sum, the reforms introduced since 2002 enabled French companies to maintain a 39-hour week with "no massive extra cost."[103]

As described in Chapter 8, the United States never introduced a legal limit to overtime working. The Fair Labor Standards Act (FLSA) only required employers to pay an overtime premium for hours exceeding the 40-hour norm. The architects of the FLSA believed that the overtime penalty would allow employers to use overtime whenever needed, but to avoid it if not absolutely necessary. In the immediate postwar decades, overtime hours, indeed, tended to fluctuate according to the business cycle, increasing during periods of high demand and falling back during subsequent slumps. Despite strong fluctuations, average weekly overtime hours put in by US manufacturing workers never exceeded 4.1 hours. The situation started to change in the 1980s: average weekly overtime hours of production workers increased over an entire business cycle from 3.3 hours in 1979 to 3.8 hours in 1989. And they continued to grow at an even higher pace in the 1990s, taking off at 3.3 hours in 1991 and reaching a record 4.9 hours in 1998. This meant that overtime had increased by almost 50 percent over a seven-year period. "Unlike in previous expansions," as Ron Hetrick notes, "manufacturing employers in the 1990s were more likely to increase overtime hours among existing employees than to hire new employees."[104]

After the work time "givebacks" of the 1970s and 1980s, union resistance against overtime working was weak (perhaps also because workers needed the additional income due to very modest wage increases in the 1980s). Among the few examples where workers stood up against mandatory overtime working in the 1990s was a strike at General Motors' Buick City Plant. Workers temporarily shut down production in 1994 to force the company to hire additional permanent staff, after management had refused to hire new workers on permanent contracts over the previous eight years.[105] The surge of overtime hours in the 1990s resulted in a growing proportion of American workers working extremely long work hours. The share of male workers who worked more than 48 hours a week grew from 16.6 percent in 1980 to 24.3 percent in 2005.[106] In 2000, 19.4 percent of all US workers (men and women) worked more than 40 hours, and those who worked overtime on average put in an additional 11.8 overtime hours per week.[107] Together with shorter vacations, the growth in overtime and the subsequent extension of the work week means that American workers put in significantly more hours per year than their European counterparts (see Chapter 4).

Workfare

The erosion of collective work standards and the individualization of the employment contract were complemented by a workfarist restructuring of welfare states. In the postwar period the expansion of welfare states aimed to protect workers from the risks of labor markets and, in the most developed versions, to even free individuals from the coercion of selling their labor power to maintain a social existence. Gøsta Esping-Andersen has pointed to the decommodifying effects of welfare allowing individuals "freely, and without potential loss of job, income, or general welfare, [to] opt out of work when they themselves consider it necessary."[108] Particularly important in this regard was the availability of public pensions, shortening the proportion of their lives that workers needed to spend at work.

In contrast, most welfare reforms introduced since the 1980s have aimed at improving workers' employability and (re)integrating individuals as quickly as possible into paid employment.[109] In addition, a series of pension reforms increased the official retirement age, forcing workers who still have a job to stay longer in employment. While early retirement was used in the 1980s to fight soaring unemployment, the regular retirement age has been increased in spite of the high unemployment levels of the 1990s and after 2000. In Britain the retirement age of women will gradually increase from 2010 onwards to match the male retirement age of 65 by 2020. At the same time, the earliest age for claiming a private or occupational pension was raised from 50 to 55. In Germany, the age for eligibility to a state pension will be increased from 65 to 67 between 2012 and 2035. A conservative president in France increased the retirement age to 62 in 2010, but his social democratic successor reinstated the 60-year threshold.

The change in welfare policies has been described as a shift from welfare to workfare. Initially, workfare referred to a series of coercive programs introduced in the United States – and later in Britain and Canada among other countries – which demanded that welfare recipients work for their welfare payments.[110] Welfare-to-work programs were promoted by the same political forces which also set out to remove "red tape" such as collectively agreed work hours. But workfare programs were only the most visible change in a more fundamental and comprehensive reform of welfare systems. As Jamie Peck notes, workfare in the broader sense refers to "a movement away from entitlement programs, an increased reliance on market-oriented social policies, a focus on the encouragement of work and work-related values, an emphasis on mandatory job-search and job placement for welfare recipients."[111] In short, the shift from welfare to workfare social policy is no longer considered an alternative or corrective to labor markets; instead it is an instrument to encourage and push individuals to find paid employment and to stay as long as possible in the labor market.[112] The OECD, the International Monetary Fund, and the European Commission have welcomed these policies as an improvement of "labor utilization." Even though there is no clear measure of labor utilization, the term is intended to reflect the intensity of work and the number of hours put in by a certain population. If we assume that the respective populations have comparable living standards, then this notion comes close to what Marxists understand as the rate of exploitation.[113]

Outcome

In sum, neoliberalism slowed and partly reversed the "secular decline in labor utilization" – that is, the partial mitigation of growing productivity and increasing labor market participation by decreasing individual work hours (both as weekly hours and as the number of hours worked over a lifetime).[114] In some countries the change can be seen in an increase in average work hours, but more often average hours have stagnated while the total number of workers, and productivity, have increased. In the United States the average work week in 2000 was 1.6 hours longer than it was in 1970.[115] By the end of the 1990s American workers were putting in more than an additional week per year than they had in the early 1980s. In manufacturing, where the part-time rate is traditionally low, the difference between 1975 and 2000 amounted to more than two weeks. Sweden also showed a strong upward trend in yearly work hours, especially during the 1980s. The difference between 1990 and 2000 is 80 hours. According to Dominque Anxo, the growth is partly explained by a growing number of women working full-time hours. Average work weeks of women increased by four hours between 1981 and 2001. But tax cuts for those on higher incomes have also favored longer hours.[116] In Britain yearly hours increased substantially in the 1980s (by 70 hours between 1981 and 1989), but fell back in the 1990s. Average yearly hours in 2001 were virtually the same as in 1981. Canada experienced a surge in work hours in the 1990s with the effect that in 1999 workers put in 13 hours more per year than they had in 1991. In contrast to Britain, hours fell back only slightly after 2000. In France and Germany average yearly hours were still falling in the 1980s and 1990s, but either stagnated or slightly increased between 2003 and 2008.

Average yearly work hours include part-time work. If we look only at full-time hours, work time more or less stagnated between 1992 and 2006 in Germany, and between 2003 and 2008 in France.[117] But there are remarkable changes within full-time hours. In Germany, for example, the proportion of male workers who put in between 36 and 39 hours per week decreased from 53 percent in 1995 to 21 percent in 2008, while the proportion of those working 40 hours increased from 31 percent to 46 percent over the same period.[118]

The halt of the secular decline in labor utilization can also be seen in the development of per capita work hours (including those without a job). In the United

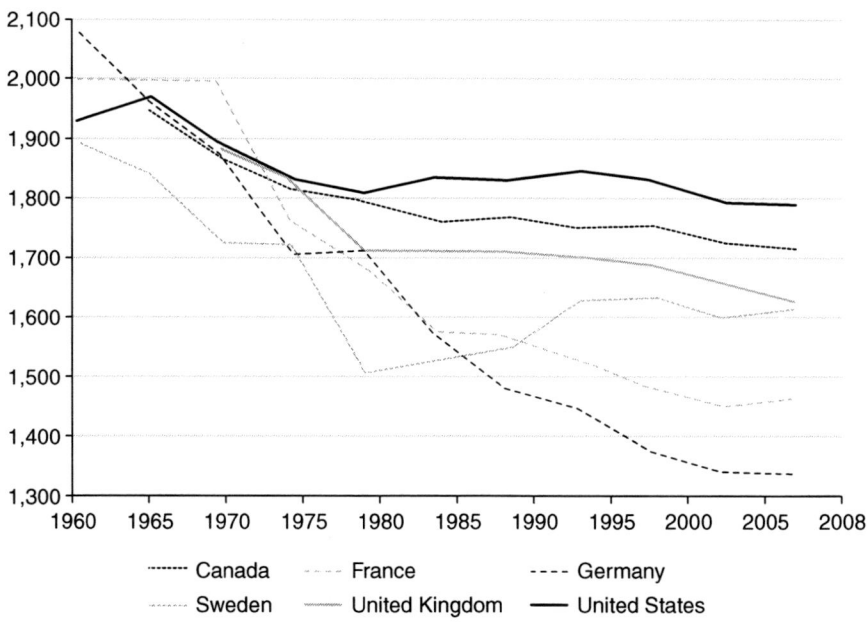

Figure 10.1 Average yearly work hours (1960–2008) (source: OECD).

Notes
* Until 1990 West Germany.
** All workers; otherwise dependent employees.

Table 10.1 Average weekly full-time hours

	1983	1985	1990	1995	2000	2005	2008
France	42.4	42.6	42.4	42.3	41.8	39.6	39.5
Germany	43.0	43.3	42.5	42.6	42.4	42.7	42.1
Sweden	n/a	n/a	n/a	38.0	40.5	39.8	39.6
UK	41.4	41.9	42.3	42.6	41.8	41.3	41.0

Source: Eurostat.

States per capita hours have increased by 18 percent between 1985 and 2000, while Canada recorded the same growth over an even longer period: 1970 to 2008. In Britain per capita hours virtually stagnated between 1980 and 2008; so too in Sweden between 1985 and 2008. In sum, "the reversal of the long-term decline in hours per capita in the 1990s was widespread across OECD countries and regions, with only few exceptions still recording significant falls."[119] Among the few countries that still recorded falling per capita hours in the 1990s were France and Germany. But in both countries the development came to a halt in the mid-1990s, with per capita hours largely stagnating between 1995 and 2008. Another way of looking at the same development is the comparison of work hours spent by households rather than by individual workers. The combined (paid) work week of married couples in the United States increased from 52.2 hours in 1970 to 63.1 hours in 2000. This is an increase of almost 20 percent.[120]

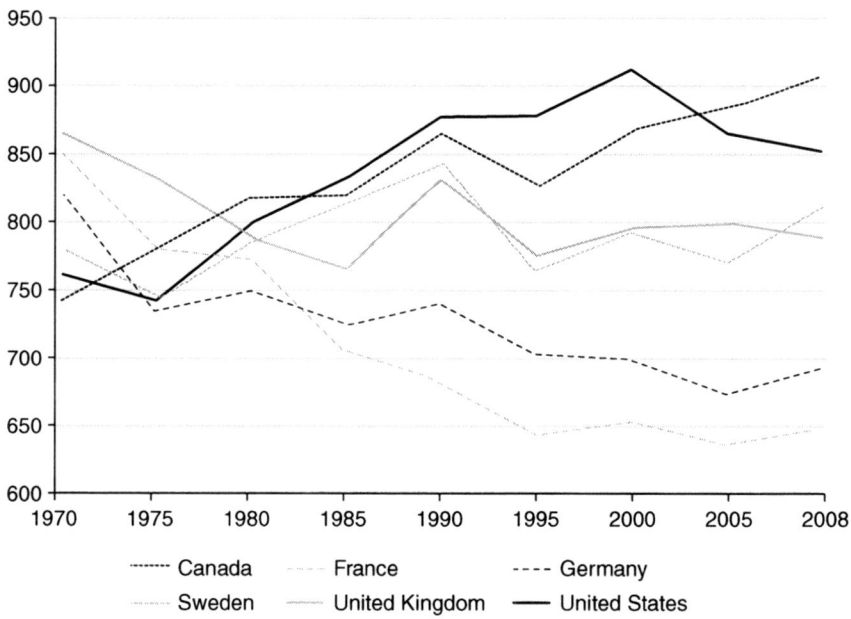

Figure 10.2 Per capita work hours (1970–2008) (source: OECD. Own calculations).

Some scholars have argued that the increase in paid work put in by American families is compensated for by an equal reduction of time spent on domestic labor.[121] Yet according to figures from American time studies compiled by Liana Sayer, men and women together spent almost two hours (117 minutes) more per day for paid and unpaid work in 1998 than in 1975. The combined free time fell by more than an hour (66 minutes) over the same time period. The brunt of this growth has been felt by women, who have added an average of 100 minutes per day in paid work, while cutting their unpaid work by only 20 minutes. Men, on the other hand, have reduced paid work by 20 minutes, but have extended unpaid work by 60 minutes.[122] According to Valerie Ramey and Neville Francis, the average weekly free time per person aged 14 years and older in the United States was five hours less in 2000 than it was in 1980.[123]

Work time has not only increased, it has also become more intense. David Maume and David Purcell found that the pace of work increased significantly in the United States between 1977 and 1997, mainly because of increasingly complex tasks.[124] The European Working Conditions Survey also shows a persistent intensification of work measured since the first survey was conducted in 1990.[125] Intensity here is measured with indicators such as "working at high speed" or "working to tight deadlines." In the United States, higher work intensity, together with accelerating automation, increased productivity by 20 percent between 1985 and 2000. In France and Germany productivity soared by roughly 40 percent over the same time period.[126] Together the growth in work hours and productivity meant that labor utilization in the US has surged by at least 40 percent since the mid-1980s. And according to the European Commission, labor utilization since the 1990s has grown at a faster pace in Europe than in the US.[127] Particularly impressive is the increase in the employment rate of older workers. In Germany the proportion of those aged between 55 and 64 who still held a job increased by 20 percent between 1992 and 2009, in France and Britain by 10 percent, while in Sweden it remained at 70 percent – 10 percent higher than in the US. If we take into account that average wages were stagnant or increased only modestly for many workers, the result is what Marxists call a substantial augmentation in surplus labor.

Neoclassical economists may argue that longer work hours are the result of higher living standards, reflecting workers' consumption choices. Growing consumption results in higher GDP; and GDP per capita has, indeed, increased to a similar extent to work hours. However, GDP per capita is not the appropriate measurement because it makes no account of the difference between work-related and non-work-related income. A crucial outcome of neoliberal restructuring was precisely the redistribution of wealth from wages to profits – as can be seen in the falling wage share (wages as a proportion of GDP). If we look at the development of wages and work hours, quite a different picture emerges: in the US real hourly wages grew more or less in line with productivity until the end of the 1970s. But from 1979 onwards a gap emerged between real wages and productivity growth. As Simon Mohun points out, "productivity growth resumed after 1980, but the real hourly wage rate showed no growth at all for two decades."[128] Given that during the same period work hours increased rather than decreased, workers could have hardly traded shorter hours for higher incomes. US workers and their interest organizations obviously failed to turn the productivity gains they captured into higher wages or shorter hours. If anything, Americans had to work more and longer hours to compensate for the stagnation or fall in real wages. As Samuel Bowles, David Gordon and Thomas Weisskopf note, the

> increase in average annual hours per capita reflects an increase in the number of household members working outside the home.... Faced with stagnating and then declining real spendable earnings, additional family members, particularly married women sought to work.... This extra labor helped sustain total household earnings.[129]

In Europe the situation was less dramatic, but since the 1980s, here, too, real wage growth lags behind the growth in productivity, after real wage growth, had temporarily exceeded the productivity gains of the late 1960s.[130] In some countries like Germany and France, the unions and their political allies could still win shorter work hours, but a slow-down in shorter work hours did not cause a greater rise in wages in other countries.[131] And the fact that wages hardly increased while workers' hours remained long made it difficult for trade unions to convince workers to make shorter work hours a bargaining priority to fight high unemployment after the Great Recession.

It should also be borne in mind that official statistics do not include the contribution of undocumented workers, many of them unauthorized migrants. Because the work is undocumented it is inherently difficult to measure. Estimates suggest that the informal economy equals between 8 percent and 10 percent of GDP in the United States, with undocumented workers accounting for 5 percent of the American workforce.[132] The real figures are probably significantly higher. Given their low wages and poor working conditions, undocumented workers are among those most exploited in developed countries. Migration more generally has played an important role in sustaining surplus labor. Official immigration, together with increasing employment rates and a lengthening of the work day, meant that the total number of hours worked in Canada grew by 50 percent between 1970 and 2008. In the US the increase amounts to 40 percent over the same period. At 16 percent, Sweden also recorded a significant increase, while total hours were more-or-less stagnant in Britain between 1975 and 2008 as they were in Germany and France between 1985 and 2008, after falling in Western Europe over the preceding decades.

Beneath the growth and stagnation of work hours lies an increasing polarization of work time. While the proportion of those working "normal" hours – that is, between 35 and 40 hours per week – has tended to diminish, the proportion of those working long and short hours has increased since the 1970s. As mentioned in Chapter 2, Britain stands out for its highly unequal distribution of work hours. Although this polarization has diminished somewhat in recent years, it is still the case that less than a third of British employees worked between 30 and 40 hours in 2008; 30 percent of male workers put in more than 45 hours per week, while 12 percent of women worked fewer than 16 hours per week.[133] In Germany, 46 percent of male workers still worked 40 hours a week in 2008, but the proportion of male workers who worked between 41and 48 hours more than doubled between 1995 and 2008; while the proportion of women working fewer than 20 hours increased by 60 percent over the same period.[134] In the United States the proportion of workers who worked 40 hours a week decreased from 48 percent in 1970 to 41 percent in 2000. Here the proportion working 50 and more hours a week increased from 21 percent to 26.5 percent over the same period.[135] Canada also recorded a growing polarization of work hours between the early 1980s and mid-1990s, but this was reversed somewhat between 1997 and 2006.[136] In France and Sweden work hours are distributed more evenly with a comparably small proportion of the workforce working fewer than 30 hours a week. But in France the proportion of men working 40 hours or more has increased from 20 percent in 2002 to more than 35 percent in 2008.[137]

Summary

Neoliberalism was foremost a political response to the crisis of postwar capitalism, and an attempt to roll back some of the gains the working classes had won during years of high growth and full employment. Increasing market dependence and accelerating (global) competition were crucial in undermining working class solidarity and increasing pressure to make work hours longer and more flexible. However, a prolongation of the legal or collective agreed work day or week was an exception. What happened instead was an erosion of collective work time regulations through measures such as the granting of concessions and exemptions, the weakening of collective bargaining, new forms of work time flexibility, opt-out clauses, and the growing use of overtime. The erosion of collective work time regulations was coupled with a shift from welfare to workfare policies. As the chapter shows these developments were not confined to a single country; they took place across a range of countries operating different models of capitalism.

The cumulative outcome was a stagnation of average work hours, a widespread increase in per capita hours, and more work hours put in by working families. However, because the changes were based on an acceleration of markets and competition rather than an outright prolongation of the work day or week, the result was also a growing polarization of work time.

Table 10.2 Distribution of weekly work hours in 2008 (percent)

Hours	1–19	20	21–9	30–5	36–9	40	41–8	49+
France	8.5	3.5	10.0	35.2	20.7	8.1	6.3	5.4
Germany	20.8	9.2	8.2	12.4	17.5	28.8	4.1	2.0
Sweden	7.2	6.0	5.4	20.7	17.9	38.1	4.1	0.4
UK	17.5	4.6	12.8	14.1	21.7	9.4	12.3	6.3

Source: Eurostat.

Notes

1 Harvey (2005: 9ff.).
2 Duménil and Lévy (2004: 44–50). See also Schulten (2004: 188–9).
3 Albo (2007: 356).
4 Altvater (2007).
5 Glyn (2006: 25–45).
6 Robert Brenner, for example, argues that the Reagan and Bush administrations stimulated the American economy through a combination of tax cuts for the rich, and military spending – even though the policy resulted in record public deficits. See Brenner (2006: 36).
7 Albo (2005: 70).
8 Hay (2007: 53–5).
9 This is epitomized in Margaret Thatcher's famous statement: "There is no alternative." See Hermann (2007: 68).
10 Gindin (2000: 349).
11 Fletcher and Gapasin (2008: 9–10).
12 Albo and Fast (2003: 39).
13 Boyer (2004: 56–61).
14 Hermann (2008: 85).
15 Cologne Institute for Economic Research, 19 June 2003. See also Bartsch (2005).
16 Gindin (1995: 183).
17 Cited in Greis (1984: 47).
18 Paid holidays and paid vacation were also reduced in other sectors including the rubber industry and retail and food stores. Ibid.: 273–6.
19 Dribbusch (2003).
20 Ibid.
21 Ibid.
22 The threat of relocation is a powerful tool to pressure workers into making concessions. A representative survey conducted after the conflicts at Siemens and Daimler-Chrysler found that about one-third of German workers feared losing their jobs as a result of their employer's shifting of production to a cheaper location. See Dribbusch and Schulten (2008: 182–3).
23 Funk (2004).
24 Haipeter (2009: 240).
25 Bispinck (2006: 124).
26 See Funk (2004) and Bispinck (2006: 125).
27 Haipeter and Lehndorff (2005: 147).
28 Ibid.: 152.
29 Lehndorff (2003: 279).
30 Haipeter (2009: 239). See also Bispinck (2006: 124–5).
31 Haipeter, ibid.: 242.
32 Ibid.: 243–5.
33 Haipeter (2010: 296). See also Bispinck (2006: 126–7).
34 Haipeter (2010: 298).
35 Lehndorff (2010: 79).
36 Dribbusch (2006).
37 Dribbusch (2005).
38 Beese (2006). See also Bispinck (2006: 125–8).
39 Dribbusch (2007).
40 Ibid.
41 Dribbusch and Schulten (2008: 189). See also Bispinck, (2006: 127).
42 Kümmerling *et al.* (2009).
43 Ibid. See also Lehndorff (2010: 84–5).

44 Lehndorff (2009: 10).
45 Bureau of Labor Statistics (2011).
46 Brown *et al.* (2009: 24). See also Blanchflower and Bryson (2009: 49).
47 Milner (1995: 85).
48 Dickens and Hall (2009: 336–7).
49 Ibid.
50 Ibid.: 337–78.
51 Blanchflower and Bryson (2009: 50). See also Brown *et al.* (2009: 24).
52 Brown *et al.* (2009: 26).
53 Ibid.: 34.
54 Fagan (2009: 44).
55 Bispinck and Schulten (2009: 202).
56 Brandt and Schulten (2008).
57 Bispinck and Schulten (2009: 204).
58 Ibid.: 203.
59 Bispinck and Schulten (2005: 467).
60 Ellguth and Kohaut (2008: 515).
61 Hassel (1999).
62 Workers have a right to elect a work council in companies with five or more employees.
63 Ellguth (2006: 50).
64 Ellguth and Kohaut (2008: 518).
65 Lehndorff (2009: 4).
66 Herrmann *et al.* (1999: 35–6).
67 Bispinck and Schulten (2001).
68 Promberger *et al.* (2002: 163).
69 Ibid.: 161.
70 Lehndorff (2007: 15).
71 Kümmerling *et al.* (2009: 75).
72 Michon (2009: 15–16).
73 Ibid.: 13.
74 Groß *et al.* (2000: 217–18).
75 Haipeter and Lehndorff (2005: 145). See also Lehndorff (2009).
76 Groß (2010: 28–9.
77 Bauer et al. (2002: 161).
78 Ibid.
79 Haipeter and Lehndorff (2005: 147).
80 Jänicke *et al.* (2008: 105).
81 Lehndorff describes the changes as the establishment of a "grey zone of work time extension" (2003: 280).
82 Fuchs *et al.* (2010).
83 Meilland (2005).
84 Thomas (2009: 97).
85 Ibid.: 109–14.
86 Ibid.: 122.
87 Ibid.: 124.
88 Thomas (2007)
89 In an extreme case, a worker could work 60 hours in week one, 60 hours in week two, 56 hours in week three, and zero hours in week four, and still get no overtime pay.
90 Thomas (2009: 127–8).
91 Ibid.: 136.
92 Brown *et al.* (2009: 26).
93 Dickens and Hall (2009: 342–3).

94 Barnard *et al.* (2003: 237).
95 The TUC believes that the proportion is significantly higher. See Exell (2006: 274).
96 Ibid.: 275–6.
97 Dickens and Hall (2009: 341).
98 Braud (2002).
99 In 2005, regulations on work time accounts were relaxed (see below), while companies were granted the possibility to compensate their managers if they agreed to work on the old schedule (235 instead of 218 days per year). See Husson (2004).
100 Meilland (2005).
101 In the case of agreements applicable to a sector or company, overtime supplements can be reduced to a minimum of 10 percent. See Husson (2004).
102 Michon (2009: 16–17).
103 Askenazy (2007: 10). See also Concialdi *et al.* (2009: 140).
104 Hetrick (2000: 33).
105 Rosenberg (2009: 75)
106 Kuhn and Lozano (2008: 311–2).
107 Golden and Jorgensen (2002: 6).
108 Esping-Andersen (1990: 23).
109 Esping-Andersen, in his more recent work, has advocated an activating social policy.
110 Peck (2001).
111 Peck (2003: 85).
112 Lessenich (2008: 85–117). Lessenich focuses on the German case, but his conclusions hold for other welfare systems.
113 Greater American labor utilization can, consequently, be interpreted as the superior capability of American capital to exploit US workers.
114 See the first chapter, "Recent labor market developments and prospects," in OECD (2004).
115 McGrattan and Rogerson (2004: 17).
116 Anxo (2009: 62, 69).
117 In Sweden full-time hours have increased by 1.6 hours between 1995 and 2008; in Britain full-time hours also increased between 1985 and 1995, but in 2006 they were roughly the same as in 1984. European Commission (2007: 135).
118 Lehndorff *et al.* (2010: 124).
119 OECD (2004: 46–7).
120 Jacobs and Gerson (2004: 29–31).
121 Robinson and Godbey (1999).
122 Sayer (2005: 292–3, Table 2).
123 Ramey and Francis (2009: 209, Table 6).
124 Maume and Purcell (2007).
125 One of the clearest trends since the first *European Working Conditions Survey* was carried out 15 years ago, is a rise in the levels of perceived work intensity. This rise, already evident in 2000, is confirmed by national working conditions surveys in most member states. In almost all countries in the EU15, there has been a clear and consistent increase in the levels of perceived work intensity over the last 15 years. Parent-Thrion *et al.* (2007: 58–9).
126 Figures from the OECD.
127 Mainly because of a "remarkable turnaround" in the development of the employment rate (European Commission 2009: 127–8).
128 Mohun (2005: 358).
129 Bowles *et al.* (1990: 39–40).
130 Schulten (2004: 183–5).
131 Ibid.
132 See Passel *et al.* (2004) and Schneider (2002).

133 Fagan (2009: 41).
134 Eurostat data. See also Lehndorff *et al*. (2010: 120, 124).
135 Jacobs and Gerson (2004: 28).
136 In 1993, 22 percent of workers put in particularly long hours and 8 percent particularly short hours, compared to 19 percent and 4 percent respectively in 1981. See Sunter and Morissette (March 2008).
137 Lehndorff *et al*. (2010: 125).

11 Capitalism and work time

Introduction

This chapter takes up the evidence from Chapters 5–10 and revisits some of the theoretical assumptions laid out in Chapters 1–3 in order to present a number of conclusions with regard to the nature and role of work time in capitalist societies. The chapter starts with a discussion of the persistence of long work hours despite very substantial gains in productivity and living standards. Among other questions it asks why existing institutions have often proved insufficient in defending working people from long and flexible work hours, and especially from the growing polarization of work time. One insight, discussed in the following section, is that solidarity is an essential precondition for a shorter work day and week, and for a more equal distribution of paid and unpaid work, whereas markets promote the interests of employers and capital owners. The next section describes how the search for surplus labor has transformed production systems and resulted in a simultaneous compression, extension, and variation of work time. Here, too, markets played a pivotal role in enforcing the changes. The following part discusses the tension between standardization and flexibilization and argues that in neoliberal capitalism flexibilization is a form of commodification and as such an erosion of working class achievements. In contrast the promotion of worker-based flexibility demands for a severe limitation of competition and more workplace democracy. The next part links consumption to ecological degradation and explores the role of shorter work hours in a more sustainable economy and society. The chapter ends with a discussion of the concept of necessary work time as an alternative to growing and increasingly intense and polarized work hours, and a list of arguments in favor of a 30-hour week.

The persistence of long work hours

John Maynard Keynes expected in the 1930s that in 2030 people would only work 15 hours a week, despite much higher living standards. Others made similar predictions. In the mid-1960s, Jean Fourastié still anticipated the introduction of the 30-hour week in 2000 when productivity would continue to grow at the established pace. Even in the 1990s, Jeremy Rifkin stated that the high-technology revolution could liberate millions of workers from long work hours. However, Rifkin conceded that a lot depended on how the productivity gains of the Information Age were distributed. In 2014 we are still far away from the 30-hour week and unless there is a radical transformation of our economic and social system no serious academic believes that the weekly work time could fall to 15 hours in the foreseeable future. The knowledge economy did not bring about a jobless future or a world without work as predicted by some scholars. With few exceptions work hours have hardly fallen in the last four decades, and if anything people work more not less. Manufacturing workers and working families in the United States put in 20 percent more hours in 2000 than they did in the 1970s. In other countries the increase was not as steep, but only in a few countries in Europe were (full-time) work hours still decreasing in the 1990s. And where they still fell this process came to an end after 2000. The trend towards more rather than less work is even clearer if we look at per capita work hours rather than hours per person in employment. Because of the increase in female labor market participation, per capita hours have increased since the mid-1970s, in some countries quite substantially. However, work has not only become longer; it has also become more intense.

Hence, it not only was Keynes who wrong in predicting a radical cut in work hours; it was all scholars who assumed that leisure time would increase in line with growing productivity and/or rising living standards. While productivity has increased by more than 18 times, and per capita GDP by more than 26 times since 1870, work time has only been halved over the same period.[1] And even though productivity and GDP growth slowed down somewhat in the 1980s and 1990s, both still increased by 60 percent between 1979 and 2009 – which means that Americans would in theory have to work less than 20 hours a week to reach the living standard of the 1970s. It is important to note that these are average values. Because of the increase in inequality in the past 40 years, many US workers actually work more hours than before to maintain their living standards. For low wage workers and their families, hence, the main problem is income; shorter hours are seen as secondary issue.

It is no accident that the growth or stagnation in work hours coincided with the ascendance of neoliberalism as the ruling ideology and political practice in the Western world and beyond. Neoliberalism halted and partly reversed the secular decline in work time. In a revealing example for neoliberal hegemony, work time reduction played no role in the discussions about solving the unemployment problem of the Great Recession, even though a number of European countries had successfully used short time working schemes to avoid unemployment in the early phase of the crisis.[2] With the shift to austerity and structural adjustment, governments reduced holidays and overtime supplements in the face of record-high unemployment – an attempt to increase weekly work hours by the Portuguese government failed due to fierce trade union opposition – following the assumption that longer work hours would create additional jobs.[3] This is a complete reversal of earlier policies adopted during the 1930s and 1970s crises, when work hours were cut in order to share the reduced amount of work among a larger number of workers. Obviously 30 years of neoliberal rule has succeeded in discrediting the cause for shorter work hours. Even those who have proposed a Green New Deal to cope with the current ecological and economic crisis have left out shorter work hours from their list of adequate countermeasures.[4] However, the change in work hours was rarely based on a formal extension of the work day or week. As shown by the Portuguese example, such policies tend to provoke resistance. What we have seen instead is the weakening of collective regulations through the granting of concessions and exemptions, the erosion and fragmentation of bargaining structures, and the introduction of new forms of flexibility that make it difficult to maintain control over work hours, as well as provisions for opting out and letting overtime grow. Per capita hours were also fueled by a shift from welfare to workfare, forcing more people into paid employment and requiring them to work longer before they retire.

From a Marxist view the growth or stagnation in work hours can be explained by the decreasing power of trade unions and other working class organizations. Rather than falling gradually, in line with growing productivity and increasing living standards – as one could expect from mainstream theories – the reduction of work time took place in phases, following major surges in power for either trade unions and/or working class parties. The manifestation of working class power took different forms including popular uprisings, militant strikes, and the expansion of trade union membership. A first cycle spanned roughly the second half of the nineteenth century and resulted in the introduction of the ten-hour work day. A second phase started in the late nineteenth century and ended with the establishment of the eight-hour work day or the 48-hour work week after the end of the First World War. A third phase began in the 1930s and in some countries led to the adoption of the 40-hour week before the Second World War or shortly thereafter. Devastated by the war, most European countries lagged behind and introduced the 40-hour week in the 1960s and 1970s. A fourth phase of work time reductions evolved in the 1980s and 1990s and led to the introduction of the 35-hour week, but only a few countries took part in this movement. Depending on the nature of conflict and the form of struggle, reductions were enforced through collective bargaining or government interventions, or through a combination of both. Once in place, institutions played an important role in channeling conflicts, including attempts to undermine existing work time norms. However, institutions are not insulated from struggles and change over time. Britain, now notorious for its culture of long hours, spearheaded the struggle for shorter work hours in the nineteenth century. And while the United States, meanwhile, has some of the longest work hours in the developed world, it was the country with the shortest work hours after the Second World War.

From the Marxist perspective neoliberalism is a systematic attempt by capital to roll back some of the gains the working classes made during the postwar boom, including shorter work hours. As the statistics show, the attempt was highly successful. Yet because the changes were based on an acceleration of market forces, the result was not a uniform increase in work hours experienced by all workers. The result, instead, was a growing polarization of work time, with some workers putting in particularly long (and others particularly short) hours, but with an overall increase in per capita hours. Institutions are important in defending established work time standards. However, to be effective institutions have to be backed by working class power. Without it they can quickly be eroded internally even if they still look the same on the surface. A country, for example, may still have a comprehensive collective bargaining system, but the bargaining institutions may no longer protect workers from capital's infringements because the unions have conceded to the logic of competition bargaining. So while institutionalists emphasize the varieties of capitalism to explain differences in work hours, what they deal with in many regards actually looks more like varieties of neoliberalism. No country has withstood the pressure to flexibilize work time and very few were still cutting work hours in the 1990s and after 2000.

The erosion of collective work time standards was partly caused by employer offensives against trade unions and collective bargaining and by the adoption of anti-trade union legislation. But trade unions themselves indirectly supported the transformation when they sacrificed shorter hours as part of concession bargaining, or accepted that work hours are negotiated on the company level rather than the sector level. With the acceptance of longer hours, even as a temporary exception, trade unions surrendered to the logic of competition bargaining and at least implicitly acknowledged that longer hours could save employment. In addition to making it difficult for working people to contemplate alternative ways of working and living, and the political strategies necessary to realize them, longer hours fueled unemployment rather than solving it. As a result the power of the trade union movement further deteriorated, leaving workers even more vulnerable to the demands of capital. In some countries workers' representatives were still able to win shorter work hours in the 1990s, but with flexibilization and a shift towards company-based bargaining they paid a heavy price. From flexibilization it was not far to individualization, the granting of exemptions, and the erosion of collective bargaining. Because flexibilization went hand-in-hand with marketization, the combination of short and flexible work hours was increasingly replaced by a combination of long and unpredictable hours. Even the introduction of individual sabbaticals and educational leave – welcomed by shorter hour activists as an effective response to individual needs – turned out to be ineffective in a situation of increasing competition and growing insecurity.

Solidarity versus markets

The crucial factor for the development of work time is not the search for new institutional compromises. More important is the extent and depth of solidarity among working people. While capitalists use competition to make sure that their interests prevail over those of their workforces, workers rely on solidarity to limit the amount of time they are expected to spend working. Marx has pointed out that individually workers cannot withstand the power of capital – one may add, unless they have specific skills making them difficult to be replaced. It is only through collective action that workers can confront capital. Even highly skilled workers who have no problem putting in long work hours, and who believe it is their individual choice to do so because they like their job, are limited as to what individual action they can take when they decide they want to spend more time with their families.

The struggle for shorter hours in several regards played an important role in fostering working class solidarity and promoting the trade union movement. Shorter hours gave workers and their families the time to develop a collective working class consciousness and culture – whereas higher wages integrated them even more into the system of capitalist accumulation, including the emerging capitalist leisure industry. Another difference is that wages depend a great deal on local costs of living, while work hours are easily comparable across borders. This is the reason why the eight-hour work day became a symbol of international solidarity for national labor movements that were still consolidating at the end of the nineteenth century. However, the failure of several countries to transpose the agreement into national law in the 1920s also shows how competition between different nation states can undermine international solidarity. Long and flexible hours, together with lower wages, play an important role in international competition. It is one way technologically less developed countries can compete with the technologically more advanced ones (some technologically advanced countries respond to such pressures by combining short work hours with long machine-operating times).

Most importantly, a reduction in work time also strengthens wider class solidarity because shorter hours also benefit those looking for a job. Not surprisingly, progressive trade unions have been hostile to overtime working even if employers offer overtime premiums and even if workers welcome the possibility to boost their wages. In the long run the coexistence of large amounts of overtime and high unemployment erodes solidarity and weakens working class power. In the same way, competition bargaining undermines solidarity and weakens trade union power, even if bargaining structures and codetermination procedures remain in place. Coordinated or regulated flexibilization may be preferable to union-busting and outright individualization, but accommodating workers' lives to market needs is not exactly a victory from the perspective of trade unions (even though the emptying of overtime accounts helped Germany and other countries avert unemployment during the Great Recession, the prospect of working and living according to the business cycle is not very tempting).

The importance of solidarity should not obscure the fact that different groups of workers can have different interests when it comes to the reduction of work time. Different interests correspond to different forms of work time reduction. Women usually have an interest in a reduction of daily work time as many of them struggle to combine paid work with unpaid domestic labor, extending the work day far beyond eight hours. In contrast young men may prefer longer vacations to a shorter work day, and older men, especially those close to retirement, favor a reduction of the retirement age because they suffer from severe physical and mental degradation after decades of strenuous and exhausting work. While initially the reduction of work time and the introduction of paid vacation often took place simultaneously – see, for example, the introduction of the 40-hour week and one week of paid vacation in Ontario in 1944 – shorter hours were repeatedly traded for more vacation, and occasionally even for early retirement during the postwar period. Employers were quick to offer more vacation or early retirement instead of shorter hours because they had a smaller effect on the organization of production and hence on the system of surplus extraction. In order to balance out the different interests of different member groups, union democracy is extremely important. This conflicts with the structure of many unions that were rebuilt after the Second World War as highly centralized and hierarchical organizations in the belief that this organizational structure would maximize the effectiveness of interest representation vis-à-vis capital.

Solidarity frequently reaches its limits when it comes to the distribution of household labor. Even though men have increased their share in domestic work in the 1960s and 1970s in response to growing female labor market participation and demands from the women's movement, the bulk of housework is still carried out by women. This is even true for households where both partners work full-time hours. More often, however, women work part-time while men put in over-time hours to boost the family budget. The result is an unequal distribution of paid and unpaid work – and since one form of work is paid and the other not women are disadvantaged in both cases. In the 1970s feminists demanded the introduction of the 30-hour week as a measure to distribute paid work more evenly. Even though a shorter work week does not guarantee that men spend more time on domestic tasks, experience has shown that men's domestic hours tend to increase when their paid hours fall and decrease when their paid hours rise. Instead of reducing the work time to 30 hours per week, employers and conservative politicians have promoted part-time employment as a solution to the double shift of women. As predicted by some feminists, part-time work served only to fortify gender differences. The unequal distribution of work hours has, meanwhile, become a major factor in explaining growing income inequality in the developed countries. Because they earn less than their male partners, women also receive lower unemployment and pension entitlements.

Some gender activists have advocated the introduction of paid leave as an alternative to shorter weekly work hours. The idea is that extended leave schemes allow individuals to adjust their work time more accurately to changing needs over the course of their lifetime. The most prominent example is parental leave, which allows parents to spend time with their newborn children before returning to work. However, although parental leave has certainly helped women with children stay in the labor market, it has hardly broken up the gender-specific bias of paid and unpaid labor. Only a fraction of the time devoted to parental leave is actually utilized by fathers. With few exceptions it is still women who stay at home and look after the children. However, shorter work hours are not only a strategy to alleviate women's double burden of paid and unpaid work, and encouraging men to take up a greater share of domestic work. "Beyond creating time for people to fulfill their duties of the family," as Kathi Weeks argues "a feminist time movement should also enable them to imagine and explore alternatives to the dominant ideals of family form, function, and division of labor." In other words, "the demand for shorter hours should not only speak in the name of existing commitments but also spark the imagination and pursuit of new ones."[5]

The struggle over the remuneration and distribution of paid and unpaid labor not only takes place in the household and at the workplace, but also in the sphere of the welfare state. Welfare states affect the relationship between paid and unpaid work in two specific ways: first, welfare states provide care and supervision for children and other dependent family members and thereby give women the possibility to take up a job outside the home. Second, welfare states transform unpaid work into paid employment, and in this way they provide job opportunities for women in sectors such as healthcare, education, and social services.

It is not by accident that the most developed welfare states tend to have particularly high female employment rates. Institutionalists are right when they argue that different institutional settings promote different work time patterns, especially when it comes to women's work hours and the distribution of work time over the life course. In less developed conservative and liberal welfare states, women often reduce work hours to combine a paid job with unpaid domestic labor. In southern Europe women even withdraw from the labor market after marriage or giving birth to a child. But welfare states also depend on solidarity between the various members of society, and it is difficult to maintain a high level of welfare benefits when the rich are no longer willing to pay taxes. As a result welfare benefits have been cut in many countries – including Sweden – while welfare recipients have been forced to take up any available employment opportunity, even if the job in question provides little security and does not pay enough to sustain a reasonable standard of living. The promotion of "mini jobs" in Germany is a good example of the link between workfarist welfare state restructuring and the flexibilization and casualization of labor markets. Other welfare state and labor market reforms show similar tendencies, consolidating existing work time differences not only with respect to gender but also to class and social status.

The simultaneous compression, extension, and variation of work time

For Marxists the struggle over work time is closely linked to the struggle over surplus labor time. The general assumption is that workers have to work longer than they would need to acquire the means for their own subsistence in order to generate a surplus that can be obtained by capital and turned into profit. Without surplus labor time capitalism would cease to exist. There are two ways to increase surplus labor: the prolongation of the work day and the intensification of work. Marx has described the two tendencies as the simultaneous extension and compression of work time, and marked it as one of the major contradictions of capitalist social systems. With the establishment and subsequent reduction of maximum work time limits, capital had to focus on the intensification of work as a source of surplus labor time. To do so, capital had to seize control over workers and the work day. The shift from the putting out to the factory system not only allowed for a greater division of labor and growing productivity, it also enabled capital to impose a strict separation between work time and free time to make sure that workers showed up for work when they were supposed to.

Taylor greatly improved control by separating the planning from the execution of work. He and his disciples used time and motion studies to redesign labor processes and speed up work. Ford adopted Taylorist principles of work organization and combined them with a far-reaching mechanization of work. Yet Ford's moving assembly line not only saved time by converting "dead time" into "productive time"; it also gave him and fellow capitalists a highly effective tool to speed up work. As a result of continuous intensification and mechanization the proportion of work time inherent in mass produced commodities fell to a fraction of what was needed before the invention of mass production.

However, for capital the substitution of machines for living labor has a major downside: machines do not produce surplus value. One way of maintaining surplus labor time in the face of rising productivity is to increase output. This is exactly what happened in the postwar period: the time saved on making individual goods was more than compensated for by a multiplication of the number of commodities that could be produced with the new mass production techniques. Given the massive expansion of output, surplus maximization primarily followed the maximization of output per unit of work time. And because of the focus on maximizing output per unit of time, manufacturers used fragmentation, standardization, and (rigid) automation to increase productivity. While this approach granted unprecedented productivity gains in the postwar decades – some manufacturers even dreamed of the "workerless factory" – there was a point where the surplus could no longer be increased by simply producing larger quantities of the same product.

Mass producers had already introduced yearly model changes to maintain high sales numbers, despite the fact that a growing number of households were already in possession of a car or other such products of mass consumption. When these minor changes no longer did the trick, mass producers had to invent new techniques to find consumers for their products. The invention of flexible technology made it possible to use the same machines for the production of a variety of models or even products. However, in the existing production paradigm smaller output numbers meant an increase of work time per unit of output. The challenge was to vary output while at the same time limiting work time expended per good or service. In the 1980s mass producers introduced new technology and started to reintegrate tasks and install teams of workers, even on the assembly line. However, the changes were not introduced to improve the working conditions of an increasingly dissatisfied and frustrated workforce that had demonstrated its disapproval through an upsurge in labor action in the 1960s and 1970s. No, the changes were introduced to limit work time per unit of output. Task enrichment and team working allowed capital to burden the same amount of work on a smaller number of workers, with the result that the same or more output could be produced with a significantly "downsized" workforce. In a nutshell this is the success of lean production. Far from improving working conditions, the changes amounted to a further intensification of work. Workers feel the changes primarily as growing lack of time. Instead of struggling with ever-shorter work cycles, they cope with an increasing number of tasks to be completed in the same or shorter amounts of time.

The changes not only resulted in a veritable intensification of work. Lean and just-in-time production also demanded changes in the length and distribution of work hours. While the maximization of output per unit of time facilitated a gradual standardization of work hours, the limitation of time according to unit of output demanded a far-reaching flexibilization of work time. Thus, flexible work hours were not only and perhaps not even primarily the result of increasingly volatile markets; they were also the result of systematic constraints in increasingly lean production systems. European producers responded to the need for more flexibility by introducing new work time systems; North American manufacturers, in contrast, reverted to overtime to cope with temporary labor shortages caused by downsized workforces. While in the European case work hours became more flexible, US workers not only suffered from growing flexibility but also from longer work hours.

Long hours in production stand in contrast with short hours in services. Precisely because of the success of Fordism in reducing production time per unit of industrial output, services have become more important as a source of surplus labor. Yet services differ from production insofar as the potential to increase output per unit of work time has always been limited. Human interactions can be standardized, especially with the help of new information and communication technologies, and they can be externalized in form of self-servicing; but they cannot be routinized and intensified to the same extent as assembly line work. The front line is still different from the assembly line. Service providers, therefore, always had a greater focus on reducing work time per unit of output and they did so primarily by adjusting work time as closely as possible to varying demand. Yet while manufacturers resort to overtime and averaging periods to adjust work hours to changing production volumes, service providers largely rely on part-time work to adjust work hours to fluctuations during the day and week. As an additional benefit, part-time jobs pay lower wages and are sometimes exempted from social security contributions. It is no wonder that most of them are held by women.

In knowledge-intensive services the situation is different: here employers lack direct control over work, since it is difficult to intensify knowledge-intensive work especially when the workers are expected to be innovative. Rather than increasing output per unit of time or limiting input per unit of output, knowledge workers are therefore encouraged to put in unpaid overtime. Skilled workers have an intrinsic motivation to use their skills and knowledge and they are often curious to master new challenges. As a result, highly skilled workers, at least for some amount of time, accept unpaid overtime in exchange for the privilege of getting intrinsic satisfaction from their jobs and for the freedom to make decisions without prior consent from their superiors. The introduction of new forms of work organization, such as project work, promoted greater autonomy and was therefore welcomed even though it meant greater workloads and more stress. However, the willingness to disregard work time regulations should not be confused with an alleged aversion to collective organizations and a desire for individuality. It is not the individualism of knowledge workers that transforms the freedom to choose one's own work hours into the freedom to choose long hours. It is capital's desire for surplus labor. Anyway, long work days make it difficult for women with family responsibilities to pursue a career in knowledge-intensive occupations, fortifying gender inequalities in the so-called knowledge economy.

In sum, the expansion of surplus labor time does not always lead to an extension of the work day. Because of the tension between absolute and relative surplus value, and between expanding output per unit of work time and reducing work time per unit of output, the expansion of surplus labor promotes a simultaneous compression, extension, and variation of work time. In addition the combination of marketization and flexibilization meant that work hours became increasingly polarized, with some workers – usually men – putting in particularly long hours, while others – usually women – put in particularly short hours. However, while some workers put in long and others short hours, work with very few exceptions has become more intense. This is an experience shared by men and women, by production and service sector workers, and by workers in North America and Europe and other parts of the world.

Long work hours and growing work intensity are increasingly threatening the health of workers. As Robert LaJeuness notes, a "growing body of empirical research is suggesting that excessive work hours adversely impact the health, well-being and longevity of workers."[6] Among the diseases frequently linked to long work hours and over-work are hypertension, cardiovascular disorders, mental health problems, and reproductive disorders. However, among the costs of work-related health conditions are not only individual pain but also family distress and ultimately burgeoning healthcare expenses.[7]

Technological change and the increase in productivity had a much more limited impact on the duration of domestic work. Although there is a vivid debate about the concrete impact of washing machines, microwaves, and dishwashers on the time spent on domestic labor – some argue that certain household appliances such as electrical dryers have even *increased* the time women spend on household tasks – there is little doubt that the time saved in household production is marginal compared to the time new technology has saved in the production of commercial goods and services. This is not surprising: domestic production creates use value but no exchange value, and use values cannot be measured – they have no price. Without a cost factor attached to it, there is little pressure to compress domestic work. Furthermore, even if technology has helped to save time in the household, the additional time has hardly been used as more free time; instead most parents spend the additional time caring for their children (it is hard to imagine how time spent with children can be compressed without eroding the essential function of childcare). As the bulk of domestic work, including childcare, is still carried out by women, this means that their work days do not end when they go home.

Markets, in several regards, played a decisive role in the shift from Fordism to post-Fordism and neoliberal capitalism. Far from just responding to market needs, producers actively deployed markets to squeeze more surplus labor out of their workforces. The breaking up of integrated production complexes and the creation of independent departments gave managers the possibility to force individual units to meet certain targets. Outsourcing and globalization, at the same time enabled them to compare different production sites and make workers of the same company compete for internal contracts. The pressure from internal and external marketization caused local workforces to accept longer and more flexible work hours – along with lower wages – in an attempt to defend their jobs. In a similar way, just-in-time production not only allowed lean manufacturers to save costs in their inventories; the prolongation of the market into the heart of the production process also greatly increased pressure on workers to meet short notice production targets. Workers can actually feel the market pressure when they have to work harder and stay longer to deliver in time. The Japanese founders of lean production borrowed the idea of just-in-time delivery from large American supermarkets. Early on, supermarkets installed a supply system that connected orders to actual sales. Today's supermarkets go even further: they not only order products when they are needed, they also require workers to come in and work for a few hours according to changing customer fluctuations. With the deployment of flexible part-timers – who work for few and frequently changing hours per day or week – modern supermarkets reach a degree of flexibility which the inventors of the flexible firm could only have dreamed of.

Employer versus worker flexibility

Variation in work time per se is not a bad thing. Workers live under very different circumstances and have different interests, which, in addition, may change over time. Gösta Rehn has rightly argued that the goal must be a society of free choice. The critical question, however, is choice for whom; or put differently, who decides about who works when. Initially it was capital that imposed a rather rigid industrial order of time against what can be described as pre-industrial flexibility of work hours. As the new order properly defined the border between work and non-work time and, as far as possible, eliminated disruptions and irregularities such as religious festivities, it was also a form of homogenization and standardization. Standardization was necessary to keep increasingly complex production processes running. However, at the same time the industrial time regime also fostered capital's power over the time of workers. Not long afterwards, capital took this power to order ever-longer work days, partly to rapidly amortize the costs for new machinery. Marx has called the ten-hour day introduced in mid-nineteenth century England a normal work day because it put an official end to an otherwise limitless source of surplus labor. However, the normal work day not only puts a limit on the amount of (absolute) surplus value. Because standardisation implies that work hours are decided outside the factory it is, as Karl Polyani pointed out, also a form of decommodification.[8] The fight for shorter work hours was, early on, linked to a struggle over standardization and decommodification. In the confrontations after the First World War and in the 1930s, trade unions not only demanded the introduction of an eight-hour day and a 40-hour week, but also for what critics have called a schematic or overly rigid work schedule. The revolutionary government in France issued a series of industry codes fixing detailed timetables for each industry. The NRA codes adopted for various industries in the United States during the New Deal also imposed rather rigid work time limits. And while these codes allowed for a variety of exemptions, the fact that the work day had a legal limit went beyond the compromise that was finally adopted in 1938. For capital the inflexibility of time was a greater threat than the reduction of work hours because it challenged capital's authority in the factory.

The compromise that evolved in the 1930s and after the Second World War was that work time should indeed be standardized, but that capital retained the flexibility to schedule time outside the normal limits as long as it was prepared to pay overtime premiums. Yet standardization not only imposed an upper limit for the work day and week; the concept of standard work hours (and the standard employment relationship more generally) meant that workers would normally also work no less than 40 hours a week. For women who entered the labor markets in the 1960s and 1970s, and who could not work 40 hours because of family responsibilities, this meant that they were confined to the sphere of non-standard employment. While initially a response to women's needs, employers quickly realized the potential of part-time and other forms of atypical work to pay lower wages and save social security costs. The right to order overtime, frequently used by employers at the height of the postwar boom, made it even more difficult for women to take on a full-time job. Yet while in the US the use of overtime accelerated in the 1980s and 1990s, some European countries adopted a new work time compromise. Weekly work time decreased to 35 hours, while employers could order overtime without having to pay overtime premiums as long as work time averaged out over a certain averaging period. In addition, workers could save work time on overtime accounts to take time off (without overtime supplements) when there was less work to do.

However, while flexibilization promises greater choice for workers, what really takes place is a subjugation of individual time to market constraints. According to a German survey 90 percent of variations in weekly work hours is the result of workplace constraints, while 5 percent is caused by family emergencies and another 5 percent by non-emergency related private interests.[9] Even those workers who think they can determine their own work time quickly discover the limits of their own discretion when their interests collide with those of the employers (often employees have internalized the interests of the company to the extent that they perceive them as external constraints rather than employer interests).

In short, in its current form flexibilization amounts to nothing less than a recommodification of labor power and as such must be seen as part of an advanced system of exploitation. As Sam Gindin notes, "management pressures for worker flexibility – essentially the deeper commodification of labor power – must be countered with an alternative notion of 'worker flexibility' that speaks to accommodating work and work schedules to the rhythms of active lives beyond work."[10] In a similar way André Gorz suggests that "all forms of passively suffered ... flexibility of work hours and staffing levels ... should be transformed into opportunities to choose and self-manage discontinuity and flexibility."[11] The problem is that all such attempts have failed in the wake of accelerating competition. It is not by accident that countries with strong product market regulations also tend to have shorter work hours.[12] Hence the limitation or abolition of competition is a precondition for worker-based flexibility. In the current situation this demands, above all, for an abolition of neoliberalism. In the long term it also demands for greater worker participation in the management of production and a return to workers' control over labor processes. As long as management decides what is produced, when, and under what conditions, workers will have little choice other than to insist on collective work time regulations and to demand for collective work time reductions.

Consumption versus free time

Workers have two possibilities to limit surplus labor – they can either reduce work hours or increase wages. Marx assumed that there was not much room in capitalism for rising wages. Workers would get merely enough to reproduce themselves and their dependents. Max Weber argued that workers, accustomed to a certain standard of living, would respond to a pay rise by working fewer hours. Neoclassical economists also assumed that work hours tend to fall with rising living standards, but insisted that in principle the decision between more consumption and more free time was open. History shows that work hours have not fallen at the same rate as living standards have risen. Workers repeatedly traded shorter hours for more income. They bought houses, cars, TV sets, and household appliances with the premiums they received from overtime working. Walter Reuther, president of the United Auto Workers, argued in 1949 that "our fight isn't between having too many material goods and not having enough leisure. Our fight is we still don't have enough material goods." And he further noted that "when we get to the point we have got everything we need, we can talk about the shorter work week, but we are a long way from that place."[13] While Reuther envisioned a future time when workers would have enough commodities to start cutting back work hours, from the 1970s onwards growing pressure on wages made sure that working families in America put in more rather than fewer hours so as to maintain their living standards. In neoliberal capitalism workers are not trading shorter hours for higher incomes; they work longer to counterbalance the decline in real wages. In Europe this development was less dramatic, but here too, very moderate (real) wage growth and the expansion of low-wage sectors made it increasingly difficult for working class families to maintain their living standards. In this situation it became even more difficult to convince workers to reduce work hours – this was one reason why it was so difficult to persuade workers to fight for shorter hours in the Great Recession. As a result, average weekly free time per person aged 14 years and older in the United States was only 3.7 hours longer in 2005 than in 1900 – and it was five hours shorter in 2000 than in 1980.[14]

In the 1970s two consecutive oil price shocks temporarily disrupted the Western mode of living and its reliance on resource-intensive mass production and consumption. Ecologists warned that one day in the not too distant future the limit of natural resources, including fossil fuel, would endanger the existing growth model. In Britain the combination of an industrial conflict in the coal industry and rising oil price caused the conservative government to introduce a three-day work week in early 1974 in order to save energy.[15] Since the 1970s ecological problems have further accelerated. Meanwhile, it is no longer only the problem of peak oil, i.e., the high point after which world oil reserves start to decline; growing carbon dioxide emissions are boosting average world temperatures and unleashing a process of climate change with potentially dramatic consequences for ecosystems and for human development.[16] Weather disasters, droughts, and increasing sea levels are threatening existing infrastructures, settlements, and agrarian output. Scientists have shown that Western societies, with their consumption patterns, live beyond their ecological means.[17] The United States is one of the countries with the largest carbon footprint, but Canada and the European countries are also using more resources than their territories can reproduce. As Serge Latouche notes, "if everyone had the same life style as the French we would need three planets; if we all followed the example of ... America we would need six."[18]

Following Gorz's lead, a number of authors have emphasized the link between shorter work hours and environmental sustainability. Comparing the US and 15 EU member states, David Rosnick and Mark Weisbrot argue that if Europeans worked as many hours in 2003 as workers in the United States, the EU-15 would have consumed 18 percent more energy.[19] According to their calculations every 1 percent increase in work time per worker results in a 0.32 percent increase in energy consumed per work hour.[20] Latouche goes further and argues that the only way to avoid an ecological disaster is a fundamental break with the existing growth paradigm.[21]

However, for a break with the existing growth and accumulation paradigm it is not enough to reduce work hours and promote sustainable consumption; a radical transformation of current society must also include a radical redistribution of wealth. The Wuppertal Institute for Climate Change has revealed that people with high levels of education, income, and environmental awareness use significantly more natural resources than low income earners who care little about the environment.[22] Hence it is as hypocritical of the well-off to demand the less well-off restrain their consumption, as it is for the Global North to ask the Global South to abstain from a Western mode of living.[23]

The question of necessary social work time

Ecologist, feminist, and neo-Marxist critiques of the current length and distribution of work hours share the insight that what is at stake is a redefinition of necessary work time. Marx understood as necessary work time the time proletarians have to work for a wage that allows them to acquire the means of their existence, or to live at a certain standard of living (actual work time is necessary work time plus surplus labor time). Thanks to feminist interventions we know that paid work is only one part of the work day; the other part consists of unpaid domestic work mainly carried out by women in the household. Living standards, as generally understood, reflect the level of consumption attained by the working classes in a specific country or point in time. While Marx has assumed that in capitalism there is not much room for the improvement of working class living standards, the postwar decades have shown that living standards can increase quite substantially along with economic growth (the past decades, however, have also shown that the benefits of growth can be distributed quite unequally). In any case, insofar as goods and services are based on resource extraction, including most notably the extraction of fossil fuel, growing consumption has proved harmful for the environment. In past decades, Western consumption patterns have clearly become unsustainable. At the same time workers suffer from increasingly long and flexible work hours, and from growing work intensification. With accelerating inequality low income families are forced to put in long work hours while still struggling to make ends meet. In this situation it is high time to take a break and start discussing what living standards we want and how much time, including paid and unpaid time, we collectively want to spend working for it. In other words, it is necessary to discuss the length and distribution of necessary social labor time. European work time surveys show that workers would like to work between 30 and 35 hours per week.[24] If desired, work hours can vary during different phases of life and they can be accumulated in life time work accounts. Some workers could also work more years than others because their jobs are less strenuous and/or more socially rewarding. The important step forward is that the length and distribution of work time, including domestic and non-domestic work time, should be decided collectively and democratically rather than leaving the decision to the market and related forces.

Arguments for a 30-hour week

- *More equal distribution of work, especially between men and women*: Neoliberalism has led to an increasing polarization of work time with a growing proportion of the workforce working particularly long and particularly short hours. The polarization has further aggravated gender inequality since it is mainly men that work full-time and women that work part-time hours.

- *Reduction of unemployment*: Although the employment effect of shorter work hours is partly cancelled out by improvements in productivity, a number of studies show that shorter work hours have a positive effect on employment. In contrast, evidence that long hours increase employment is extremely weak. Recent experience has also shown that short time working helps to maintain jobs in the face of an economic downturn.
- *Relief for those who have to combine paid and unpaid work:* Many women perform work in their paid job but also unpaid work in family households. Even though shorter work hours do not guarantee a more equitable distribution of domestic work between men and women, at least they shorten the total work day of women in paid employment. Furthermore, experience shows that men tend do more in the household when they work less in their paid jobs.
- *Improvement of health:* Many workers suffer from long work hours and high stress levels. Shorter work hours make sure that workers have enough time to recover from work-related strains and that they are still able to do their job when they are old and less able to work under pressure. Of course free time should be spent it a way that does not endanger the health of those who are enjoying time off work.
- *Ecological sustainability*: More free time instead of more consumption means less pollution and environmental degradation. Shorter work hours are therefore also a contribution to ecological sustainability. More free time also means that people can spend time on local initiatives or practices that have a positive impact on the environment.
- *Democratic participation, culture, and the search for alternatives:* Shorter work hours give people more time for participation in initiatives or decision-making processes that go beyond casting a vote every four or five years. It also gives individuals who are not professional artists the possibility to make art, promote culture, and engage with people with similar ideas and interests. Most importantly, more free time enables citizens to engage in a range of communal activities and to commonly develop ideas and strategies about how to tackle current economic and social challenges and how to create alternatives to the status quo.
- *Solidarity and equity:* Shorter work hours promote solidarity by sharing employment and by creating time to develop collective cultures and identities. By distributing work more evenly, shorter work hours also reduce income inequality.

Notes

1 US figures based on Maddison's time series between 1870 and 1998; for the period between 1998 and 2008 2 percent increases in productivity and living standards are assumed.
2 Messenger and Ghoseh (2013).
3 Hermann (2014a: 115).
4 Hermann (2014b).

5 Weeks (2010: 170).
6 LaJeunesse (2009: 169–170).
7 Ibid.
8 Polanyi (1957: 157).
9 Bauer *et al.* (2004: 136).
10 Gindin (2013: 45).
11 Gorz (1999: 96).
12 Causa (2009).
13 Edsforth (1995: 170).
14 Ramey and Francis (2009: 209, Table 6).
15 The three-day week lasted from December 31, 1973, to March 8, 1974.
16 Altvater (2006). Mahnkopf (2013).
17 Rees (2000: 371–4).
18 Latouche (2009: 21).
19 Rosnick and Weisbrot (2006: 5).
20 Ibid.
21 Ibid.: 40–1. See also: Jackson (2009: 180–1).
22 Wuppertal Institute for Climate Change (2008: 144–5).
23 Brandt and Wissen (2013: 690).
24 Bielenski *et al.* (2002: 67, Table 15).

Bibliography

Abel, Jörg. "Shifting Patterns of Labor Regulation: Highly Qualified Knowledge Workers in German New Media Companies." *Critical Sociology* 33, nos. 1–2, 2007: 101–25.

Abendroth, Wolfgang. *Sozialgeschichte der Europäischen Arbeiterbewegung.* Frankfurt am Main: Suhrkamp Verlag, 1965.

Adam, Barbara. *Time and Social Theory.* Oxford: Polity Press, 1990.

Adam, Barbara. "When Time Is Money: Contested Rationalities of Time and Challenges to the Theory and Praxis of Work." Cardiff University, School of Social Science Working Paper 16, 2001.

Advisory Group on Working Time and the Distribution of Work. "Report of the Advisory Group on Working Time and the Distribution of Work." Ottawa, 1994.

Aglietta, Michel. *A Theory of Capitalist Regulation: The US Experience.* London: NLB Books, 1979.

Albo, Gregory. "Contesting the 'New Capitalism.'" In *Varieties of Capitalism, Varieties of Approaches*, ed. David Coates. Basingstoke: Palgrave Macmillan, 2005: 63–82.

Albo, Gregory. "Neoliberalism and the Discontented." In *Socialist Register 2008*, eds. Leo Panitch and Colin Leys. London: Merlin Press, 2007: 346–53.

Albo, Gregory, and Travis Fast. "Varieties of Neoliberalism: Trajectories of Workfare in Advanced Capitalist Countries." Paper presented at the Annual Meetings of the Canadian Political Science Association Congress of the Humanities and Social Sciences, Dalhousie University, Halifax, Nova Scotia, May 2003.

Albritton, Robert. *Economics Transformed: Discovering the Brilliance of Marx.* London: Pluto Press, 2007.

Alesina, Alberto, Edward Glaeser, and Bruce Sacerdote. "Work and Leisure in the U.S. And Europe: Why So Different?" NBER Working Paper 11278, 2005.

Altman, Norbert. "Japanese Work Policy: Opportunity, Challenge or Threat?" In *Enriching Production: Perspectives on Volvo's Uddevalla Plant as an Alternative to Lean Production*, ed. Åke Sandberg. Aldershot, Brookfield, VT: Avebury, 1995: 329–68.

Altvater, Elmar. *Das Ende des Kapitalismus wie wir ihn kennen. Eine radikale Kapitalismuskritik.* Münster: Westfälisches Dampfboot, 2006.

Altvater, Elmar. "The Roots of Neoliberalism." In *Socialist Register 2008*, eds. Leo Panitch and Colin Leys. London: Merlin Press, 2007: 346–53.

Altvater, Elmar. "Mit Green New Deal aus dem Wachstumsdilemma?" *Widerspruch*, no. 60 (2011): 119–32.

Altvater, Elmar, and Birgit Mahnkopf. *Grenzen der Globalisierung: Ökonomie, Ökologie und Politik in der Weltgesellschaft.* Münster: Westfälisches Dampfboot, 1996.

Andrew, Ed. *Closing the Iron Cage: The Scientific Management of Work and Leisure.* Montreal: Black Rose Books, 1999.

Andrews, Christoph, Craig Lair, and Bart Landry. "The Labor Process in Software Start-ups: Production on a Virtual Assembly Line?" In *Management, Labor Process and Software Development: Reality Bytes*, ed. Rowena Barrett. London, New York: Routledge, 2005: 45–75.

Anxo, Dominique. "Politique et évolution du temps de travail en Suéde." In *Le temps de travail en Europe: Organisation et réduction*, eds. Reiner Hoffmann and Jean Lapeyre. Paris: Syros, 1995: 126–42.

Anxo, Dominique. "Working Time Policy in Sweden." In *Working Time – in Search for New Research Territory Beyond Flexibility Debates*. Tokyo: The Japan Institute for Labor Policy and Training, 2009: 55–70.

Anxo, Dominique. "Towards an Active and Integrated Life Course Policy: The Swedish Experience." In *The Welfare State and Life Transitions: A European Perspective*, eds. Dominque Anxo, Gerhard Bosch and Jill Rubery. Cheltenham: Edward Elgar, 2011: 104–27.

Anxo, Dominique, and Jacqueline O'Reilly. "Working-Time Regimes and Transitions in Comparative Perspective." In *Working-Time Changes: Social Integration through Transitional Labour Markets*, eds. Jacqueline O'Reilly, Inmaculada Cebrián, and Michel Lallement. Cheltenham: Edward Elgar, 2000: 61–90.

Anxo, Dominque, Gerhard Bosch, and Jill Rubery, eds., *The Welfare State and Life Transitions: A European Perspective*. Cheltenham: Edward Elgar, 2011.

Anxo, Dominique, Jean-Yves Boulin, and Colette Fagan. "Decent Working Time in a Life-Course Perspective." In *Decent Working Time: New Trends, New Issues*, eds. Jean-Yves Boulin, Michel Lallement, Jon C. Messenger, and François Michon. Geneva: International Labour Organisation, 2006: 93–120.

Armstrong, Philip, Andrew Glyn, and John Harrison. *Capitalism since World War II: The Making and Breakup of the Great Boom*. London: Fontana, 1984.

Aronowitz, Stanley, and Jonathan Cutler. *Post-Work: The Wages of Cybernation*. London, New York: Routledge, 1998.

Aronowitz, Stanley, and William DiFazio. *The Jobless Future: Sci-Tech and the Dogma of Work*. Minneapolis: University of Minnesota Press, 1994.

Askenazy, Philippe. "A Primer on the 35-Hour in France, 1997–2007." IZA Discussion Paper No. 3402. Bonn: Institute for the Study of Labor, 2007.

Askenazy, Philippe. "Working Time Regulation in France from 1996 to 2012." *Cambridge Journal of Economics*, no. 37, 2013: 323–47.

Askenazy, Philippe, Catherine Bloch-London, and Muriel Roger. "La réduction du temps de travail 1997–2003: Dynamique de construction des lois 'Aubry' et Premières Évaluations." *Économie et Statistique*, no. 376–7, 2004: 153–71.

Atkinson, John. "Emerging UK Work Patterns." Institute for Manpower Studies Report No. 88/1984. Brighton, 1984.

Atkinson, John, and Nigel Meager. "Changing Working Patterns: How Companies Achieve Flexibility to Meet New Needs." Institute of Manpower Studies, National Economic Development Office, London, 1986.

Avrich, Paul. *The Haymarket Tragedy*. Princeton: Princeton University Press, 1984.

Bahnmüller, Reinhard. *Der Streik. Tarifkonflikt um Arbeitszeitverkürzung in der Metallindustrie*. Hamburg: VSA Verlag, 1985.

Bakker, Isabella. "Neoliberal Governance and the Reprivatization of Social Reproduction: Social Provisioning and Shifting Gender Orders." In *Power, Production, and Social Reproduction: Human In/Security in the Global Political Economy*, eds. Isabella Bakker and Stephen Gill. Basingstoke: Palgrave Macmillan, 2003: 66–80.

Baret, Christophe, Jean Gadrey, and Camal Gallouj. "France, Germany, Great Britain: The Organization of Working Time in Large Retail Food Stores." In *European Journal of Industrial Relations*, issue 5, no. 1, 1999: 27–48.

Barnard, Catherine, Simon Deakin, and Richard Hobbs. "Opting out of the 48-Hour Week: Employer Necessity or Individual Choice? An Empirical Study of the Operation of Article 18(1)(B) of the Working Time Directive in the UK." In *Industrial Law Journal*, issue 32, no. 4, 2003: 223–52.

Bartsch, Klaus. "Durch Arbeitszeitverlängerung aus der Beschäftigungskrise?" In *WSI-Mitteilungen*, no. 2, 2005: 90–6.

Basso, Pietro. *Modern Times, Ancient Hours: Working Lives in the Twenty-First Century*. London, New York: Verso, 2003.

Batchelor, Ray. *Henry Ford, Mass Production, Modernism, and Design*. Manchester: Manchester University Press, 1994.

Bauer, Frank, Hermann Groß, Eva Munz, and Suna Sayin. "Arbeits- und Betriebszeiten 2001. Neue Formen des betrieblichen Arbeits- und Betriebszeitmanagements. Ergebnisse einer repräsentativen Betriebsbefragung." Institut zur Erforschung Sozialer Chancen (ISO): Cologne, 2002.

Bauer, Frank, Hermann Groß, Klaudia Lehmann, and Eva Munz. "Arbeitszeit 2003. Arbeitszeitgestaltung, Arbeitsorganisation und Tätigkeitsprofile." Institut zur Erforschung sozialer Chancen (ISO): Cologne, 2004.

Baumol, William J., and Wallace E. Oates. "The Cost Disease of the Personal Services and the Quality of Life." In *Baumol's Cost Disease: The Arts and Other Victims*, ed. Ruth Towse. Cheltenham: Edward Elgar, 1997.

Baxter, Janeen. "Gender Equality and Participation in Housework: A Cross-National Perspective." In *Journal of Comparative Family Studies*, issue 28, no. 3, 1997: 220–47.

Becker, Gary Stanley. *A Treatise on the Family*. Cambridge, MA: Harvard University Press, 1991.

Beechey, Veronica. *Unequal Work*. London, New York: Verso, 1987.

Beechey, Veronica, and Tessa Perkins. *A Matter of Hours: Women, Part-Time Work and the Labour Market*. Cambridge: Polity Press, 1987.

Beese, Birgit. "New Collective Agreement for [the] Public Sector." European Industrial Relations Observatory Online, 2006, www.eurofound.europa.eu/eiro/2006/06/articles/de0606029i.htm [accessed Jannuary 10, 2012].

Bell, Daniel. *The Coming of Post-Industrial Society*. New York: Basic Books, 1973.

Bell, Linda, and Richard B. Freeman. "Why Do Americans and Germans Work Different Hours?" NBER Working Paper No. 4808, 1994.

Bell, Linda, and Richard B. Freeman. "The Incentive for Working Hard: Explaining Hours Worked Differences in the US and Germany." NBER Working Paper No. 8051, 2000.

Bellofiore, Riccardo. "After Fordism, What? Capitalism at the End of the Century: Beyond the Myths." In *Global Money, Capital Restructuring, and the Changing Patterns of Labour*, ed. Riccardo Bellofiore. Cheltenham: Edward Elgar, 1999: 10–32.

Bendix, Reinhard. *Work and Authority in Industry; Ideologies of Management in the Course of Industrialization*. New York: Harper & Row, 1963.

Berggren, Christian. *Alternatives to Lean Production: Work Organization in the Swedish Auto Industry*. Ithaca: ILR Press, 1992.

Bergmann Nadja, Marcel Fink, Nikolaus Graf, Christoph Hermann, Ingrid Mairhuber, Claudia Sorger, and Barbara Willsberger. "Qualifizierte Teilzeitbeschäftigung in Österreich. Bestandsaufnahme und Potentiale." Research Report. Vienna: Federal Ministry for Women and Equal Opportunities, 2004.

Berrebi-Hoffmann, Isabelle, Damian Grimshaw, Michel Lallement, and Marcela Miozzo. "Employment Challenges to the Knowledge Economy in Europe: The Case of IT Services." In *Work Organisation, Labour and Globalisation*, issue 4, no. 1, 2010: 84–103.

Beynon, Huw. *Working for Ford*. Harmondsworth: Penguin, 1984.

Bianchi, Suzanne. "Maternal Employment and Time with Children: Dramatic Change or Surprising Continuity?" In *Demography*, issue 37, no. 4, 2000: 401–14.

Bielenski, Harald, Gerhard Bosch, and Alexandra Wagner, *Wie die Europäer arbeiten wollen. Erwerbs- und Arbeitszeitwünsche in 16 Ländern*. Frankfurt am Main: Campus Verlag, 2002.

Bienefeld, M. A. *Working Hours in British Industry: An Economic History*. London: London School of Economics and Political Science, 1972.

Bispinck, Reinhard. "Germany: Working Time and Its Negotiation." In *Collective Bargaining on Working Time: Recent European Experiences*, eds. Maarten Keune and Bela Galgoczi. Brussels: European Trade Union Institute, 2006: 111–29.

Bispinck, Reinhard, and Thorsten Schulten. "Zur Kritik der wettbewerbsorientierten Tarifpolitik". In *Interventionen wider den Zeitgeist. Für eine emanzipatorische Gewerkschaftspolitik im 21. Jahrhundert*, ed. Hilde Wagner. Hamburg: VSA, 2001: 209–25.

Bispinck, Reinhard, and Thorsten Schulten. "Deutschland vor dem tarifpolitischen Systemwechsel?" In *WSI-Mitteilungen*, no. 8, 2005: 466–72.

Bispinck, Reinhard, and Thorsten Schulten. "Re-Stabilisierung des deutschen Flächentarifvertragssystems." In *WSI-Mitteilungen*, no. 4, 2009: 201–9.

Bittman, Michael. "Parenting and Employment: What Time-Use Surveys Show." In *Family Time. The Social Organization of Care*, eds. Nancy Folbre and Michael Bittman. New York: Routledge, 2004: 152–70.

Bittman, Michael, James Mahmud Rice, and Judy Wajcman. "Appliances and their Impact: The Ownership of Domestic Technology and Time Spent on Household Work." In *The British Journal of Sociology*, issue 55, no. 3, 2004: 401–23.

Blanchflower, David, and Alex Bryson. "Trade Union Decline and the Economics of the Workplace." In *The Evolution of the Modern Workplace*, eds. William Arthur Brown, Alex Bryson, Jon Forth, and Keith Whitfield. Cambridge: Cambridge University Press, 2009: 48–73.

Blaug, Mark. *Economic Theory in Retrospect*. Homewood: R. D. Irwin, 1968.

Bloch-London, Catherine. "Les normes du temps de travail à l'épreuve de la négociation: Le cas des lois Aubry de réduction du temps de travail." In *Travail et Emploi*, no. 83, 2000: 27–45.

Block, Fred L. *Postindustrial Possibilities: A Critique of Economic Discourse*. Berkeley: University of California Press, 1990.

Böhm-Bawerk, Eugen von. *The Positive Theory of Capital*. New York: G. E. Stechert, 1923.

Boltanski, Luc, and Eve Chiapello. *The New Spirit of Capitalism*. London, New York: Verso, 2005.

Bosch, Gerhard. "The Dispute over the Reduction of the Working Week in West Germany." In *Cambridge Journal of Economics*, issue 10, no. 3, 1986: 271–90.

Bosch, Gerhard. "From 40 to 35 Hours: Reduction and Flexibilisation of the Working Week in the Federal Republic of Germany." *International Labor Review*, issue 129, no. 5, 1990: 611–27.

Bosch, Gerhard. "Working Time and the Standard Employment Relationship." In *Decent Working Time: New Trends, New Issues*, eds. Jean-Yves Boulin, Michel Lallement, Jon C. Messenger, and François Michon. Geneva: International Labour Office, 2006: 41–57.

Bosch, Gerhard, and Steffen Lehndorff. "Working-Time Reduction and Employment: Experiences in Europe and Economic Policy Recommendations." In *Cambridge Journal of Economics*, issue 25, no. 2, 2001: 209–43.

Bosch, Gerhard, and Alexandra Wagner. "Why Do Countries Have Such Different Service Sector Employment Rates?" In *Working in the Service Sector: A Tale from Different World*, eds. Steffen Lehndorff and Gerhard Bosch. London, New York: Routledge, 2005: 74–102.

Bosch, Gerhard, Peter Dawkins, and François Michon. "Overview". In *Times Are Changing: Working Time in 14 Industrialised Countries*, eds. Gerhard Bosch, Peter Dawkins and François Michon. Geneva: International Institute for Labour Studies, 1994: 1–45.

Botwinick, Howard. *Persistent Inequalities: Wage Disparity under Capitalist Competition*. Princeton: Princeton University Press, 1993: 170–200.

Boulin, Jean-Yves, Michel Lallement, and Silvera Rachel. "Working Times in France: Institutional Methods of Regulating and New Practices." In *Labour Markets and Employment Policy*, ed. Jacqueline O'Reilly. Cheltenham: Edward Elgar, 2003.

Bowles, Samuel, and Yongjin Park. "Emulation, Inequality, and Work Hours: Was Thorsten Veblen Right?" In *The Economic Journal*, issue 115, no. 507, 2005: 397–412.

Bowles, Samuel, David Gordon, and Thomas Weisskopf, *After the Wasteland. A Democratic Economic for the Year 2000.* Armonk, NY: M. E. Sharp, 1990.

Boyer, Robert. *The Search for Labour Market Flexibility: The European Economies in Transition.* Oxford, New York: Oxford University Press, 1988.

Boyer, Robert. *Théorie de la régulation.* Paris: Editions la découverte, 2004.

Boyer, Robert, and Jean-Pierre Durand. *After Fordism.* Basingstoke: Palgrave Macmillan, 1997.

Brandeis, Elizabeth. "Organized Labor and Protective Legislation." In *Labor and the New Deal*, eds. Milton Derber and Edwin Young. Madison: University of Wisconsin Press, 1957: 195–237.

Brandt, Torsten. "Bilanz der Minijobs und Reformperspektiven." In *WSI-Mitteilungen*, no. 8, 2006: 446–52.

Brandt, Torsten, and Thorsten Schulten. "Liberalisierung und Privatisierung öffentlicher Dienstleistungen und die Erosion des Flächentarifvertrags." In *WSI-Mitteilungen*, no. 10, 2008: 570–6.

Brandt, Ulrich and Markus Wissen. "Crisis and Continuity of Capitalist Society-Nature Relationships: The Imperial Mode of Living and the Limits to Environmental Governance." In *Review of International Political Economy*, issue 20, no. 4, 2013: 687–711.

Braud, Maurice. "Bill Issued on Wages, Working Time and Job Creation." European Industrial Relations Observatory Online, 2002. www.eurofound.europa.eu/eiro/2002/09/feature/fr0209105f.htm [accessed Jannuary 10, 2012].

Braverman, Harry. *Labor and Monopoly Capital: The Degradation of Work in the Twentieth Century.* New York: Monthly Review Press, 1974.

Brenner, Robert. *The Economics of Global Turbulence: The Advanced Capitalist Economies from Long Boom to Long Downturn, 1945–2005.* London, New York: Verso, 2006.

Brentano, Lujo. *Über das Verhältnis von Arbeitslohn und Arbeitszeit zu Arbeitsleistung.* Leipzig: Duncker und Humboldt, 1893.

Brinkman, Ulrich, and Klaus Dörre. "Wissensarbeit im Neuen Marktregime." In *Informatisierung der Arbeit – Gesellschaft im Umbruch*, eds. Andreas Baukrowitz, Thomas Berker, Andreas Boes, Sabine Pfeiffer, Rudi Schmiede, and Mascha Will. Berlin: Edition Sigma, 2006: 132–44.

Brody, David. *Workers in Industrial America: Essays on the Twentieth Century Struggle.* Oxford, New York: Oxford University Press, 1980.

Brown, William, Alex Bryson, and John Forth. "Competition and the Retreat from Collective Bargaining." In *The Evolution of the Modern Workplace*, eds. William Arthur Brown, Alex Bryson, Jon Forth and Keith Whitfield. Cambridge, New York: Cambridge University Press, 2009: 22–47.

Bureau of Labor Statistics. "Union Members 2010." News Release, no. USDL-11–0063, 2011.

Burgoon, Brian, and Phineas Baxandall. "Three Worlds of Working Time: The Partisan and Welfare Politics of Work Hours in Industrialized Countries." In *Politics & Society*, issue 32, no. 4, 2004: 439–68.

Burkett, Paul. *Marx and Nature: A Red and Green Perspective.* New York: St Martin's Press, 1999.

Canada Deptartment of Labour. "The Labour Gazette." Ottawa, January 1956.

Castel, Robert. *Les métamorphoses de la question sociale: Une chronique du salariat.* Paris: Fayard, 1995.

Castells, Manuel. *The Rise of the Network Society.* Cambridge, MA: Blackwell, 1996.

Causa, Orsetta. "The Policy Determinants of Hours Worked across OECD Countries." In *Economic Studies (OECD Journal)*, 2009.

Cette, Gilbert, and Dominique Taddei. *Temps de travail, modes d'emplois. Vers la semaine de quatre jours?* Paris: Editions la découverte, 1994.

Chasserio, Stéphanie, and Marie-Josée Legaul. "Strategic Human Resources Management Is Irrelevant When It Comes to Highly Skilled Professionals in the Canadian New Economy." In *The International Journal of Human Resource Management*, issue 20, no. 5, 2009: 1113–31.

Chatriot, Alain. "Débats internationaux, rupture politique et négociations sociales: Le bond en avant des 40 heures 1932–1938." In *La France et le temps de travail 1814–2004*, eds. Patrick Fridenson and Bénédicte Reynaud. Paris: Odile Jacob, 2004: 83–102.

Chatriot, Alain, Patrick Fridenson, and Éric Pezet. "La réduction du temps de travail en France entre réglementation tutélaire et négociation encadrée (1814–1978)." In *Revue de l'IRES*, issue 42, no. 2, 2003: 9–40.

Chinoy, Ely. "Control and Resistance on the Assembly Line." In *Social Class and the Division of Labour: Essays in Honour of Ilya Neustadt*, eds. Anthony Giddens and Gavin Mackenzie. Cambridge: Cambridge University Press, 1982: 87–100.

Clark, Alice. *Working Life of Women in the Seventeenth Century.* London: Routledge, 1919.

Coates, David. *The Crisis of Labour: Industrial Relations and the State in Contemporary Britain.* Oxford: Philip Allan, 1989.

Coates, David. *Models of Capitalism: Growth and Stagnation in the Modern Era.* Cambridge: Polity Press, 2000.

Cologne Institute for Economic Research. "Wieder in die Hände spucken: Arbeitszeitverlängerung." In *IWD – Informationsdienst des Instituts der deutschen Wirtschaft.* 19 June 2003: 6–7.

Compston, Hugh. *The New Politics of Unemployment: Radical Policy Initiatives in Western Europe.* London, New York: Routledge, 1997.

Concialdi, Pierre Noélie Delahaie, Alexandre Fabre and Annie Jolivet. *La France du travail. Données, analyses, débats.* Paris: Editions l'Atelier, 2009.

Copeland, Morris A. "Economic Theory and the Natural Science Point of View." *The American Economic Review*, issue 21, no. 1, 1931: 67–79.

Coriat, Benjamin. *L'atelier et le chronomètre essai sur le Taylorisme, le Fordisme et la production de masse*. Paris: C. Bourgois, 1979.

Coulson, Margaret, Branka Magas, and Hilary Wainwright. " 'The Housewife and Her Labour under Capitalism' – a Critique." In *New Left Review*, no. 89 (January–February) 1975: 59–71.

Crompton, Rosemary. *Employment and the Family. The Reconfiguration of Work and Family Life in Contemporary Societies*. Cambridge: Cambridge University Press, 2006.

Cross, Gary. *A Quest for Time: The Reduction of Work in Britain and France, 1840–1940*. Berkeley: University of California Press, 1989.

Cross, Gary. *An All-Consuming Century: Why Commercialism Won in Modern America*. New York: Columbia University Press, 2000.

Crouch, Colin. *Industrial Relations and European State Traditions*. Oxford, New York: Clarendon Press, 1993.

Cutler, Jonathan. *Labor's Time: Shorter Hours, the UAW, and the Struggle for the American Unionism*. Philadelphia: Temple University Press, 2004.

Dalla Costa, Mariarosa, and Selma James. *The Power of Women and the Subversion of Community*. Bristol: Falling Wall Press, 1972.

Dankbaar, Ben. "New Production Concepts, Management Strategies and the Quality of Work." In *Work, Employment & Society*, issue 2, no. 2, 1988: 25–50.

Dassbach, Carl "Lean Production in North America: Myth and Reality." In *Global Money, Capital Restructuring, and the Changing Patterns of Labour*, ed. Riccardo Bellofiore. Cheltenham: Edward Elgar, 1999: 111–24.

Daune-Richard, Anne-Marie. "How does the 'Societal Effect' Shape the Use of Part-Time Work in France, Sweden and the UK." In *Part-Time Prospects*, eds. Jacqueline O'Reilly and Collete Fagan. New York: Routledge, 1998: 214–31.

Davis, Mike. *Prisoners of the American Dream: Politics and Economy in the History of the U.S. Working Class*. London, New York: Verso, 1986.

Delsen, Lei. *Operating Hours and Working Times: A Survey of Capacity Utilisation and Employment in the European Union*. Heidelberg: Physica Verlag, 2007.

Deutschmann, Christoph. "Zeitflexibilität und Arbeitsmarkt. Zur Entstehungsgeschichte und Funktion des Normalarbeitstages." In *Arbeitszeitpolitik: Formen und Folgen einer Neuverteilung der Arbeitszeit*, eds. Claus Offe, Karl Hinrichs, and Helmut Wiesenthal. Frankfurt am Main: Campus Verlag, 1982: 32–45.

Dickens, Linda, and Mark Hall. "Legal Regulation and the Changing Workplace." In *The Evolution of the Modern Workplace*, eds. William Arthur Brown, Alex Bryson, Jon Forth, and Keith Whitfield. Cambridge, New York: Cambridge University Press, 2009: 332–52.

Dribbusch, Heiner. "IG Metall Suffers Defeat over 35-Hour Week in East German Metalworking." European Industrial Relations Observatory Online (2003). www.eurofound. europa.eu/eiro/2003/07/feature/de0307204f.htm [accessed Jannuary 10, 2012].

Dribbusch, Heiner. "New Agreement on Job Security Signed for Railway Employees." European Industrial Relations Observatory Online (2005). www.eurofound. europa.eu/ eiro/2005/04/feature/de0504205f.htm [accessed Jannuary 10, 2012].

Dribbusch, Heiner. "Union Agrees to More Working Hours to Safeguard Jobs at Volkswagen." European Industrial Relations Observatory Online (2006). www.eurofound.europa.eu/eiro/2006/10/articles/de0610039i.htm [accessed January 10, 2012].

Dribbusch, Heiner. "Agreement Ends Dispute over Employee Relocation at Deutsche Telekom." European Industrial Relations Observatory Online (2007). www. eurofound. europa.eu/eiro/2007/07/articles/de0707019i.htm [accessed January 10, 2012].

Dribbusch, Heiner. "Germany: Flexible Forms of Work: 'Very Atypical' Contractual Arrangements." European Industrial Relations Observatory Online (2010). www.eurofound.europa.eu/ewco/studies/tn0812019s/de0812019q.htm [accessed January 10, 2012].

Dribbusch, Heiner, and Thorsten Schulten. "German Trade Unions between Neoliberal Restructuring, Social Partnership and Internationalism." In *Labour and the Challenges of Globalization: What Prospects for Transnational Solidarity?* eds. Andreas Bieler, Ingemar Lindberg and Devan Pillay. London: Pluto Press, 2008: 178–98.

Dufour, Christian. "35-Stunden-Frage in Frankreich – Verhandlung oder Zwang?" Kurswechsel, no. 4, 1999: 79–89.

Dufour, Christian. "Reduction of Working Time in France: A Lone Knight." In *Collective Bargaining on Working Time: Recent European Experiences*, eds. Maarten Keune and Bela Galgoczi. Brussels: European Trade Union Institute, 2006: 93–103.

Dumazedier, Joffre. *Toward a Society of Leisure*. New York: Free Press, 1967.

Duménil, Gérard, and Dominique Lévy. *Capital Resurgent: Roots of the Neoliberal Revolution*. Cambridge, MA: Harvard University Press, 2004.

Durand, Jean-Pierre. *The Invisible Chain: Constraints and Opportunities in the New World of Employment*. Basingstoke: Palgrave Macmillan, 2007.

Durbin, Susan. "Who Gets to Be a Knowledge Worker? The Case of UK Call Centers." In *Gendering the Knowledge Economy: Comparative Perspectives*, eds. Sylvia Walby, Heidi Gottfried, Karin Gottschal, and Mari Osawa. Basingstoke: Palgrave Macmillan, 2007: 228–47.

Dymond, W. R., and George Saunders. "Hours of Work in Canada." In *Hours of Work*, eds. Clyde Edward Dankert, Floyd Christopher Mann, and Herbert Roof Northrup. York: Harper & Row, 1965: 54–75.

Edelman, Murray. "New Deal Sensitivity to Labor Interests." In *Labor and the New Deal*, eds. Milton Derber and Edwin Young. Madison: University of Wisconsin Press, 1957: 159–91.

Edsforth, Ronald. "Why Automation Didn't Shorten the Work Week." In *Autowork*, eds. Robert Asher, Ronald Edsforth, and Stephen Merlino. Albany: State University of New York Press, 1995: 155–80.

Edwards, Richard. *Contested Terrain: The Transformation of the Workplace in the Twentieth Century*. New York: Basic Books, 1979.

Elam, Mark. "Puzzling out the Post-Fordist Debate: Technology, Markets and Institutions." In *Post-Fordism: A Reader*, ed. Ash Amin. Oxford; Cambridge, MA: Blackwell, 1994: 43–70.

Ellguth, Peter. "Betriebe ohne Betriebsrat – Verbreitung, Entwicklung und Charakteristika – unter Berücksichtigung betriebsspezifischer Formen der Mitarbeitervertretung." In *Betriebe ohne Betriebsrat. Informelle Interessenvertretung in Unternehmen*, eds. Ingrid Artus, Sabine Böhm, Stefan Lücking and Rainer Trinczek. Frankfurt am Main: Campus Verlag, 2006: 43–80.

Ellguth, Peter, and Susanne Kohaut. "Tarifbindung und betriebliche Interessenvertretung: Aktuelle Ergebnisse aus dem IAB-Betriebspanel 2007." In *WSI-Mitteilungen*, no. 8, 2008: 515–19.

Esping-Andersen, Gøsta. *The Three Worlds of Welfare Capitalism*. Cambridge: Polity Press, 1990.

European Commission. "Employment in Europe 2007." ed. the Social Affairs and Equal Opportunities Directorate-General for Employment. Brussels: European Commission, 2007.

European Commission. "Employment in Europe 2009." ed. the Social Affairs and Equal Opportunities Directorate-General for Employment. Brussels: European Commission, 2009.

Evans, Archibald A. *Hours of Work in Industrialised Countries*. Geneva: International Labour Office, 1975.

Exell, Richard. "Collective Bargaining on Working Time: UK." In *Collective Bargaining on Working Time: Recent European Experiences*, eds. Maarten Keune and Bela Galgoczi. Brussels: European Trade Union Institute, 2006: 273–87.

Fagan, Colette. "Working Time in the UK – Developments and Debates." In *Working Time – in Search for New Research Territory Beyond Flexibility Debates*. Tokyo: The Japan Institute for Labor Policy and Training, 2009: 37–54.

Faggio, Giulia, and Stephen Nickell. "Patterns of Work Across the OECD." In *The Economic Journal*, issue 117, no. 521, 2007: 416–40.

Ferlemann, Erwin. "Bilanz des Arbeitskampfes 1984 – aus der Sicht der IG Druck und Papier". In *Gewerkschaftliche Monatshefte*, no. 11, 1984: 671–82.

Ferlemann, Erwin. "Erfolge und Probleme des Tarifabschlusses in der Druckindustrie. Existenz sichern, Arbeit ändern, Leben gestalten". In *Leben gestalten. Gewerkschaften im Kampf um Arbeitszeitverkürzung*, eds. Erwin Ferlemann and Hans Janssen, Hamburg: VSA Verlag, 1985: 63–93.

Fine, Ben. *Women's Employment and the Capitalist Family*. London, New York: Routledge, 1992.

Fine, Ben. *Labour Market Theory: A Constructive Reassessment*. London, New York: Routledge, 1998.

Flecker, Jörg. "Not-Wendigkeit? Zum Zusammenhang von flexiblen Unternehmensformen, Qualifikationsanforderungen und Arbeitsmarktregulierung." In *Flexibilisierung – Problem oder Lösung?*, eds. Hans-Georg Zilian and Jörg Flecker. Berlin: Edition Sigma, 1998: 207–22.

Flecker, Jörg, Annika Schönauer, Christoph Hermann, and Bernadette Allinger. "Arbeitszeitverkürzung zur Umverteilung von Arbeit – internationale Beispiele." FORBA-Research Report 1/2010, Vienna.

Fletcher, Bill, and Fernando Gapasin. *Solidarity Divided: The Crisis in Organized Labor and a New Path toward Social Justice*. Berkeley: University of California Press, 2008.

Flohr, Bernd. *Arbeiter nach Maß: Die Disziplinierung der Fabrikarbeiterschaft während der Industrialisierung Deutschlands im Spiegel von Arbeitsordnungen*. Frankfurt am Main: Campus Verlag, 1981.

Folbre, Nancy. "Exploitation Comes Home: A Critique of the Marxian Theory of Family Labour." In *Cambridge Journal of Economics*, issue 6, vol. 4, 1982: 317–29.

Folbre, Nancy. "A Patriarchal Mode of Production." In *Alternatives to Economic Orthodoxy: A Reader in Political Economy*, eds. Randy Pearl Albelda, Christopher Eaton Gunn, and William Waller. Armonk, NY: M. E. Sharpe, 1987: 323–38.

Folbre, Nancy, Jayoung Yoon, Kade Finnoff and Allison Sidle Fuligni. "By What Measure? Family Time Devoted to Children in the US." University of Massachusetts Amherst Economic Department Working Paper 73, 2004.

Foley, Duncan K. *Understanding Capital: Marx's Economic Theory*. Cambridge, MA: Harvard University Press, 1986.

Ford, Henry, and Samuel Crowther. *My Life and Work*. Garden City: Garden City Publisher, 1926.

Fourastié, Jean. *Les 40 000 Heures*. Paris: R. Laffont, 1965.

Fox, Liana, Wen-Jui Han, Christopher Ruhm and Jane Waldfogel. "Time for Children: Trends in the Employment Patterns of Parents, 1967–2009." In *Demography*, issue 50, no. 1, 2013: 25–49.

Freeman, Richard B., and Ronald Schettkat. "Marketization of Production and the US–Europe Employment Gap." NBER Working Paper 8797, 2002.

Freyssinet, Jacques. *Le temps de travail en miettes. Vingt ans de politique de l'emploi et de négociation collective*. Paris: Editions l'Atelier, 1997.

Freyssinet, Jacques. "France: A Recurrent Aim, Repeated near-Failures and a New Law." In *Transfer: European Review of Labour and Research*, issue 4, no. 4, 1998: 641–56.

Freyssenet, Michel. "The Current Social Form of Automation and a Conceivable Alternative: French Experience." In *Transforming Automobile Assembly: Experience in Automation and Work Organization*, eds. Kōichi Shimokawa, Ulrich Jürgens, and Takahiro Fujimoto. New York: Springer Verlag, 1997; 305–17.

Fridenson, Patrick. "La multiplicité des processus de réduction de la durée du travail de 1814 à 1932: Négociations, luttes, textes et pratiques." In *La France et le temps de travail 1814–2004*, eds. Patrick Fridenson and Bénédicte Reynaud. Paris: Odile Jacob, 2004: 55–70.

Frieden, Jeffry A. *Global Capitalism: Its Fall and Rise in the Twentieth Century*. New York: Norton, 2006.

Friedman, Andrew L. *Industry and Labour: Class Struggle at Work and Monopoly Capitalism*. London: Macmillan, 1977.

Fuchs, Johann, Markus Hummel, Sabine Klinger, Eugen Spitznagel, Susanne Wanger, and Gerd Zika. "Die Spuren der Krise sind noch länger sichtbar." IAB Kurzbericht, no. 3, Institute for Employment Research, Nuremberg, 2010. Online. http://doku.iab.de/kurzber/2010/kb0310.pdf [accessed January 10, 2012].

Fuchs, Victor Robert. *The Service Economy*. New York: National Bureau of Economic Research, 1968.

Fucini, Joseph J., and Suzy Fucini. *Working for the Japanese: Inside Mazda's American Auto Plant*. New York: Free Press, 1990.

Funk, Lothar. "Cost-Cutting Deal Signed at Daimlerchrysler." European Industrial Relations Observatory Online, 2004. www.eurofound.europa.eu/eiro/2004/08/inbrief/de0408102n.htm. [accessed Jannuary 10, 2012].

Funk, Lothar. "Siemens Deal Launches Debate on Longer Working Hours." European Industrial Relations Observatory Online, 2004, www.eurofound.europa.eu/eiro/2004/07/feature/de0407106f.htm [accessed January 10, 2012].

Gadrey, Jean. *New Economy, New Myth*. London, New York: Routledge, 2003.

Gadrey, Jean. *Socio-économie des services*. Paris: Editions la découverte, 2003.

Gadrey, Jean, Steffen Lehndorff, and Thierry Ribault. "A Societal Interpretation of the Differences and Similarities in Working Time Practices." In *Flexible Working in Food Retailing: A Comparison between France, Germany, the United Kindom and Japan*, eds. Christophe Baret, Steffen Lehndorff, and Leigh Sparks. London and New York: Routledge, 2000: 143–66.

Galbraith, John Kenneth. *The Affluent Society*. Boston: Houghton Mifflin, 1969.

Galbraith, John Kenneth. *The New Industrial State*. Harmondsworth: Penguin, 1969.

Gardiner, Jean. "Domestic Labour Revisited: A Feminist Critique of Marxist Economics." In *Inside the Household: From Labour to Care*, ed. Susan Himmelweit. Basingstoke: Macmillan, 2000: 80–101.

Gardiner, Jean. "Women's Domestic Labour." *New Left Review*, no. 89, January–February 1975: 47–58.

Gardiner, Jean, Susan Himmelweit, and Maureen Mackintosh. "Women's Domestic Labor." In *Inside the Household: From Labour to Care*, ed. Susan Himmelweit. Basingstoke: Macmillan 2000: 25–40.

Gauthier, Anne, Timothy Smeeding, and Frank Furstenberg. "Are Parents Investing Less Time in Children? Trends in Selected Industrialized Countries." In *Population and Development Review*, issue 30, no. 4, 2004: 674–71.

Geist, Claudia. "The Welfare State and the Home: Regime Differences in the Domestic Division of Labour." In *European Sociological Review*, issue 21, no. 1, 2005: 23–41.

Gerlmaier, Anja. "Nachhaltige Arbeitsgestaltung in der Wissensökonomie?" In *Das Politische in Der Arbeitspolitik*, ed. Steffen Lehndorff. Berlin: Edition Sigma, 2005: 71–98.

Gershuny, Jonathan. *After Industrial Society?: The Emerging Self-Service Economy*. Atlantic Highlands, NJ: Humanities, 1978.

Gershuny, Jonathan. *Changing Times. Work and Leisure in Postindustrial Society*. Oxford: Oxford University Press, 2000.

Gilbert, G. Nigel, Roger Burrows, Anna Pollert. *Fordism and Flexibility: Divisions and Change, Explorations in Sociology*. Basingstoke: Macmillan, 1992.

Gindin, Sam. *The Canadian Auto Workers: The Birth and Transformation of a Union*. Toronto: James Lorimer, 1995.

Gindin, Sam. "Turning Points and Starting Points." In *Socialist Register 2001*, eds. Leo Panitch and Colin Leys. London: Merlin, 2000: 343–66.

Gindin, Sam. "Rethinking Unions, Registering Socialism." In *Socialist Register 2014*, eds. Leo Panitch, Greg Albo, and Vivek Chibber. London: Merlin Press, 2013: 26–51.

Glyn, Andrew. *Capitalism Unleashed: Finance Globalization and Welfare*. Oxford, New York: Oxford University, 2006.

Golden, Lonnie. "Overemployment in the United States: Which Workers Are Willing to Reduce Their Work-Hours and Income?" In *Decent Working Time: New Trends, New Issues*, eds. Jean-Yves Boulin, Michel Lallement, Jon C. Messenger, and François Michon. Geneva: International Labor Office, 2006: 209–34.

Golden, Lonnie, and Helene Jorgensen. "Time after Time: Mandatory Overtime in the U.S. Economy." Economic Policy Institute Briefing Paper 120, Washington DC, 2002.

Goldfield, Michael. *The Decline of Organized Labor in the United States*. Chicago: University of Chicago, 1987.

Gordon, David M., Richard Edwards, and Michael Reich. *Segmented Work, Divided Workers: The Historical Transformation of Labor in the United States*. Cambridge, New York: Cambridge University Press, 1982.

Gorz, André. "Work and Consumption." In *Towards Socialism*, eds. Perry Anderson and Robin Blackburn. Ithaca, NY: Cornell University Press, 1966: 317–53.

Gorz, André. *Strategy for Labor: A Radical Proposal*. Boston: Beacon Press, 1969.

Gorz, André. "Technology, Technicians and Class Struggle." In *The Division of Labour: The Labour Process and Class-Struggle in Modern Capitalism*, ed. André Gorz. Atlantic Highlands, NJ: Humanities Press, 1976: 159–80.

Gorz, André. *Ecology as Politics*. Boston: South End, 1980.

Gorz, André. *Farewell to the Working Class: An Essay on Post-Industrial Socialism*. London: Pluto Press, 1982.

Gorz, André. *Critique of Economic Reason*. London, New York: Verso, 1989.

Gorz, André. *Capitalism, Socialism, Ecology*. London, New York: Verso, 1994.

Gorz, André. *Reclaiming Work: Beyond the Wage-Based Society*. Cambridge: Polity Press, 1999.

Goul Andersen, Jørgen. "A Note on the Termination of the Danish Job Leave Programmes." Working Paper, University of Aalborg, 2002.

Gould, Arthour. "Study Leave in Sweden." In *Studies in the Education of Adults*, issue 35, no. 1, 1993: 68–84.

Graham, Laurie. "How Does the Japanese Model Transfer to the United States? A View from the Line." In *Global Japanization?: The Transnational Transformation of the Labour Process*, eds. Tony Elger and Chris Smith. London, New York: Routledge, 1994: 123–51.

Graham, Philip, and Paul Stewart. "Thinking Smarter to Work Harder? Einige Probleme der 'Lean Production' in der Automobilindustrie im Vereinigten Königreich." In *Zwischen Schweden und Japan. Lean Production aus europäischer Sicht*, eds. Bruno Cattero, Gerd Hurrle, Stefan Lutz, and Rainer Salm. Münster: Westfälisches Dampfboot, 1995: 139–55.

Green, David I. "Pain-Cost and Opportunity-Cost." In *The Quarterly Journal of Economics*, issue 8, no. 2, 1894: 218–29.

Greenbaum, Joan M. *Windows on the Workplace: Technology, Jobs, and the Organization of Office Work*. New York: Monthly Review Press, 2004.

Greis, Theresa Diss. *The Decline of Annual Hours Worked in the United States since 1947*. Philadelphia: University of Pennsylvania Press, 1984.

Groß, Hermann. "Vergleichende Analyse der Arbeits- und Betriebszeitenentwicklung im Zeitraum von 1987 bis 2007." SFS Beiträge aus der Forschung 176. Sozialforschungsstelle Dortmund: 2010.

Groß, Hermann, Eva Munz, and Hartmut Seifert. "Verbreitung und Struktur von Arbeitszeitkonten." In *Arbeit*, issue 9, no. 3, 2000: 217–29.

Guedj, François, and Gérard Vindt. *Le temps de travail, une histoire conflictuelle*. Paris: Syros, 1997.

Hagen, Elisabeth, and Jane Jenson. "Paradoxes and Promises: Work and Politics in the Postwar Years." In *Feminization of the Labour Force: Paradoxes and Promises*, eds. Jane Jenson, Elisabeth Hagen, and Ceallaigh Reddy. Cambridge: Polity Press 1988: 3–16.

Haipeter, Thomas. "Can Norms Survive Market Pressures in Germany?" In *Decent Working Time: New Trends, New Issues*, eds. Jean-Yves Boulin, Michel Lallement, Jon C. Messenger, and François Michon. Geneva: International Labor Office, 2006: 319–41.

Haipeter, Thomas. "Kontrollierte Dezentralisierung? Abweichende Tarifvereinbarungen in der Metall- und Elektroindustrie." In *Industrielle Beziehungen*, issue 16, no. 3, 2009: 232–53.

Haipeter, Thomas. "Tarifauseianandersetzung im Betrieb: Neue Herausforderung für Gewerkschaften und Betriebsräte". In *Zeitkonflikte. Renaissance der Arbeitszeitpolitik*, eds. Hermann Groß and Hartmut Seifert. Berlin: Edition Sigma, 2010: 289–312.

Haipeter, Thomas, and Steffen Lehndorff. "Decentralised Bargaining of Working Time in the German Automotive Industry." In *Industrial Relations Journal*, issue 36, no. 2, 2005: 140–56.

Haipeter, Thomas, Steffen Lehndorff, Gabi Schilling, Dorothea Voss-Dahm and Alexandra Wagner. "Vertrauensarbeit. Analyse eines neuen Rationalisierungskonzepts." In *Leviathan*, issue 30, no. 3, 2002: 360–83.

Hall, Peter A., and Daniel W. Gingerich. "Varieties of Capitalism and Institutional Complementaries in the Political Economy: An Empirical Analysis." In *Debating Varieties of Capitalism: A Reader*, ed. Bob Hancké. Oxford, New York: Oxford University Press, 2009: 135–79.

Hall, Peter A., and David W. Soskice. "Varieties of Capitalism: The Institutional Foundations of Comparative Advantage." In *Varieties of Capitalism: The Institutional Foundations of Comparative Advantage*, eds. Peter A. Hall and David W. Soskice. Oxford, New York: Oxford University Press, 2001: 1–68.

Hartz, Peter. *The Company That Breathes: Every Job Has a Customer*. New York: Springer Verlag, 1996.

Harvey, David. *Spaces of Hope*, California Studies in Critical Human Geography. Berkeley: University of California Press, 2000.

Harvey, David. *A Brief History of Neoliberalism*. Oxford, New York: Oxford University Press, 2005.

Hassan, Robert. "Network Time and the New Knowledge Epoch." In *Time & Society*, issue 12, no. 2–3, 2003: 226–41.

Hassan, Robert, and Ronald E. Purser. *24/7: Time and Temporality in the Network Society*. Stanford: Stanford Business Books, 2007.

Hassel, Anke. "The Erosion of the German System of Industrial Relations." In *British Journal of Industrial Relations*, issue 37, no. 3, 1999: 483–505.

Hay, Colin. "The Genealogy of Neoliberalism." In *Neoliberalism: National and Regional Experiments with Global Ideas*, eds. Ravi K. Roy, Arthur Denzau, and Thomas D. Willett. London, New York: Routledge, 2007: 51–69.

Hayden, Anders. *Sharing the Work, Sparing the Planet: Work Time, Consumption, and Ecology*. Toronto: Between the Lines, 1999.

Hayden, Anders. "France's 35-Hour Week: Attack on Business? Win–Win Reform? Or Betrayal of Disadvantaged Workers?" In *Politics & Society*, issue 34, no. 4, 2006: 503–42.

Heinrich, Michael. *Die Wissenschaft vom Wert: Die marxsche Kritik der politischen Ökonomie zwischen wissenschaftlicher Revolution und klassischer Tradition*. Münster: Westfälisches Dampfboot, 2001.

Henwood, Doug. *After the New Economy*. New York: New Press, 2003.

Hermann, Christoph. "Arbeitszeitverkürzung in Frankreich." In *Wirtschaft und Gesellschaft*, issue 26, no. 4, 2000: 561–78.

Hermann, Christoph. "Neoliberalism in the European Union." In *Studies in Political Economy*, no. 79, 2007: 61–89.

Hermann, Christoph. "Kampf um die Arbeitszeit. Ein Überblick." In *Prokla*, no. 150, 2008: 83–102.

Hermann, Christoph. "Value and Knowledge: Insights from Marxist Value Theory for the Transformation of Work in the Digital Economy." In *Rethinking Marxism*, issue 21, no. 2, 2009: 275–89.

Hermann, Christoph. "Structural Adjustment and Neoliberal Convergence in Labor Markets and Welfare: The Impact of the Crisis and Austerity Measures on European Social Models." In *Competition and* Change, issue 18, no. 2, 2014a: 109–128.

Hermann, Christoph. "Green New Deal, Green Economy and Green Jobs: Consequences for Environmental and Social Justice." Paper presented at the 9th Global Labour University Conference, 15–17 May 2014b, Berlin, Germany.

Hermann, Christoph, Torsten Brandt, and Thorsten Schulten. "Commodification, Casualization and Intensification of Work in Liberalized European Postal Markets." In *Work Organization, Labor & Globalization*, issue 2, no. 2, 2008: 40–55.

Heron, Craig. "National Contours: Solidarity and Fragmentation." In *The Workers' Revolt in Canada, 1917–1925*, ed. Craig Heron. Toronto: University of Toronto Press, 1998: 268–304.

Herrmann, Christa, Markus Promberger, Susanne Singer, and Rainer Trinczek. *Forcierte Arbeitszeitflexibilisierung. Die 35-Stunden-Woche in der betrieblichen und gesellschaftlichen Praxis.* Berlin: Edition Sigma, 1999.

Hetrick, Ron L. "Analyzing the Recent Upward Surge in Overtime Hours." In *Monthly Labor Review*, issue 123, no. 2, 2000: 30–3.

Hicks, John Richard. *Value and Capital: An Inquiry into Some Fundamental Principles of Economic Theory.* Oxford, New York: Oxford University Press, 1946.

Himmelweit, Susan. "The Discovery of 'Unpaid Work': The Social Consequences of the Expansion of 'Work.'" *Feminist Economics*, issue 1, no. 2, 1995: 1–19.

Himmelweit, Susan. *Inside the Household: From Labour to Care.* Basingstoke: Macmillan, 2000.

Himmelweit, Susan, and Simon Mohun. "Domestic Labour and Capital." In *Cambridge Journal of Economics*, issue 1, no. 1, 1977: 15–31.

Hinrichs, Karl. *Motive und Interessen im Arbeitszeitkonflikt. Eine Analyse der Entwicklung von Normalarbeitszeitstandards.* Frankfurt am Main: Campus Verlag, 1988.

Hinrichs, Karl. "Working Time Development in West Germany: Departure to a New Stage." In *Working Time in Transition. The Political Economy of Working Hours in Industrial Nations*, eds. Karl Hinrichs, William Roche, and Carmen Sirianni. Philadelphia: Temple University Press, 1991: 27–59.

Hinrichs, Karl, Claus Offe, and Helmut Wiesenthal. "Der Streit um die Zeit. Die Arbeitszeit im gesellschaftspolitischen und industriellen Konflikt." In *Arbeitszeitpolitik. Formen und Folgen einer Neuverteilung der Arbeitszeit*, eds. Claus Offe, Hinrichs Karl, and Helmut Wiesenthal. Frankfurt am Main: Campus Verlag, 1982: 8–31.

Hirsch, Joachim, and Roland Roth. *Das neue Gesicht des Kapitalismus. Vom Fordismus zum Postfordismus.* Hamburg: VSA Verlag, 1986.

Holtgrewe, Ursula. "Restructuring Gendered Flexibility in Organizations: A Comparative Analysis of Call Centers in Germany." In *Gendering the Knowledge Economy: Comparative Perspectives*, eds. Sylvia Walby, Heidi Gottfried, Karin Gottschal, and Mari Osawa. Basingstoke: Palgrave Macmillan, 2007: 248–70.

Hooker, Clarence. *Life in the Shadows of the Crystal Palace, 1910–1927: Ford Workers in the Model T Era.* Bowling Green, OH: Bowling Green State University Popular Press, 1997.

Hörning, Karl H., Anette Gerhard, and Matthias Michailow. *Time Pioneers: Flexible Working Time and New Lifestyles.* Cambridge: Polity Press, 1995.

Hounshell, David A. *From the American System to Mass Production, 1800–1932: The Development of Manufacturing Technology in the United States.* Baltimore: Johns Hopkins University Press, 1984.

Howell, Chris. *Regulating Labor: The State and Industrial Relations Reform in Postwar France.* Princeton: Princeton University Press, 1992.

Hubermann, Michael. "Working Hours of the World Unite? New International Evidence of Worktime, 1870–1913." In *The Journal of Economic History*, issue 64, no. 4, 2004: 964–1001.

Humphries, Jane, and Jill Rubery. "The Reconstitution of the Supply Side of the Labour Market: The Realtive Autonomy of Social Reproduction" In *Cambridge Journal of Economics*, issue 8, no. 4, 1984: 331–46.

Hunnicutt, Benjamin Kline. *Work without End: Abandoning Shorter Hours for the Right to Work.* Philadelphia: Temple University Press, 1988.

Hunt, E. K. *History of Economic Thought: A Critical Perspective.* Armonk, NY: M. E. Sharpe, 2002.

Husson, Michel. "Le temps de travail." In *Le monde du travail*, eds. Jacques Kergoat, Danièle Linhart, and Josiane Boutet. Paris: Editions la découverte, 1998: 180–8.

Husson, Michel. "Pressure Mounts on 35-Hour Week." European Industrial Relations Observatory Online, 2004. www.eurofound.europa.eu/eiro/2004/08/feature/fr0408108f. htm [accessed Jannuary 10, 2012].

Huws, Ursula. *The Making of a Cybertariat: Virtual Work in a Real World*. New York: Monthly Review Press, 2003.

Huws, Ursula. "The Underpinnings of Class in the Digital Age: Living, Labor and Value." In *Socialist Register 2014*, eds. Leo Panitch, Greg Albo, and Vivek Chibber. London: Merlin Press, 2013: 80–107.

Hyman, Jeff, and Abigail Marks. "Frustrated Ambitions: The Reality of Balancing Work and Life for Call Center Employees." In *Work Less, Live More? A Critical Analysis of the Work-Life Boundary*, eds. Christopher Warhurst, Doris R. Eikhof, and Axel Haunschild. Basingstoke: Palgrave Macmillan, 2008: 191–209.

Hyman, Jeff, Chris Baldry, Dora Scholarios, and Dirk Bunzel. "Work-Life Imbalance in Call Centers and Software Development." In *British Journal of Industrial Relations*, issue 41, no. 2, 2003: 215–39.

Hyman, Richard. "The Historical Evolution of British Industrial Relations." In *Industrial Relations, Theory and Practice in Britain*, ed. Paul Edwards. Oxford, New York: Oxford University Press, 2003: 37–57.

Hyman, Richard. *Industrial Relations: A Marxist Introduction*. London: Macmillan, 1975.

International Monetary Fund. "Euro Area Policies: Selected Issues." IMF Country Report No. 04/235. Washington DC, 2004.

Jacobs, Jerry A., and Kathleen Gerson. "Understanding Changes in American Working Time." In *Fighting for Time: Shifting Boundaries of Work and Social Life*, eds. Cynthia Fuchs Epstein and Arne L. Kalleberg. New York: Russel Sage, 2004: 25–45.

Jacobs, Jerry A., and Kathleen Gerson. "Who Are the Overworked Americans?" In *Working Time: International Trends, Theory, and Policy Perspectives*, eds. Lonnie Golden and Deborah M. Figart. London, New York: Routledge, 2000: 89–105.

Jackson, Tim. *Prosperity without Growth. Economies for a Finite Planet*. London: Earthscan, 2009.

Jamieson, Stuart Marshall. *Industrial Relations in Canada*. Ithaca, NY: Cornell University Press, 1957.

Jänicke, Sophie, Kay Ohl, and Hildegard Wagner. "Es wird Zeit! Ansätze einer neuen Arbeitszeitdebatte in der IG Metall." In *Prokla*, no. 150, 2008: 103–12.

Jany-Catrice, Florence, and Steffen Lehndorff. "Work Organization and the Importance of Labor Markets in the European Retail Trade." In *Working in the Service Sector: A Tale from Different Worlds*, eds. Gerhard Bosch and Steffen Lehndorff. London, New York: Routledge, 2005: 190–212.

Jefferys, Stephen. "Western European Trade Unionism at 2000." In *Socialist Register 2001*, eds. Leo Panitch and Colin Leys. London: Merlin Press, 2000: 143–70.

Jefferys, Stephen. "A 'Copernican Revolution' in French Industrial Relations: Are the Times a' Changing?" In *British Journal of Industrial Relations*, issue 38, no. 2, 2002: 241–60.

Jefferys, Stephen. "Critical Times for French Employment Regulation: The 35-Hour Week and the Challenge to Social Partnership." In *Challenging the Market: The Struggle to Regulate Work and Income*, eds. Jim Stanford and Leah F. Vosko. Montreal: McGill-Queen's University Press, 2004: 346–64.

Jensen, Per. "Die dänische Freistellungsmodelle und ihre Gleichstellungsdimensionen." In *Zukunft der Arbeit und Geschlecht. Diskurse, Entwicklungspfade und Reformoptionen internationalen Vergleich*, eds. Karin Gotschall and Birgit Pfau-Effinger. Opladen: Leske and Budrich, 2002: 267–80.

Jenson, Jane. "'Different' but Not 'Exceptional': Canada's Permeable Fordism." In *Canadian Review of Sociology – Revue canadienne de sociologie*, issue 26, no. 1, 1989: 69–94.

Jenson, Jane, and Rianne Mahon. "Legacies for Canadian Labor of Two Decades of Crisis." In *The Challenge of Restructuring: North American Labor Movements Respond*, eds. Jane Jenson and Rianne Mahon. Philadelphia: Temple University Press, 1993: 72–91.

Jevons, H. Stanley. *The Theory of Political Economy*. London: Macmillan, 1888.

Jürgens, Ulrich. "Rolling Back Cycle Times: The Renaissance of the Classic Assembly Line in Final Assembly." In *Transforming Automobile Assembly: Experience in Automation and Work Organization*, eds. Kōichi Shimokawa, Ulrich Jürgens, and Takahiro Fujimoto. New York: Springer Verlag, 1997: 255–71.

Jürgens, Ulrich, Thomas Malsch, and Knuth Dohse. *Breaking from Taylorism: Changing Forms of Work in the Automobile Industry*. Cambridge, New York: Cambridge University Press, 1993.

Kalleberg, Arne L. "Nonstandard Employment Relations: Part-Time, Temporary and Contract Work." In *Annual Review of Sociology*, no. 26, 2000: 341–65.

Kenney, Martin, and Richard L. Florida. *Beyond Mass Production: The Japanese System and Its Transfer to the U.S.* Oxford, New York: Oxford University Press, 1993.

Kern, Horst, and Michael Schumann. "Limits of the Division of Labour: New Production and Employment Concepts in West German Industry." In *Economic and Industrial Democracy*, issue 8, no. 2, 1987: 151–70.

Kern, Horst, and Michael Schumann. *Das Ende der Arbeitsteilung?: Rationalisierung in der industriellen Produktion: Bestandsaufnahme, Trendbestimmung*. Munich: Beck Verlag, 1990.

Keynes, John Maynard. "Economic Possibilities for Our Grandchildren." In *Essays in Persuasion*, ed. John Maynard Keynes. New York: Norton, 1963: 358–73.

Keynes, John Maynard. "Letter to T.S. Eliot, 5 April 1945." In *The Collected Writings of John Maynard Keynes. Activities 1940–1946: Shaping the Postwar World, Employment and Commodities*, eds. Donald Moggride. Basingstoke and Cambridge: Macmillan and Cambridge University Press, 1980: 383–4.

Killmann, Claudia, and Martina Klein. "Part-Time Work in Germany: Gender-Specific Structures of Work Hours." In *Part-Time Work in Europe*, ed. Martina Klein. Frankfurt am Main: Campus Verlag 1997: 81–94.

Kinley, John. *Evolution of Legislated Standards on Hours of Work in Ontario*. Toronto: Ontario Task Force on Hours of Work and Overtime, 1988.

Kirsch, Johannes, Martina Klein, Steffen Lehndorff, and Dorothea Voss-Dahm. "The Organization of Working Time in Large German Food Retail Firms." In *Flexible Working in Food Retailing: A Comparison between France, Germany, the United Kindom and Japan*, eds. Christophe Baret, Steffen Lehndorff and Leigh Sparks. London, New York: Routledge, 2000: 58–82.

Klug, Thomas. "Employers' Strategies in the Detroit Labor Market 1900–1929". In *On the Line: Essays in the History of Auto Work*, eds. Nelson Lichtenstein and Stephen Meyer, Urbana: University of Illinois Press, 1989.

Knight, Frank H. *Risk, Uncertainty and Profit*. Boston, New York, London: Houghton Mifflin, 1921.

Knight, Kyle, Eugene Rosa and Juliet Schor. "Reducing Growth to Achieve Environmental Sustainability: The Role of Work Hours." PERI Working Paper 304, 2012.

Kochan, Thomas, Harry Charles Katz, and Robert McKersie. *The Transformation of American Industrial Relations*. New York: Basic Books, 1986.

Kolehmainen, Sirpa. "Dynamics of Control and Commitment in IT Firms." In *Information Society and the Workplace: Spaces, Boundaries and Agency*, eds. Tuula Heiskanen and Jeff Hearn. London, New York: Routledge, 2004: 83–102.

Kuhn, Peter, and Fernando Lozano. "The Expanding Workweek? Understanding Trends in Long Work Hours among U.S. Men, 1979–2006." In *Journal of Labor Economics*, issue 26, no. 2, 2008: 311–43.

Kümmerling, Angelika, Andreas Jansen, and Steffen Lehndorff. "Die Veränderung der Beschäftigungs- und Arbeitszeitstrukturen in Deutschland 2001 Bis 2006." Institute for Work, Skills and Training (IAQ), Duisburg Essen, 2009. Online. www.iaq.uni-due.de/aktuell/veroeff/2009/kuemmerling01.pdf [accessed Jannuary 10, 2012].

Kurz-Scherf, Ingrid. "Chancen, Risken und Tendenzen der neuen Arbeitszeitbestimmungen." In *Leben gestalten. Gewerkschaften im Kampf um Arbeitszeitverkürzung*, eds. Erwin Ferlemann and Hans Janssen. Hamburg: VSA Verlag, 1985: 94–141.

LaJeunesse, Robert. *Work Time Regulation as a Sustainable Full Employment Strategy: The Social Effort Bargain*. London, New York: Routledge, 2009.

Lallement, Michel. *Temps, travail et modes de vie*. Paris: Presses Universitaires de France, 2003.

Lallement, Michel. "Une antinomie durkheimienne … et au-delà.". In *Temporalités*, no. 8, 2008.

Lash, Scott, and John Urry. *The End of Organized Capitalism*. Madison: University of Wisconsin Press, 1987.

Latouche, Serge. *Farewell to Growth*. Cambridge: Polity Press, 2009.

Lazonick, William. *Business Organization and the Myth of the Market Economy*. Cambridge, New York: Cambridge University Press, 1991.

Lebowitz, Michael A. *Beyond Capital: Marx's Political Economy of the Working Class*. Basingstoke: Palgrave Macmillan, 2003.

Legault, Marie-Josée. "IT Firms' Working Time (De)Regulation Model: A By-Product of Risk Management Strategy and Project-Based Work Management." In *Work Organisation Labour & Globalisation*, issue 7, no. 1, 2013: 76–94.

Lehndorff, Steffen. *Zeitnot und Zeitsouveränität in der just-in-time Fabrik*. Munich: Rainer Hampp Verlag, 1997.

Lehndorff, Steffen. "Working Time and Operating Hours in the European Automotive Industry." Institut für Arbeit und Technik Gelsenkirchen, 2000.

Lehndorff, Steffen. *Weniger ist mehr. Arbeitszeitverkürzung als Gesellschaftspolitik*. Hamburg: VSA Verlag, 2001.

Lehndorff, Steffen. "The Governance of Service Work – Changes in Work Organisation and New Challenges for Service-Sector Trade Unions." In *Transfer: European Review of Labour and Research*, issue 8, no. 3, 2002: 415–34.

Lehndorff, Steffen. "The Long Good-Bye? Tarifvertragliche Arbeitszeitregulierung und gesellschaftlicher Arbeitszeitstandard." In *Industrielle Beziehungen*, issue 10, no. 2, 2003: 273–95.

Lehndorff, Steffen. "Flexibility and Control: New Challenges for Working-Time Policy in the European Union." In *Labor & Industry*, issue 17, no. 3, 2007: 9–28.

Lehndorff, Steffen. "Before the Crisis, in the Crisis, and Beyond: The Upheaval of Collective Bargaining in Germany." Working Paper, Institute for Work, Skills and Qualification, University of Duisburg-Essen, 2009.

Lehndorff, Steffen. "Normalität jenseits der Normen. Der deutsche Sonderweg in der Arbeitszeitentwicklung". In *Zeitkonflikte. Renaissance Der Arbeitszeitpolitik*, eds. Hermann Groß and Hartmut Seifert. Berlin: Edition Sigma, 2010: 71–99.

Lehndorff, Steffen, and Dorothea Voss-Dahm. "The Delegation of Uncertainty: Flexibility and the Role of the Market in the Service Economy." In *Working in the Service Sector: A Tale from Different Worlds*, eds. Gerhard Bosch and Steffen Lehndorff. London, New York: Routledge, 2005: 289–315.

Lehndorff, Steffen, Alexandra Wagner, and Christine Franz. "Development of Working Time in the EU." Report commissioned by the European United Left/Nordic Green Left, 2010. Online. www.iaq.uni-due.de/aktuell/veroeff/2010/lehndorff01_en.pdf [accessed January 10, 2012].

Lessenich, Stephan. *Die Neuerfindung des Sozialen. Der Sozialstaat im flexiblen Kapitalismus*. Bielefeld: Transcript Verlag, 2008.

Lewchuk, Wayne. *American Technology and the British Vehicle Industry*. Cambridge, New York: Cambridge University Press, 1987.

Lewis, Jane. "Gender and the Development of Welfare Regimes." In *Journal of European Social Policy*, issue 2, no. 3, 1992: 159–73.

Lichtenstein, Nelson. *Labor's War at Home: The CIO in World War II*. Cambridge, New York: Cambridge University Press, 1982.

Lichtenstein, Nelson. *State of the Union: A Century of American Labor*. Princeton: Princeton University Press, 2002.

Lichtenstein, Nelson. *The Retail Revolution: How Wal-Mart Created a Brave New World of Business*. New York: Metropolitan Books, 2009.

Linder, Marc. *The Autocratically Flexible Workplace: A History of Overtime Regulation in the United States*. Iowa City: Fanpihua Press, 2002.

Lipietz, Alain. "Die Welt des Postfordismus." In *Supplement der Zeitschrift Sozialismus*, nos. 7 and 8, 1997.

Lipietz, Alain. *Towards a New Economic Order: Postfordism, Ecology, and Democracy*. Oxford, New York: Oxford University Press, 1992.

Littler, Craig R. *The Development of the Labour Process in Capitalist Societies: A Comparative Study of the Transformation of Work Organization in Britain, Japan, and the USA*. London: Heinemann Educational, 1982.

Lorwin, Val R. *The French Labor Movement*. Cambridge, MA: Harvard University Press, 1954.

Lüscher, Rudolf. *Henry und die Krümelmonster – Versuch über den fordistischen Sozialcharakter*. Tübingen: Konkursbuch Verlag Claudia Gehrke, 1987.

Macdonald, Martha "Post-Fordism and the Flexibility Debate." In *Studies in Political Economy*, no. 31 (Fall 1991): 177–201.

MacDuffe, John, and Frits K. Pil. "From Fixed to Flexible: Automation and Work Organization Trends from the International Assembly Plant Study." In *Transforming Automobile Assembly: Experience in Automation and Work Organization*, eds. Kōichi Shimokawa, Ulrich Jürgens, and Takahiro Fujimoto. New York: Spring Verlag, 1997: 238–54.

Maddison, Angus. *The World Economy: A Millennial Perspective*. Paris: OECD, 2001.

Madsen, Per Kongshoj. "Working Time Policy and Paid Leave Arrangements: The Danish Experience in the 1990s." In *Transfer*, issue 4, no. 4, 1998: 692–716.

Mahnkopf, Birgit. "Peak Everything? Folgen der sozialökologischen Krise für die Dynamik des historischen Kapitalismus." Friedrich-Schiller Universität Jena, Kolleg Postwachstumsgesellschaft, Working Paper no. 2, 2013.

Malsch, Thomas. "Konzernstrategien und Arbeitsreform in der Automobilindustrie am Beispiel der Arbeitsintegration." In *Die Zukunft der Arbeit in der Automobilindustrie*, eds. Ben Dankbaar, Ulrich Jürgens, and Thomas Malsch. Berlin: Edition Sigma, 1988: 62–82.

Mankiw, Gregory N., and Matthew Weinzierl. "The Optimal Taxation of Height: A Case Study of Utilitaraian Income Redistribution." Harvard Business School Working Paper 09–139, Cambridge, MA, 2009.

Marglin, Stephen A. "What Do Bosses Do? The Origins and Functions of Hierarchy in Capitalist Production." In *Radical Political Economy: Explorations in Alternative Economic Analysis*, ed. Victor D. Lippit. Armonk, NY: M. E. Sharpe, 1996: 19–59.

Maruani, Margaret. "Part-Time Work in France: A Time of Crisis." In *Part-Time Work in Europe*, ed. Martina Klein. Frankfurt am Main: Campus Verlag 1997: 70–80.

Maruani, Margret. *Travail et emploi des femmes*. Paris: Editions la découverte, 2000.

Marx, Karl. *Capital. A Critique of Political Economy*, New World Paperbacks. New York: International Publishers, 1967.

Marx, Karl. *Theories of Surplus Value*. Vol. 3. London: Lawrence & Wishart, 1969.

Marx, Karl. Grundrisse. Foundations of the Critique of Political Economy. New York: Vintage Books, 1973.

Marx, Karl. "Inaugural Address and Provisional Rules of the International Working Men's Association." In *The Portable Marx*, ed. Eugene Kamenka. Harmondsworth: Penguin, 1983: 355–65.

Maume, David, and David Purcell. "The 'Over-Paced' American: Recent Trends in the Intensification of Work." In *Research in the Sociology of Work*, no. 17, 2007: 251–82.

Mayer-Ahuja, Nicole, and Harald Wolf. "Beyond the Hype: Working in the German Internet Industry." In *Critical Sociology*, issue 33, nos. 1–2, 2007.

Mayr, Hans. "Der Kampf um die 35-Stunden-Woche – Erfahrungen und Schlußfolgerungen aus der Tarifbewegung 1984." In *Gewerkschaftliche Monatshefte*, no. 11, 1984: 661–70.

McDonald, Angus. "Labor Provisions and the NRA Codes." In *Proceedings of the Oklahoma Academy of Science*. Oklahoma City: Oklahoma Academy of Science, 1935: 105–8.

McGrattan, Ellen R., and Richard Rogerson. "Changes in Hours Worked, 1950–2000." In *Federal Reserve Bank of Minneapolis Quarterly Review*, issue 28, no. 1, 2004: 14–33.

Meadows, Donella H., Jørgen Randers, Dennis L. Meadows and William W. Behrens. *The Limits to Growth: A Report for the Club of Rome's Project on the Predicament of Mankind*. New York: Universe Books, 1972.

Meilland, Christèle. "Reform of 35-Hour Week Law under Way." European Industrial Relations Observatory Online, 2005. www.eurofound.europa.eu/eiro/2005/02/feature/fr0502109f.htm [accessed Jannuary 10, 2012].

Messenger, Jon C., and Naj Ghoseh, eds. *Work Sharing during the Great Recession. New Developments and Beyond*. Cheltenham: Edward Elgar, 2013.

Meyer, Stephen. *The Five Dollar Day: Labor Management and Social Control in the Ford Motor Company, 1980–1921*. Albany: State University of New York Press, 1981.

Michon, François. "From 'Working Less for More Jobs' to 'Working More for More Money' – Recent Development and Issues on Working Time in France." In *Working Time – in Search for New Research Territory Beyond Flexibility Debates*. Tokyo: The Japan Institue for Labor Policy and Training, 2009: 3–20.

Milner, Simon. "The Coverage of Collective Pay-Setting Institutions in Britain, 1895–1990." In *British Journal of Industrial Relations*, issue 33, no. 1, 1995: 69–91.

Mincer, Jacob. "Labor Force Participation of Married Women: A Study of Labor Supply." In *The Economics of Women and Work*, ed. Alice H. Amsden. New York: St. Martin's Press, 1980: 41–51.

Mincer, Jacob, and Solomon Polachek. "Family Investments in Human Capital: Earnings of Women." In *The Economics of Women and Work*, ed. Alice H. Amsden. New York: St. Martin's Press, 1980: 169–205.

Ministère de l'emploi et de la solidarité. "Les enseignements des accords sur la réduction du temps de travail. Eté 1998 – Eté 1999". Paris: Ministry of Employment and Solidarity, 1999.

Mohun, Simon. "Distributive Shares in the US Economy, 1964–2001." In *Cambridge Journal of Economics*, issue 30, no. 3, 2005: 347–70.

Moody, Kim. *An Injury to All: The Decline of American Unionism*. London, New York: Verso, 1988.

Moody, Kim. *Workers in a Lean World: Unions in the International Economy*. London, New York: Verso, 1997.

Mörtvik, Roger, and Åsa Regnér. "The Labor Market and Part-Time Work in Sweden." In *Part-Time Work in Europe*, ed. Martina Klein. Frankfurt am Main: Campus Verlag: 187–194.

Nätti, Jouko, Timo Anttila, and Mia Väisänen. "Managers and Working Time in Finland." In *Decent Working Time: New Trends, New Issues*, eds. Jean-Yves Boulin, Michel Lallement, Jon C. Messenger, and François Michon. Geneva: International Labour Office, 2006: 289–317.

Negt, Oskar. *Arbeit und menschliche Würde*. Göttingen: Steidl Verlag, 2001.

Nelson, Daniel. *Managers and Workers: Origins of the New Factory System in the United States, 1880–1920*. Madison: University of Wisconsin Press, 1975.

Nelson, Daniel. *Shifting Fortunes: The Rise and Decline of American Labor, from the 1820s to the Present*, The American Ways Series. Chicago: Ivan R. Dee, 1997.

Nowotny, Helga. *Time: Modern and Postmodern Experience*. Cambridge: Polity Press, 1994.

Nyland, Chris. *Reduced Worktime and the Management of Production*. Cambridge, New York: Cambridge University Press, 1989.

Oakely, Ann. *Woman's Work. The Housewife Past and Present*. New York: Vintage Books, 1976.

OECD. *Employment Outlook 1998*. Paris: OECD, 1998.

OECD. *The Service Economy*. Paris: OECD, 2000.

OECD. *Employment Outlook 2001*. Paris: OECD, 2001.

OECD. *Employment Outlook 2004*. Paris: OECD, 2004.

OECD. *Divided we Stand. Why Inequality Keeps Rising*. Paris: OECD, 2011.

Offe, Claus, and John Keane. *Disorganized Capitalism: Contemporary Transformations of Work and Politics*. Cambridge: Polity Press, 1985.

Office of National Statistics. "Women in the Labor Market." London: Office of National Statistics, September 25, 2013.

Ono, Taiichi. *Toyota Production System: Beyond Large-Scale Production*. Portland: Productivity Press, 1988.

Parent-Thrion, Agnès, Enrique Fernández Macías, John Hurley, and Greet Vermeylen. *Fourth European Working Conditions Survey*. Dublin: European Foundation for the Improvement of Working and Living Conditions, 2007.

Parker, Mike, and Jane Slaughter. "Unions and Management by Stress." In *Lean Work: Empowerment and Exploitation in the Global Auto Industry*, ed. Steve Babson, Detroit: Wayne State University Press, 1995: 41–53.

Passel, Jeffrey S., Randy Capps, and Michael Fix. *Undocumented Immigrants: Facts and Figures*. Washington, DC: Urban Institute, 2004.

Peck, Jamie. *Work-Place: The Social Regulation of Labor Markets*. New York: Guilford, 1996.

Peck, Jamie. *Workfare States*. New York: Guilford, 2001.

Peck, Jamie. "The Rise of the Workfare State." In *Kurswechsel*, no. 3, 2003: 75–87.

Perkins, Frances. *The Roosevelt I Knew*. New York: Viking, 1946.

Philip, Bruce. "Marxism, Neoclassical Economics and the Length of the Working Day." In *Review of Political Economy*, issue 13, no. 1, 2001: 27–39.

Philip, Bruce, Gary Slater, and David Harvie. "Preferences, Power, and the Determination of Work Hours." In *Journal of Economic Issues*, issue 39, no. 1, 2005: 75–90.

Phillips, Paul. "Labour in the New Canadian Political Economy". In *Understanding Canada. Building on the New Canadian Political Economy*, ed. Clement Wallace. Montreal, Kingston: McGill-Queen's University Press, 1997: 64–84.

Pigou, A. C. *A Study in Public Finance*. London: Macmillan, 1947.

Piore, Michael J., and Charles F. Sabel. *The Second Industrial Divide: Possibilities for Prosperity*. New York: Basic Books, 1984.

Plantenga, Janneke, and Chantal Remery. "Work Hard, Play Hard? Work in Software Engineering." In *Working in the Service Sector: A Tale from Different Worlds*, eds. Gerhard Bosch and Steffen Lehndorff. London, New York: Routledge, 2004: 189–201.

Polanyi, Karl. *The Great Transformation: The Political and Economic Origins of Our Time*. Boston: Beacon Press, 1957.

Pollert, Anna. "Dismantling Flexibility." In *Capital & Class*, no. 34, 1988: 42–75.

Pollert, Anna. "The 'Flexible Firm': Fixation or Fact?" In *Work Employment & Society*, issue 2, no. 3, 1988: 281–316.

Pollert, Anna. *Farewell to Flexibility?* Oxford: Basil Blackwell, 1991.

Prasch, Robert E. *How Markets Work: Supply, Demand and the 'Real World.'* Cheltenham: Edward Elgar, 2008.

Prescott, Edward. "Why Do Americans Work So Much More Than Europeans?" NBER Working Paper 10316, 2004.

Price, John. *Japan Works: Power and Paradox in Postwar Industrial Relations*. Ithaca, NY: ILR Press, 1997.

Price, John. "Lean Production at Suzuki and Toyota: A Historical Perspective." *Studies in Political Economy*, no. 45, 1994: 66–99, 1994.

Promberger, Markus, Sabine Böhm, Thilo Heyder, Susanne Pamer, and Katharina Strauss. *Hochflexible Arbeitszeiten in der Industrie. Chancen, Risiken und Grenzen für Beschäftigte*. Berlin: Edition Sigma, 2002.

Ramey, Valerie. "Time Spent in Home Production in the Twentieth Century: New Estimates from Old Data." NBER Working Paper 13985, 2008.

Ramey, Valerie, and Neville Francis. "A Century of Work and Leisure." In *American Economic Journal: Macroeconomics*, issue 1, no. 2, 2009: 189–224.

Rasmussen, Benete, and Brigitte Johansen. "Trick or Treat? Autonomy as Control in Knowledge Work." In *Management, Labour Process and Software Development: Reality Bytes*, eds. Rowena Barrett. London, New York: Routledge, 2005: 100–22.

Ray, Rebecca, and John Schmitt. "No-Vacation Nation USA – a Comparison of Leave and Holiday in OECD Countries." ETUI Policy Brief 3, 2007. Brussels: European Trade Union Institute, 2007.

Rees, William. "Eco-Footprint Analysis: Merits and Brickbats." In *Ecological Economics*, issue 32, no. 3, 2000: 347–9.

Rehn, Gösta. "Die Gesellschaft der freien Wahl." In *Beiträge zu einer Theorie der Sozialpolitik*, eds. Bernhard Külp and Wofgang Stützel. Berlin: Duncker and Humbolt, 1973: 317–52.

Resnick, Stephen A., and Richard D. Wolff. *New Departures in Marxian Theory*. London, New York: Routledge, 2006.

Revelli, Marco. "Vom 'Fordismus' zum 'Toyotismus'. Das Kapitalistische Wirtschafts- und Sozialmodell im Übergang." In *Supplement der Zeitschrift Sozialismus*, no. 4, 1997.

Revelli, Marco. *Die Gesellschaftliche Linke. Jenseits der Zivilisation von Arbeit*. Münster: Westfälisches Dampfboot, 1999.

Reynolds, Lloyd George, Stanley H. Masters, and Collette Moser. *Readings in Labor Economics and Labor Relations*. Englewood Cliffs, NJ: Prentice-Hall, 1974.

Rifkin, Jeremy. *Time Wars: The Primary Conflict in Human History*. New York: H. Holt, 1987.

Rifkin, Jeremy. *The End of Work: The Decline of the Global Labor Force and the Dawn of the Post-Market Era*. New York: Putnam, 1995.

Rigaudiat, Jacques. *Réduire le temps de travail*. Paris: Syros, 1993.

Rinehart, James, Christopher Victor Huxley, and David Robertson. *Just Another Car Factory?: Lean Production and Its Discontents*. Ithaca: ILR Press, 1997.

Rinehart, James, David Robertson, Christopher Victor Huxley, and Jeff Wareham. "Reunifying Conception and Execution of Work under Japanese Production Management? A Canadian Case Study." In *Global Japanization?: The Transnational Transformation of the Labour Process*, eds. Tony Elger and Chris Smith. London, New York: Routledge, 1994: 152–74.

Robbins, Lionel "On the Elasticity of Demand for Income in Terms of Effort." In *Economica*, no. 29, 1930: 123–9.

Roberts, Bruce. "From Lean Production to Agile Manufacturing: A New Round of Quicker, Cheaper and Better." In *Re-Shaping Work. Union Responses to Technological Change*, eds. Christopher R. Schenk and John Anderson. Don Mills: Ontario Federation of Labor, 1995: 197–214.

Roberts, Christopher. "Harnessing Competition? The UAW and Competitiveness in the Canadian Auto Industry, 1945–1990." PhD Thesis, York University, Toronto, 2002.

Robinson, Joan. *Essays in the Theory of Employment*. Oxford: Blackwell, 1947.

Robinson, John, and Geoffrey Godbey. *Time for Life: The Surprising Ways Americans Use Their Time*. University Park: Pennsylvania State University Press, 1999.

Roediger, David. "Limits of Corporate Reform: Fordism, Taylorism, and the Working Week in the United States, 1914–1929." In *Worktime and Industrialization: An International History*, ed. Gary S. Cross. Philadelphia: Temple University Press, 1988: 142–8.

Roediger, David, and Philip Sheldon Foner. *Our Own Time: A History of American Labor and the Working Day*, The Haymarket Series. London, New York: Verso, 1989.

Rose, Nikolas. *Inventing Our Selves: Psychology, Power, and Personhood*. Cambridge, New York: Cambridge University Press, 1996.

Rosenberg, Samuel. "United States of America." In, *Times Are Changing: Working Time in 14 Industrialised Countries*, eds. Gerhard Bosch, Peter Dawkins, and François Michon. Geneva: International Institute for Labour Studies, 1994: 289–312.

Rosenberg, Samuel. "Long Work Hours for Some, Short Hours for Others: Working Time in the United States." In *Working Time – in Search for New Research Territory Beyond Flexibility Debates*. Tokyo: The Japan Institue for Labor Policy and Training, 2009: 71–86.

Rosnick, David, and Mark Weisbrot. "Are Shorter Work Hours Good for the Enviornment?" Center for Economic and Policy Research, Washington DC, 2006.

Rubery, Jill. "Working Time in the UK." In *Transfer: European Review of Labour and Research*, issue 4, no. 4, 1998: 657–77.

Rubery, Jill. "Part-Time Work: A Threat to Labour Standards?" In *Part-Time Prospects*, eds. Jacqueline O'Reilly and Collete Fagan. New York: Routledge, 1998: 137–55.

Rubery, Jill, and Collete Fagan. "Part-Time Work in Britain." In *Part-Time Work in Europe*, ed. Martina Klein. Frankfurt am Main: Campus Verlag 1997: 213–333.

Rubery, Jill, and Damian Grimshaw. "ICTs and Employment: The Problem of Job Quality." In *International Labour Review*, issue 40, no. 2, 2001: 165–92.

Rubery, Jill, and Damian Grimshaw. *The Organization of Employment: An International Perspective*. Basingstoke: Palgrave Macmillan, 2003.

Rubery, Jill, Simon Deakin, and Sara Horrel. "United Kingdom." In *Times Are Changing: Working Time in 14 Industrialised Countries*, eds. Gerhard Bosch, Peter Dawkins, and François Michon. Geneva: International Institute for Labour Studies, 1994: 261–88.

Rubery, Jill, Mark Smith, and Colette Fagan. "National Working-Time Regimes and Equal Opportunities." In *Feminist Economics*, issue 4, no. 1, 1998: 71–101.

Russell, Alice. *The TUC and the Working Time Question: Policy, Action and Outcomes in Twentieth-Century Britain*. Lewes: Book Guild, 2000.

Russell, Bob. *Smiling Down the Line: Info-Service Work in the Global Economy*. Toronto: University of Toronto Press, 2009.

Saad-Filho, Alfredo. *The Value of Marx: Political Economy for Contemporary Capitalism*. London, New York: Routledge, 2002.

Samuel, Howard. "Troubled Passage: The Labor Movement and the Fair Labor Standards Act." In *Monthly Labor Review*, issue 123, no. 12, 2000: 32–7.

Sandberg, Åke. *Enriching Production: Perspectives on Volvo's Uddevalla Plant as an Alternative to Lean Production*. Aldershot; Brookfield, VT: Avebury, 1995.

Sassoon, Donald. *One Hundred Years of Socialism: The West European Left in the Twentieth Century*. New York: New Press, 1996.

Saville, John. *The Labour Movement in Britain: A Commentary*. London: Faber, 1988.

Sawhill, Isabel, and John Morton. "Economic Mobility: Is the American Dream Alive and Well?" Economic Mobility Project, Washington DC, 2007.

Sayer, Liana "Gender, Time and Inequality: Trends in Women's and Men's Paid Work, Unpaid Work and Free Time." In *Social Forces*, issue 84, no. 1, 2005: 285–303.

Sayer, Liana "Trends in Housework". In *Dividing the Domestic. Men, Women and Household Work in Cross-National Perspective*, eds. Judith Treas and Sonja Drobnic. Stanford: Stanford University Press, 2010: 19–38.

Sayer, R. Andrew, and Richard Walker. *The New Social Economy: Reworking the Division of Labor*. Cambridge, MA: Blackwell, 1992.

Scharf, Günter. *Geschichte der Arbeitszeitverkürzung: Der Kampf der deutschen Gewerkschaften um die Verkürzung der täglichen und wöchentlichen Arbeitszeit*. Cologne: Bund Verlag, 1987.

Schettkat, Ronald. "Differences in US–German Time-Allocation: Why Do Americans Work Longer Hours Than Germans." IZA Discussion Paper 697. Bonn: Institute for the Study of Labor, 2003.

Schmidt, Rudi, and Rainer Trinczek. "Erfahrungen und Perspektiven gewerkschaftlicher Arbeitszeitpolitik" in *Prolka*, no. 64, 1988: 85–105.

Schmiede, Rudi. "Der 'schematische Achtstundentag' 1918 Bis 1923." In *Arbeitspolitik: Materialen zum Zusammenhang von politischer Macht, Kontrolle und betrieblicher*

Organisation der Arbeit, eds. Ulrich Jürgens and Frieder Naschold. Opladen: Westdeutscher Verlag, 1984: 365–80.

Schneider, Friedrich. "Size and Measurement of the Informal Economy in 110 Countries around the World." Linz: Johannes Kepler University, 2002. Online. www.amnet.co.il/attachments/informal_economy110.pdf [accessed January 10, 2012].

Schneider, Michael. *Streit um Arbeitszeit: Geschichte des Kampfes um Arbeitszeitverkürzung in Deutschland.* Cologne: Bund Verlag, 1984.

Schor, Juliet. *The Overworked American: The Unexpected Decline of Leisure.* New York: Basic Books, 1991.

Schor, Juliet. *The Overspent American: Upscaling, Downshifting, and the New Consumer.* New York: Basic Books, 1998.

Schor, Juliet. *Plentitude: The Economics of True Wealth.* New York: Penguin Press, 2010.

Schudlich, Edwin. "Arbeitszeitpolitik seit 1950: Interessensparallelitäten und Widersprüche." In *Arbeitspolitik: Materialen zum Zusammenhang von politischer Macht, Kontrolle und betrieblicher Organisation der Arbeit,* eds. Ulrich Jürgens and Frieder Naschold. Opladen: Westdeutscher Verlag, 1984: 381–92.

Schulten, Thorsten. *Solidarische Lohnpolitik in Europa. Zur politischen Ökonomie der Gewerkschaften.* Hamburg: VSA Verlag, 2004.

Schumann, Michael. "Frisst die Shareholder-Value-Ökonomie die Modernisierung der Arbeit?" In *Metamorphosen von Industriearbeit und Arbeiterbewußtsein,* ed. Michael Schumann. Hamburg: VSA Verlag, 2003: 51–60.

Seccombe, Wally. "The Housewife and Her Labour under Capitalism." In *New Left Review,* no. 83, January–February 1974: 3–24.

Seccombe, Wally. *Weathering the Storm. Working Class Families From the Industrial Revolution to the Fertility Decline.* London: Verso, 1993.

Segre, Sandro. "A Weberian Theory of Time." In *Time & Society,* issue 9, nos. 2–3, 2000: 147–70.

Shaiken, Harley. *Work Transformed: Automation and Labor in the Computer Age.* New York: Holt, Rinehart, and Winston, 1985.

Shaiken, Harley, Stephen Herzenberg, and Sarah Kuhn. "The Work Process under More Flexible Production." In *Industrial Relations,* issue 25, no. 2, 1986: 167–83.

Shiomi, Haruhito. "The Formation of Assembler Networks in the Automobile Industry: The Case of Toyota Motor Company (1955–80)." In *Fordism Transformed: The Development of Production Methods in the Automobile Industry,* eds. Haruhito Shiomi and Kazuo Wada. Oxford, New York: Oxford University Press, 1995: 28–48.

Shorter, Edward, and Charles Tilly. *Strikes in France, 1830–1968.* London: Cambridge University Press, 1974.

Silver, Beverly J. *Forces of Labor: Workers' Movements and Globalization since 1870.* Cambridge, New York: Cambridge University Press, 2003.

Skorstad, Egil. "Lean Production, Conditions of Work and Worker Commitment." In *Economic and Industrial Democracy,* issue 15, no. 3, 1994: 429–55.

Smith, Mark. "The Incidence of New Forms of Employment in Service." In *Working in the Service Sector: A Tale from Different Worlds,* eds. Gerhard Bosch and Steffen Lehndorff. London, New York: Routledge, 2005: 54–73.

Smith, Mark, Collete Fagan, and Jill Rubery. "Where and Why Is Part-Time Work Growing in Europe?" In *Part-Time Prospects: An International Comparison of Part-Time Work in Europe, North America and the Pacific Rim,* eds. Colette Fagan and Jacqueline O'Reilly. London, New York: Routledge, 1998: 35–56.

Smith, Tony. *Technology and Capital in the Age of Lean Production: A Marxian Critique of the "New Economy."* Albany: State University of New York Press, 2000.

Spencer, David A. "'The Labor-Less Labor Supply Model' in the Era before Philip Wicksteed." in *Journal of the History of Economic Thought*, issue 25, no. 1, 2003a: 505–13.

Spencer, David A. "Love's Labor's Lost? The Disutility of Work and Work Avoidance in the Economic Analysis of Labor Supply." In *Review of Social Economy*, issue 61, no. 2, 2003b: 235–50.

Spencer, David A. "From Pain Cost to Opportunity Cost: The Eclipse of the Quality of Work as a Factor in Economic Theory." In *History of Political Economy*, issue 36, no. 2, 2004: 387–400.

Spencer, David A. "Work for All Those Who Want It? Why the Neoclassical Labour Supply Curve Is an Inappropriate Foundation of the Theory of Employment and Unemployment." In *Cambridge Journal of Economics*, issue 30, no. 3, 2006: 459–72.

Spencer, David A. *The Political Economy of Work.* London, New York: Routledge, 2009.

Springer, Roland. "Rationalization Also Involves Workers – Teamwork in the Mercedes-Benz Lean Concept." In *Transforming Automobile Assembly: Experience in Automation and Work Organization*, eds. Kōichi Shimokawa, Ulrich Jürgens, and Takahiro Fujimoto. New York: Springer Verlag, 1997: 274–87.

Springer, Roland. *Rückkehr zum Taylorismus?: Arbeitspolitik in der Automobilindustrie am Scheideweg.* Frankfurt am Main: Campus Verlag, 1999.

Standing, Guy. *Global Labour Flexibility: Seeking Distributive Justice.* Basingstoke: Macmillan, 1999.

Stewart, Paul. *We Sell Our Time No More: Workers' Struggles against Lean Production in the British Car Industry.* London: Pluto Press, 2009.

Stiglitz, Joseph. "Towards a General Theory of Consumerism: Reflections on Keynes' Economic Possibilities for our Grandchildren." In *Revisiting Keynes: Economic Possibilities for our Grandchildren*, eds. Lorenzo Pecchi and Gustavo Piga. Cambridge: MIT Press, 2008: 41–85.

Streeck, Wolfgang. "The Uncertainties of Management in the Management of Uncertainty: Employers, Labor Relations and Industrial Adjustment in the 1980s." In *Work, Employment & Society*, issue 1, no. 3, 1987: 281–308.

Sunter, Deborah, and René Morissette. "The Hours People Work." In *Perspectives on Labor and Income*, issue 6, no. 3, 1994: 8–12.

Sward, Keith. *The Legend of Henry Ford.* New York: Russell & Russell, 1968.

Taylor, Frederick W. *The Principles of Scientific Management.* New York, London: Harper, 1911.

Taylor, Frederick W. *Scientific Management: Testimony before the Special House Committee.* New York: Harper, 1947.

Thomas, Mark. "Toyotaism Meets the 60-Hour Work Week: Coercion, Consent, and the Regulation of Working Time." in *Studies in Political Economy*, no. 80, Autumn 2007: 105–38.

Thomas, Mark. *Regulating Flexibility: The Political Economy of Employment Standards.* Montreal: McGill-Queen's University Press, 2009.

Thompson, Edward Palmer. *The Making of the English Working Class.* New York: Pantheon Books, 1964.

Thompson, Edward Palmer. "Time, Work-Discipline, and Industrial Capitalism." In *Past & Present*, no. 38, December 1967: 56–97.

Thompson, Paul. *Skating on Thin Ice: The Knowledge Economy Myth: Big Thinking.* University of Strathclyde: Glasgow, 2004.

Tilly, Chris. *Half a Job: Bad and Good Part-Time Jobs in a Changing Labor Market.* Philadelphia: Temple University Press, 1996.

Tolliday, Steven, and Jonathan Zeitlin. "Introduction: Between Fordism and Flexibility." In *Between Fordism and Flexibility: The Automobile Industry and Its Workers*, eds. Steven Tolliday and Jonathan Zeitlin. Oxford, New York: Berg, 1992: 1–26.

Tomaney, John. "A New Paradigm of Work Organization and Technology?" In *Post-Fordism: A Reader*, ed. Ash Amin. Oxford, Cambridge, MA: Blackwell, 1994: 157–94.

Touraine, Alain. *The Post-Industrial Society; Tomorrow's Social History: Classes, Conflicts and Culture in the Programmed Society.* New York: Random House, 1971.

Trauwein-Kalms, Gudrun, and Elke Ahlers. "High Potential unter Druck – Gestaltung der Arbeits- und Leistungsbedingungen von Software-Experten und IT Dienstleister." In *Dienstleistungsarbeit: Auf dem Boden der Tatsachen. Befunde aus Handel, Industrie, Medien und IT-Branche*, eds. Markus Pohlmann, Dieter Sauer, and Gudrun Trautwein-Kalms. Berlin: Edition Sigma, 2003: 244–94.

Urry, John. "Time, Leisure and Social Identity." In *Time & Society*, issue 3, no. 2, 1994: 131–49.

Usalcas, Jeannine. "Hours polarization revisited." In *Perspectives*, March 2008: 5–15.

van der Lippe, Tanja. "Women's Employment and Housework." in *Dividing the Domestic. Men, Women and Household Work in Cross-National Perspective*, eds. Judith Treas and Sonja Drobnic. Stanford: Standford University Press, 2010: 41–58.

Vanek, Joanne. "Time Spent in Housework." In *Scientific American*, issue 231, no. 5, 1974: 116–20.

Veblen, Thorstein, and Martha Banta. *The Theory of the Leisure Class.* Oxford, New York: Oxford University Press, 2007.

Visser, Jelle. "Corporatism Beyond Repair? Industrial Relations in Sweden." In *Industrial Relations in Europe: Traditions and Transitions*, eds. J. van Ruysseveldt and Jelle Visser. London: Sage Publications, 1996: 175–204.

Voss-Dahm, Dorothea. "Coming and Going at Will? Working Time Organization in German IT Companies." In *Management, Labour Process and Software Development: Reality Bytes*, eds. Rowena Barrett. London; New York: Routledge, 2005: 123–45.

Voth, Hans-Joachim. *Time and Work in England 1750–1830*, Oxford, New York: Clarendon Press, 2000.

Wagner, Alexandra. "Arbeiten ohne Ende? Über Arbeitszeiten von hochqualifizierten Angestellten." In *Institut für Arbeit Und Technik Jahrbuch 1999/2000*, Gelsenkirchen: Institut für Arbeit und Technik, 2001a: 258–75.

Wagner, Alexandra. "Entgrenzung der Arbeit und der Arbeitszeit?" In *Arbeit*, issue 10, no. 3, 2001b: 365–78.

Walby, Sylvia. *Patriarchy at Work. Patriarchal and Capitalist Relations in Employment.* Cambridge: Polity Press, 1986.

Wallis, Victor. "Beyond 'Green Capitalism.'" *Monthly Review*, issue 61, no. 9, 2010: 32–48.

Walsh, Tim J. "Flexible Labour Utilization in the Private Service Sector." In *Work Employment & Society*, issue 4, no. 4, 1990: 517–30.

Warhurst, Chris, and Paul Thompson. "Mapping Knowledge in Work: Proxies or Practices?" In *Work Employment & Society*, issue 20, no. 4, 2006: 787–800.

Weber, Max. *The Protestant Ethic and the Spirit of Capitalism.* New York, London: Scribner: G. Allen & Unwin, 1930.

Weber, Max. "Die Grenznutzenlehre und das 'Psychophysische Grundgesetz'". In *Gesammelte Aufsätze zur Wirtschaftslehre*, eds. Johannes Winckelmann. Tübingen: J. B. C. Mohr (Siebeck), 1988: 384–99.

Weber, Max. "Zur Psychophysik der Industriellen Arbeit". In *Gesammelte Aufsätze Zur Soziologie und Sozialpolitik*, ed. Marianne Weber. Tübingen: J. B. C. Mohr (Siebeck), 1988: 61–255.

Weeks, John. *Capital and Exploitation*. Princeton: Princeton University Press, 1981.

Weeks, Kathi. *The Problem with Work. Femininsm, Marxism, Antiwork Politics, and Postwork Imaginaries*. Durham: Duke University Press, 2010.

Weigelt, Ulla. "The Road to a Society of Free Choice: The Politics of Working Time in Sweden." In *Working Time in Transition: The Political Economy of Working Hours in Industrial Nations*, eds K. Hinrichs, William Roche, and Carmen Sirianni. Philadelphia: Temple University Press, 1989: 203–29.

Weinkopf, Claudia. "Call-Centre Work: Specific Characteristics and the Challenges of Work Organisation." In *Transfer: European Review of Labour and Research*, issue 8, no. 3, 2002: 456–66.

West, Edwin G. "Marx's Hypotheses on the Length of the Working Day." In *Journal of Political Economy*, issue 91, no. 2, 1983: 266–81.

Wicksteed, Philip Henry. *The Common Sense of Political Economy, Including a Study of the Human Basis of Economic Law*. London: Macmillan, 1910.

Williams, Karel, Tony Cutler, John Williams and Colin Haslam. "The End of Mass Production?" In *Economy and Society*, issue 16, no. 3, 1987: 405–39.

Williams, Karel, Colin Haslam, John Williams, Tony Cultler, Andy Adcroft and Sukhdev Johal. "Against Lean Production." In *Economy and Society*, issue 21, no. 3, 1992: 321–54.

Wolf, Harald, and Nicole Mayer-Ahuja. "'Grenzen der Entgrenzung von Arbeit' – Perspektiven der Arbeitsforschung." In *SOFI-Mitteilungen*, no. 30, 2002: 197–205.

Wolff, Richard D., and Stephen A. Resnick. *Economics: Marxian Versus Neoclassical*. Baltimore: Johns Hopkins University Press, 1987.

Womack, James P., Daniel T. Jones, and Daniel Roos. *The Machine That Changed the World: How Japan's Secret Weapon in the Global Auto Wars Will Revolutionize Western Industry*. New York: Harper Perennial, 1991.

Wood, Stephen. "The Transformation of Work?" In *The Transformation of Work?: Skill, Flexibility and the Labour Process*, ed. Stephen G. Wood. London, New York: Routledge, 1989.

Wuppertal Institute for Climate Change. *Zukunftsfähiges Deutschland in einer globalisierten Welt: Ein Anstoß zur gesellschaftlichen Debatte*. Frankfurt am Main: Fischer Verlag, 2008.

Yates, Charlotte A. B. *From Plant to Politics: The Autoworkers Union in Postwar Canada*. Philadelphia: Temple University Press, 1993.

Yates, Charlotte, Wayne Lewchuk, and Paul Stewart. "Empowerment as a Trojan Horse: New Systems of Work Organization in the North American Automobile Industry." In *Economic and Industrial Democracy*, issue 22, no. 4, 1991: 517–41.

Yerkes, Mara, and Jelle Visser. "Women's Preferences or Deliniated Policies? The Development of Part-Time Work in the Netherlands, Germany, and the United Kingdom." In *Decent Work Time*, eds. Jean-Yve Boulin, Michel Lallement, Jon C. Messenger and François Michon. Geneva: ILO, 2006: 235–56.

Zeytinoglu, Isik, Waheeda Lillevik, M. Bianca Seaton, and Josefina Moruz. "Part-Time and Casual Work in Retail Trade: Stress and Other Factors Affecting the Workplace." In *Relations Industrielles/Industrial Relations*, issue 59, no. 3, 2004: 516–44.

Index

Page numbers in *italics* denote tables, those in **bold** denote figures.